MW00829875

"*The Hollow Half* catapults every single expectation we have ever had of the memoir genre and of the settled memory. Is it a memoir? It's at least that. But Aziza both longs for and accepts radical tradition and the aches of innovation. The book is body and spirit, full and famished. I'm not sure I've read a book more unafraid of finding free." —Kiese Laymon, author of *Heavy*

"What is the vocabulary of loss? How much history can a body hold? Visceral, gutting, and stunning, *The Hollow Half* is one of those books that comes along only rarely. Sarah Aziza has found a way to make language an active witness to one woman's—and one nation's—insistence on life."
—Maaza Mengiste, author of *The Shadow King*,
short-listed for the Booker Prize

"Excruciating, to live in a nation, a culture, a moment in which one must continuously insist upon their own humanity and the humanity of those they love. And yet so many of history's greatest writers—from Mahmoud Darwish to Toni Morrison—have taken up this project, fractaling shards of unprecedented experience into something as vital, precious, undeniable, as life itself. Sarah Aziza sings herself into that chorus with clarity and tenderness, writing, 'Palestine: an orientation toward a life that names, and holds open, the ruptures loving makes.' *The Hollow Half* is inventive, propulsive testimony, a lush love letter to a place, a people, and the resilience of memory." —Kaveh Akbar, author of *Martyr!*

"If warring nations were to fall away, what would be left but bodies? Sarah Aziza's *The Hollow Half* brings a Palestinian song and body back to life from the ruins. To sing this blood song she must cross all boundaries, between people, places, histories, and languages. Here is a heart beating, not beaten. The question is, How will we hold such a sacred text?"

—Lidia Yuknavitch, author of *The Chronology of Water*

"How do we come to this life? Is it automatic, by birth? Or must we also choose it? Sarah Aziza's astonishing memoir is a record of a mystery of the self, a woman in the grip of a despair that has too many names or none at all, hiding as it seeks to erase her. To survive she must move towards being, as she says, 'ambushed by hope.' We travel with her into that place where even language abandoned her, and her effort to return, yes, alive, maybe even more than that, has lessons for us all. A blazing, hard-won triumph."

—Alexander Chee, author of *How to Write an Autobiographical Novel*

"In the breathtaking, fiercely honest *The Hollow Half*, Sarah Aziza weaves a genre-bending memoir of body and land, an unflinching look at the tyranny of emotional, physical, and intrapsychic hunger. These hungerings—complex, visceral, ever-present—frame a story of hauntings, erasures, colonization, and the metaphor and reality of Palestine. But *The Hollow Half* is not merely a dissection of absence; it is an expansion of genre itself, gorgeously blending memoir with dreamwork, ancestral secrets with reclaimed history. Through stunning, transformative prose, Aziza writes both herself—and the reader—towards liberation."

—Hala Alyan, author of *The Moon That Turns You Back*

"Sarah Aziza's writing penetrates the heart and the pulse in such a way that you are breathing with her, rapturous against the fate of a body that cannot fully contain you, nor can it be contained. *The Hollow Half* is a potent and confronting memoir about the perils of our explicable ghosts—whether that be ancestral lineages or the unsatiated dreams of our ancestors or the yearning of something that can be never tasted or quenched—this book shakes you into understanding the devastation of what it means to be alive in a time like this."

—Fariha Róisín, author of *Who Is Wellness For* and *Survival Takes a Wild Imagination*

"*The Hollow Half* is a shimmering testament to disciplined love's exigencies and transcendent possibilities. It is a book that all who seek a path beyond the brutal systems and narratives of colonial modernity will return to time and again."

—Nadia Owusu, author of *Aftershocks*

"In a world where 'survival requires a brief act of insanity,' Sarah Aziza has given us a miraculous clarity that is nothing short of catastrophic to a global order intent on paving over and dis-remembering Palestinians. Never have I read a book that has made me feel as loved, held, and cared for in my Palestinian body as *The Hollow Half.* Here is return translated, however im/permanently, into a kind of present tense. Here is a capacious dreaming, forming constellar kinship across, against, and despite borders in space-time, while never failing to return us to the body. This is a memoir we have all needed for many lifetimes."

—George Abraham, author of *Birthright*

The
Hollow
Half

❖

A MEMOIR OF BODIES AND BORDERS

❖

Sarah Aziza

CATAPULT   NEW YORK

THE HOLLOW HALF

This is a work of nonfiction. However, some names and identifying details of individuals have been changed to protect their privacy, correspondence has been shortened for clarity, and dialogue has been reconstructed from memory.

for Love
&
for Gaza

words fail.

قُلْتُ: وسِرِّي الدَّفِين؟
قَالَ: فَجُد بِهِ.

وهَا أنا فَاعِلٌ.

But what about the secret I bear? I asked.
Tell it to the world, he advised.

And that is what I am doing.

—Emile Habibi

Contents

✧

The
Hollow
Half

Translator's Note
ترجم

Ask someone to write the word *translate* in Arabic, and you will almost certainly see ترجم. A verb of rare root, a long, four-letter stem.

But here, language winks at us. The word ترجم does not fit neatly into the Western notion of *translate*. The English, coming from the Latin *translatus*, means *to remove from one place to another*. Translation as acquisition. The fiction of perfect transference, wherein nothing is lost in uprooting from origins.

نقل would be the word for this—*to transfer, to relocate, to deliver*. نقل: the book buyers dispatched from European palaces in the 1700s, sent from Europe to raid Egyptian and Ottoman libraries. *Oriental* books were objects to acquire, curios and trinkets collected by Western aristocracy.

ترجم, by contrast, is a storytelling word. Its meaning emanates from *interpret*, touches *expound, explain*. For ترجم, words are less like cargo, more like memories or dreams. Colors render in one mind, ideas quiver inside flesh. ترجم, an open window wafting aromas of the bread you will not taste.

ترجم can haunt us, with all that it withholds.

3

استهلال
Overture

My grandmother couldn't read. *She was a simple woman*, my father would say after her death. Bowed with age and unnamed illness, she lived her final decades on hands and knees. Crawling, sputtering in a tight track between the sitting room, toilet, and kitchen. Her days began with the dragging of pots and bowls off their shelves, the flickering of a propane flame. Pita bread—fresh or sometimes stale—charring over heat. A tray of tea and hunked cheese with jam or cucumber. These smells and tastes, all that remained continuous with the worlds that she once knew.

There was something of pity in the way others spoke of her—even those who revered her, like my father, her favorite son. *She's suffered so much*, he used to say, never prompted or elaborating. *Miskeenah, poor Mama.* From there, he reached for my life as a consoling corollary. *You're so lucky, habibti. She did her best, just trying to survive. But you! In this country, you can be anything.* He spun big, proud destinies for me. *Doctor, lawyer? Mashallah, first female president?* My future, American-born and unbounded, a bright sky cast in contrast to hers.

But perhaps my grandmother sheltered in that littleness. Perhaps her small peace was enough, hard won. After all, a sky can be too large. I know the longing to shrink the world to a single room.

Part I

صمت

Silence

Is this you?

The question confronts me on an endless pandemic morning, pixelated letters beaming from the palm of my hand. My iPhone has a feature that sorts faces, filing photos under names. Here, I am three people. My body, a series of transformations so drastic the algorithm fails to recognize me as a coherent being across time.

Three suggested *Sarah*s gaze up from the screen. I remember myself into these different bodies, feel the frequencies of each. I recall the wariness of the youngest version, my every move taut with self-judgment, the whir of relentless monitoring. All those shallow breaths, fearing to expand. Fingers tugging the edges of my shirt, a too-small curtain over me. I see now that I was already slim, slim enough that my body tapered beneath my waist. My hips are shrunken to a prepubescent girth, my balance forever unsteady in the absence of any ass. Yet I still appear as one who belongs to the land of the living, my eyes three dimensional, lit by a working mind.

Is this you? My phone requests me to check *yes* or *no*.

From there, my face narrows and wilts. After a certain point, my cheeks cave in, my eyes and nose suddenly uncannily large. This second version of me lingers for a year, flickering through frames of joy: rooftop parties and sunsoaked graduation gowns, an engagement ring. All those selfies with friends. We grin into the camera eagerly, evidence that we knew, beneath our self-deprecation, how beautiful we were. *Is this Sarah?* asks my phone. In these photos I am happy, but my shallowing health jars slightly with the scenes.

In my wedding dress, I beam with just-whitened teeth that take a little too much space in my face. My long curled hair falls perfectly, but my shoulders interrupt its softness, bones poking under pale skin. A few too many contours on my collarbone, rib shadowing above lace. In the frames of dance-floor mayhem, my bride-arms fly out, swaying to some forgotten song. Now, I wince at the sharpness of my elbows. I tried hard to make myself eat that day, thinking I did not want my wedding memories forever tied to hunger. Those bites of lamb still live in my mind, succulent instants of abandon.

It's not until after the honeymoon that I fall off that cliff—my face going stone, skull barely sheathed by tissue-skin. After this, my body loses its fundamental resemblance to others. It keeps no secrets, spells every organ and bone. I get tangled in the straps of my slipping tank top. My smallest pair of jeans drops abruptly, twice, in public. I begin walking with a finger through my belt loop, feeling every step through brittle feet. Once, to beat a walk sign counting down, I try bursting into a jog. I am stunned to find my legs barely lifting. My dissolved muscles no longer able to respond, a marionette with severed strings.

My iPhone asks, *Who is this?*

By this time, hunger is a state of being so beyond physical sensation, I cease to feel it. My body floats below me, a constellation of pains with silences lodged between. Bandages live on my joints, my knees or wrists always popping out of place. My head thrums with a perennial ache that brings me frequently to tears. I ask my husband, C, to knead my muscles for relief. He hesitates. Confesses he is afraid to hurt me, says he's only rubbing bone. In the morning, his eyes are bagged after a night spent checking my pulse. I make a smile with my face, slide out of bed to meet emails and deadlines. *Busy* is how I know I am not about to die.

The cliff is in my mind, too—I retain few memories of our first year of marriage, except that the space inside my head felt vast and stifling at once, an emptiness so complete it had a music all its own. The ringing of ears right before a swoon, the serene buzz I used to find tucked inside glasses of wine. A photo from this time shows me at a favorite restaurant, coyly holding two glasses of cabernet. *Take a picture of me!* I asked C, amused with myself. *I want to post this, you know, like, "How Sarah does date night."* My eyes look egg sized in cavernous sockets. My torso is shapeless, a blank slate of black fabric draped over hollow air.

My iPhone asks, *Is this you?*

In truth I will barely touch the wine that night. It is not only that I fear the calories lurking in that muddy red. My body has lost the ability to metabolize alcohol—a few sips trigger a hangover for days. Caffeine sends a dagger through my head and gut, and solid food hits like swallowed cement. Still, I delight in the delicate tapas we splurge on, C hoping to entice my appetite. Smoked carrots in yogurt sauce, ramen topped with lobster, sourdough and cheese—I photograph them with my phone, fodder for my feed. I take one to three bites a meal.

As I died, I fired off photos to the void, filtered to look like living.

As a child, I had the sense of growing up with two fathers, though only one was spoken of. The public, favored father lived in my mother's Protestant world. He loved her with his English tongue, cheered for Michael Jordan, grilled burgers each July. My other father appeared at a distance, angled toward some other place. Each morning, this father unrolled a carpet to kneel alone before Allah. Tucked between a stationary bike and my parents' mussed-up bed, a slip of holy ground. Sometimes I'd peek in, goose bumps on my neck as I watched his gentle rakat. Finishing, he glanced to his right and left with a soft *salaam*. It was a salutation to the angels on his shoulders, invisible bookkeepers of his deeds. But to me it always felt like a call to some larger crowd. A private multitude.

This multitude was always flickering in and out of view. They hovered in his Qur'an, its gilded pages and delicate script. They slept in dusty jars of dried herbs stored in a corner cabinet. And they spoke, the inaudible second half of my father's Saturday-morning calls. On these days, the sound of booming Arabic drew me to his bedroom door again. I spied him kneeling next to a plastic phone, the curly cord bouncing as he gestured in empty air. I imagined where the cord might lead. Out of his room, joining the tangled phone lines hatching the sky outside. Beyond, to the ropy, undulating wires that followed the train tracks at the edge of our small town. On, marching across fields of corn and wheat and soybeans, until it met some distant shore. Trying to picture its other end, my mind came up blank.

Instead, my parents filled my imagination with American fablery. *You can do anything you put your mind to, ruhi*, my father said. *Just look at me—I came from nothing, and now look where we are.* He cast his glance around our sitting room—umber shag carpet, lumpy couch, a wood-paneled TV. The backdoor, always drafty in the winter, facing a backyard, sandbox and swings. Our life: furnished secondhand, in a Chicago suburb in decline. But to him—first-time possessor of passport and property—it was dazzling. Catching his zeal, I conjured hyphenated dreams. Ballerina-president, astronaut-painter, pilot-rock star. *Do you think I can do it?* I'd ask, just to hear his certainty. *Of course you can.* My father, newcomer from Nothing, felt sure of Everything. *Just keep working hard.*

I was supposed to be a son; my father called me *Tariq* until my birth. Confronted with biology, they chose my name in the delivery room. *Sarah*—a woman of questionable humor, but amenable to any tongue or creed. A name chosen for what it could span, covering the gaps they could not close. Later they'd embellish: *Sarah, like princess!* Perfect for a fairy tale. I could not hear what they did not say: that I arrived after six years of marriage, each one edging on divorce. That they needed me like they needed Amreeka, *America*—a new, pure shape for their belief. One with the power to absolve.

On weekends, he raked leaves or rolled snowballs with us in the yard. In battered work boots, wide strides over the land he was making his, one mortgage payment at a time. He piled overtime hours into evenings, double-long-john winters pouring concrete, laying pipe. He clutched his exhaustion like a talisman, smiled in his sleep. Of course he murmured *hamdulilah*, but it was the country he praised. Soon, he would bring his mother to live with us, lifting her across the Atlantic, into our living room. *So much better, here.* His comparative paradise.

Better than what? I never asked, and he didn't say. He did not speak of his stillborn lives, all those murdered tries. Perhaps it was real forgetfulness. Perhaps silence was a choice made fresh each day. Yet the unspoken pressed against us, filled our hallways with its breath. It flickered on his dark skin, in the twin bites left by the smallpox vaccine they still gave *Third World* babies in his day. His crooked, cavitied tooth. The way he refused to waste food, serving himself expired yogurt and dried-out bread. *I'm used to it*, his answer to my mother's wrinkled nose as he scraped his plate, sucked marrow from chicken bones. But for his own babies, nothing but fresh food. My delicate American belly fed casserole, ketchup, toast.

Do you understand how sick you are? they asked me over and over that first day. I did not know what to say.

MENTAL STATUS EXAMINATION 10-23-2019

PT: Sarah ********

Appearance: Gaunt young woman, appearing slightly older than stated age, with blonde hair pulled back into a ponytail, wearing multiple sweaters layered on top of one another and a large scarf.

Attitude: Pleasant, cooperative

Behavior: Sitting quietly at table, occasionally gesturing with her hands. No PMR or PMA noted. Speech/Language: Normal volume, rate, and prosody. No detectable accent.

Mood: "Nervous"

Affect: Euthymic, appropriately reactive.

Thought process: Linear, goal-directed

Thought content: Focusing on answering questions about her history of disordered eating. No evidence of paranoid thought content.

Perception: Denies auditory or visual hallucinations. Does not appear internally preoccupied.

Is patient exhibiting any aggressive, threatening, or highly impulsive, paranoid behaviors?

(x) No ( ) Yes

Orientation:

Ask: **What is your name?** *Sarah --------*
Where are we right now? *Psychiatric Institute*
What is today's date? *October 23 2019*
What is the season of the year? *Fall*

Attention and Calculation:

Ask: Subtract 7 from 100 and continue to subtract 7 from each subsequent remainder until I tell you to stop. If unable start at 21 and subtract by 3's:

100-93-86-79-72

Abstraction:

How are a bird and a plane alike? *Both fly*
How are an apple and an orange alike? *Both fruit*

Fund of knowledge:

Name the presidents of the U.S. in order? Continue back as far as you can. *Trump, Obama, Bush, Clinton, Bush, Reagan, Carter, Ford.*
Who is the Mayor of New York City? *De Blasio*

Insight: Fair—recognizes that she has an eating disorder but has difficulty describing all the ways in which it impacts her eating and other behaviors.

Judgment: Fair—agreeable to voluntary inpatient treatment

Intelligence: Patient is estimated to be:
( ) Below average ( ) Average (x) Above average
As evidenced by: academic career, fund of knowledge, use of language.

PATIENT'S STRENGTHS: (List at least 2):
Intelligence, humor, supportive family

PATIENT WEAKNESSES: Limited insight, longstanding illness.

❖ ❖ ❖

On a bright day in October, my favorite month, I drifted up a city sidewalk behind C. He pulled my suitcase, dark eyes staring at the red brick tower that was his final hope for me. He had lived months of suppressed panic, trying to persuade me, gently, to get help. By the time he issued his ultimatum, I could barely grasp the words. *We're out of options, Sarah.* Anorexia had ravaged my five-ten frame down to eighty-two hobbling pounds. *It's a miracle your heart is beating,* the consulting doctor told me the week before. *Were you really still going to work?* I hung my startled head. Beside me, I felt C flinch.

My luggage, stuffed with sweaters, still bore a British Airways tag. As a journalist, I'd been reporting in London and Oslo just days before. Resting in my coat pocket, my phone held interview notes, a few photos of the Thames. Souvenirs from the fiction I'd maintained, a denial I could not yet grasp. For months, C had been carrying me up the three flights to our apartment. Each time he lowered me gingerly at our front door, I apologized, then sailed inside. Already forgetting the limp heft of me against his back. Already whirring with a frenzied productivity.

As a newcomer to the psychiatric ward, the ten other patients treated me with kindness, but I also caught frequent stares. One of the teenagers explained to me: *You don't know how you look.* She gave an anemic smile. *It's okay, none of us did at first.* I understood her meaning a month later, when a new arrival appeared and shocked me with her skeleton frame. *That's what you looked like,* my doctor said when I expressed horror at her state. In fact, she informed me, this woman was healthier than I had been.

Later, my best friend, B, will tell me that she'd already said goodbye. *I was so angry at you for leaving. After fifteen years, you'd never meet my kids.* On the morning I signed in for treatment, she texted, *Thank you for staying.* Months after this day, C will burst into sobs that shake his desk and me. Covering his face with his hands long after the tears end. *You were dead. Sarah. You were dead.*

It would be impossible to know how many times my grandmother eluded death. Did it begin with her first birthday, in a Palestinian village sometime around 1930—just as the British occupiers were noting an infant mortality rate twenty times higher than today's? Was it in 1948, when, as a teenage mother, she outran an army with her firstborn son? Was it in the Gazan refugee camp where she drank dirty water that didn't kill her and gave birth to two more boys? There, she buried her only daughter and somehow survived the grief. This, before her third displacement, when she outlasted her second war.

I met her in Amreeka, in bewilderment. A sudden world, a small woman in an embroidered robe. I was seven, she was timeless, heavy gold on drooping earlobes. From her wheelchair, she stretched bangled arms, singing blessings into the room. *This is your grandmother,* my father said, guiding my little body to hers. Engulfed in those arms, in her musk of ʿoud and cheap detergent. A moment later, a wail. I felt the first tear anoint my cheek, her soft breasts undulate. The overflow, I now imagine, of a lifetime's precarity. Of a body that had memorized how happiness adjoins grief.

PROGRESS REPORT PT Sarah ******

Patient began treatment in a behavioral plan
for anorexia nervosa. The program promotes
the **modification of behaviors related to food** by
increasing privileges based on the patient's
ability to eat 100% of her meals, gain weight in
an expected fashion and maintain weight in a
4lb. range.

The patient started with the medical
stabilization phase of 1000 kcal. From the
outset the patient ate 100% of her meals. She
received daily weight-ins, 1 hour observation
following meals. Her diet was advanced to 3000
kcal daily in addition to 2 Ensures Plus. Her
rate of weight gain slowed, requiring her to
advance to 3 Ensures Plus daily to continue
weight gain at a minimum rate of 2.25 lbs per
week.

❖ ❖ ❖

My first inpatient meal was served at noon on the dot in a windowless classroom set with a dozen trays. Around the pushed-together tables sat ten other patients and a stranger wearing a lanyard looped over his zipped coat. Around us, a silence diluted only by the whir of an aging air duct. Under sallow light, the close walls were crowded with pinned-up papers, faded acrylic and collage. *Art therapy.* Soggy latkes sweated on our plastic plates, the air filling with the scent of cheap cooking oil.

My mind had collapsed to a single thought—*I want C. I want C.* Upon arrival, after surrendering my suitcase to be searched, I was whisked to an examination room at the far end of the ward. There, I lay on a table as a phlebotomist struggled to slip a needle into my clenching vein. Next, following orders, I stripped my warm layers to be weighed. Naked, my shivers rattled the manual scale, making the number waver, hop. I returned to the front, arms now dressed in Band-Aids, my eyes searching for C. He was gone—sent off by the head nurse, who explained *there was no reason for him to stay.* I stared at her square face, the hard mouth daring me to complain. *You need to get to your paperwork.*

The clock hands clapped twelve. The man in the lanyard announced, *You may begin.* Around me, a sudden shuffle of napkins and trays. In a haze, I cut into the rubbery potato on my plate. A moment later, my mouth exploded with the long-forgotten taste of grease. I chewed and swallowed, my ears ringing with shock. By the third bite, I paused, fatigued. I looked up to distant stares, patients' jaws working grim and quick. I returned to my plate, taking the full thirty minutes to push through three damp chicken nuggets and a cup of split pea soup. When time was called, I fell back in my seat, staggered by the amount I'd just consumed.

Our supervisor stood up and slowly circled. He paused to inspect each patient's tray, lifting every napkin, shaking each carton of milk or juice. Arriving at mine, he informed me I *failed to complete*, pointing to the mustard-colored dregs of soup clinging to the bottom of the paper cup. *It was an honest mistake*, I wanted to say. But I was speechless as the head doctor arrived to give a *gentle warning*. If I failed again, I would spend the next three meals in isolation. *This is not a punishment*, he said. *We just have to keep things strict, this is the only way.*

The only way—on the ward, all speech was absolute. Our food arrived on a dented trolley pushed by a cheerful, aging man in a hairnet and chinos. We ate under the watch of one or two nurses, as an auxiliary staff member at the front desk surveilled us via live feed. Each room was equipped by a camera hooked to the same stream. Between meals, a staff member was assigned *visual checks*, roving the halls with a clipboard, noting our location four times an hour.

We slept in shared or single rooms, the doors framed by windows with a curtain on the outside. At night, I heard the swish of fabric as each quarter hour passed. I tried not to jump, tried to ignore the face pressed up to the glass, the bright hall light spilling in. For the first three weeks, a drowsing nurse sat at my open door. As a high-risk patient, I was placed under *constant observation*, or CO. I could not help but think of the carceral acronym, *correctional officer.* I could go nowhere without a nurse tailing me. I resented this, though there was nowhere for me to be, aside from a poorly lit toilet reeking of industrial bleach.

The nurse kept the door cracked while I peed. To make sure I didn't topple over. To make sure I didn't exercise or *purge.* The intense scrutiny coated my skin like accusation, threat. But we were assured it was necessary. *It's an insidious disease*, they told us, their impassive faces neutering my anger, thickening my shame. Accountability would help us make *prorecovery choices.* The staff endorsed a program plotted in discrete units of compliance. Our bodies, graphable amalgams of pulse and pounds.

Afraid, and limp after years of hunger, I warped quickly to the shape of this new world. My body sank into long-delayed exhaustion, thoughts thin, flatline gray. At meals, my mind went completely dark, overcome as my phobia of food was hurled against mounds of calories. Surfacing thirty minutes later, I'd gasp for air, somehow even more depleted after the act of nourishment. For weeks, I drifted in coarse silence, making no contact outside the ward, barely speaking within.

During C's nightly visits, I rattled tears, sputtering complaint. When had I agreed to this? Why the punishments, the rules, the too too much food? Could he please, please take me home? His apologies were tender. *Let's try a few more weeks, okay?* Through my dull, cold panic, I saw his face had changed. A new softness where I had not realized it was taut. Eyes still ringed but clearer now. His body, slowly draining of a horror I had not and could never grasp.

My grandmother's small frame held a secret gravity. The ground trembled with her inaugural kisses, a sway in the axis of our suburban home. Overnight, sumac and zaʿatar, dusted the bottom cupboards, SpaghettiOs supplanted by dried goods pulled from her ancient suitcase. Thin floor mats usurped couches in the den. The TV, suddenly displaying Egyptian channels, became a portal to new worlds.

It was in the kitchen that I was first pulled into her atmosphere— spices and steaming meat, rose water and sweat. There was a power in her corporeality, a mesmerizing contrast with the odorless, muted women I was accustomed to. Her ailments lived out loud— groaning, perspiring—yet her flesh reached for, and gave, life. To eat at her table was to submerge in sensuality, to have one's body remembered, stirred. Jostled, kissed, and copiously fed, I was delighted by the new norm of eating with our hands. Beneath the bright cloud of Arabic banter, my fingers wrapped around warm, slick sustenance—feta, maqlouba, mutabaq. Each bite an arrival. *You're eating nothing*, she repeated to each of us, tearing hunks from a chicken thigh and tossing them our way. *Kul, kuli, eat!* She continued until we all fell back, full and polished with grease.

After dinner, we planted our purring bodies on the sitting room floor. My grandmother brewed tea slowly, a ritual of ease. I leaned against her, absorbing the microlanguage of her body—gentle rocking, faint sighs—as the smell of Lipton laced with mint or sage infused my drowsy haze. Stirring, pouring, her mottled hands moved with a dexterity generations deep. I began to speak her Arabic, the فلاحي dialect of our rural roots, embroidered with poetic allusions and quirks of syntax. Her words, her recipes, her movements in the world—through them I imbibed our history. Wisdom and ways swimming through time in the channel of bodies, mothers and daughters and sons, into me.

In pictures and grainy home footage of those days, I see the sturdy self-assurance in my limbs as I flirt with my grandmother, my pudgy hand gesticulating, flecked with molokhea. An aura of similitude fills the space between us, a resemblance that is deeper than our differing forms. In these frames, I glimpse the part of me that has always known the wrap of ورق عنب, the scent of maramiya, the difference between the bright beat of the letter د and the velvety, dark depths of ض.

A moment later, I might be clamoring for pizza or one of my favorite VHS tapes—*Lion King, Winnie the Pooh*, or, unironically, *Aladdin*. My grandmother found joy in these things, too—she loved a slice of beef sausage from Domino's, slathering hers with ketchup or hot sauce. In those days, perhaps, I came closest to my parents' ideal, a *mixed* child not yet mixed up. Sitting between my father and his mother, laughing as all three of us tried to cheat at cards, I felt not Arab or American, but home.

◇ ◇ ◇

At the hospital, the sudden intake of food sent my body into shock. The doctors cut my meals down by two-thirds, trying to coax nutrients into my organs without triggering cardiac arrest. They ordered daily blood draws to track dangerous chemical swings. My heart fluttered with wild electrolytes, blood pressure dropping to a whimper, stomach seizing into knots. I fell frequently, folding against the wall, sinking into couches and chairs.

You're one of the worst cases I've ever seen, my social worker repeated as I slumped on the couch across from her. I watched her eyebrows arch under platinum bangs. *You really couldn't tell you had a problem?* It was a favorite subject of my *care team*—this absence of my *insight. Insight,* in psychiatry, is defined as the capability of psychiatric patients to recognize and accept that they are suffering from a mental illness...[it is] the reflexive awareness of oneself as a "diseased subject." Anorexia, more than many other illnesses, is defined by insight's lack. The British Airways sticker on my suitcase. All that uncanny energy. The mirror that hid death's mark from me.

In the hospital, I recognized the devastation of anorexia first in those around me—the patient with permanent heart damage. The bodies swollen with edema, the knuckles jutting like stones. Ten women, one man, twenty advanced degrees between us. Some of them joking that they were *lifers,* alone during visiting hours, their families estranged. In sweatpants we shuffled between the three common rooms, our faces shifting weather. Red-blotched outrage. Uncombed resignation. Brittle cheerfulness. Each set of eyes opaque—then flashing open. Releasing, for an instant, a glimpse of private hells.

You really couldn't tell you had a problem? I failed to share my social worker's shock. Of course I had always sensed I was an aberration. But what alarmed me was not the vise grip of compulsion, not my cage of hunger nor the lock around my throat. These were the lesser tortures, abuse that came to feel like comfort, obliteration as balm. In the haze of starvation, I could scarcely recall—how I have lived for years inside a throbbing sense of loss, a sorrow I could not explain. How it frightened me to hold palpable despair inside a life called *fortunate, beautiful.* This paradox worse, perhaps, than the sorrow itself. A secret I kept tightly, amid real and forced happiness. Feeding my body to compulsions. Chasing the violent mirage of relief until my limbs disappeared. Until I forgot every country.[1] Until I could not imagine stopping, could not remember why I ran at all.

❖ ❖ ❖

Hospital rules forbade us from our phones and limited our laptop use to an hour in the evening. In lieu of high-tech communication, family and friends sent letters and cards. Some envelopes held dried flowers, bright gold autumn leaves—*sending you a piece of fall!* I could glimpse them only for a moment, as a nurse pulled the flaking flora from envelopes and discarded it with an apology. They were under strict instructions to confiscate anything that might conceivably be eaten or used for self-harm. I wondered which of these scenarios they were imagining as they swept the oak crumbs from their desk.

They permitted the enclosed photos, though, and I soon covered my wall with snapshots of my past. In long, trickling afternoons I sat and stared at the mosaic. I saw a young woman taking hikes in Guatemala, sauntering heel-clad into the Louvre, hugging a sister in L.A. This was my story as I had learned to read it—a series of peaks, instants of legible happiness posing as an entirety. The heft of life—its inscrutable, monotonous, chaotic weight—banished from the frame.

The first letter from my parents contained three photos, all graduation days. In each, I beam in a different cap and gown— first blue, then black, then violet. In each, my parents wear the same half-delirious grins. My rosy mother, my father olive brown, dressed in their Kohl's and JCPenney best. Between them, I wear my hair long and curled in dutiful imitation of the other blonds I knew. My smile is wide with a happiness both real and rehearsed. Each milestone, foretold so long, arrived like déjà vu.

The day of my college graduation, I sat in a folding chair on the campus football field, submerged in wagging tassels, squealing selfie-takers, *Pomp and Circumstance*. My thoughts fluttered to my family. They had looked so tired after their long drive from Illinois to Philadelphia. In the packed stadium, would they find a place to sit? I worried for my parents. They always seemed fragile to me, their gentle faces so open amid a crowd. I thumbed through the ceremony program, found my name nestled at the far end of the alphabet. As always, it jutted out at the right side of the column, a jagged branch of consonants breaking uniformity. An asterisk dangled off the last of the fifteen letters, *S*████*. A dandelion seed, a mark of honors I had worked four years to attain.

The sight of my name brought both pride and a wince. By then I'd spent two-thirds of my life in the United States, each year watching people treat this name like a deformity. In Arabic, our family name comprises just five untroubling letters. A proud name, a good one, neither too grand nor obscure. But unlike my father's alias—he switched his first name from *Ziyad* to *Ed*—our family name grew long and jagged in English. Growing up, I apologized countless times—to strangers on the phone, to puzzled teachers, to Smiths and Williamses and Whites, as they butchered the pronunciation. Chuckling, face hot, my hands batting our bothersome syllables out of their way. *Oh, don't worry, that's close enough.*

My mind shot again to my father. I knew he'd stare at those letters, too, long and unabashedly. There was something hungry in his face each time he saw our name in ink. I knew he'd gather each program from my mother and siblings, stacking all five under his arm. I knew he'd carry them back home, tucked in his suitcase, between his clothes. There, he would add them to the boxes that

hold a paper trail dating to his birth in Gaza. An informal archive—
photographs, certificates, his every report card. Old rosters for his
college soccer league, his first work ID. Stacks that moved with us,
resting in garages, the bulk of a small child. His presence a truth he
could never trace enough. All that paper, dormant but prepared.[2]

In my coldest hours on the ward, the photo mosaic felt like a
mausoleum, a shrine to a dead friend. Senders had hoped the snapshots would inspire cheerfulness, reminders of my *real life*. But these
scenes stirred only the edges of my brain, like murmurs scarcely
overheard. My body barely knew the woman in the photos, who
lived in self-exile from her senses, drifting on the fringes of her flesh.
As I stared, a thick sense of absence gathered under my throat. *How
wonderful it almost was, if I had only been there.*

◇ ◇ ◇

In the hospital, our hallway ended at a pair of buzzer-locked doors facing south. Peeking through their small windows, we saw a mirror image of our ward—long linoleum, laminated doors, the dim fluorescent sky. Over there, we were told, lived *members of the community.* While our ward was highly specialized for treating eating disorders, the south end was a catchall for other mental maladies. Some of *them*, a nurse explained in hushed tones, *used to be on the street.*

Many of the staff worked on both halls, and I overheard them comparing notes. On our side were the *spoiled girls.* We were mostly white, mostly young and female; our sickness, in their telling, was more of a privileged folly.* But over there—darker skinned, less affluent, often insecurely housed—were the *real crazy ones.* They were given labels that, unfairly, made me fear. *Psychotic. Bipolar. Borderline. Dissociative.*

---

* "Large-scale studies have found that rates of all eating disorders are the same or higher in all racial and ethnic groups as compared to white individuals. Despite the lack of differences in rates, individuals with minoritized, marginalized, and other intersectional identities are less likely to receive care and services. . . given the multiple traumas that women of color are exposed to, they may be more vulnerable to eating disorders."
—National Eating Disorders Association

An extensive survey published in the *Journal of Adolescent Health* . . . found that 15% of the transgender people surveyed reported an eating disorder diagnosis within the last year, compared with 3.52% of cisgender sexual minority women, 2.06% of cisgender sexual minority men, 1.85% of cisgender heterosexual women, and 0.55% of cisgender heterosexual men."
—Baxter Ekern, *Why Transgender People Are More Likely to Develop an Eating Disorder*

Our treatment was funded by a university research program, which meant we paid nothing for care that could have cost $2,000 a day. Frequently, some well-dressed assistant appeared, a pantsuit amid white coats. They retrieved a patient, signing us out at the front desk. We were taken downstairs or downtown, to rooms that were always too cold. We signed waivers and lay in fMRI machines, or had nodes taped to us, administering small electric shocks.

Sometimes we were asked to play *decision games* as they watched our brains light up their screens. On other days we opened our mouths to be swabbed for DNA. We filled out surveys and questionnaires, becoming data they promised to anonymize. They looked for *behavioral and neurobiological underpinnings*, tried to predict *longitudinal relapse rates*. It would take years to publish any results, but we were thanked for our contribution. We were furthering science, they said, *saving future lives*.

And we spent many cold predawn mornings grouped at the far corner of the southern hallway, near those double doors. Summoned by the hoarse voice of a nurse, we took turns in the examination room, where we stripped naked to be weighed. Sleepy, sullen, nervous, we clutched our bathrobes close to resist the chill or to hide our changing, curving forms. One patient—the only man—always rose before the nurse's call. We found him sitting by the exam room door, silently insisting on going first. After, he emerged with silent eyes and raced back to his room.

Occasionally, loitering by those double doors, we glimpsed a figure in the south hall. *Look!* someone would whisper, and we'd all turn to stare. I only ever saw them obliquely—a body shuffling away from me or slipping behind a wall. Later, these fragments grew into embarrassing clichés. I imagined shadowy figures in nightgowns, all echoes of Bertha Mason—Jane Eyre's foil, Brontë's madwoman in the attic.

As a girl, I'd read the novel three times, enchanted by the elfin heroine. I aspired to be like Jane—tidy and delicate. Strong willed yet refined. In my rereads, I jumped over the parts that mentioned Bertha. I was chilled by her, the rejected Creole, *that dark-haired, clothed hyena.* I shuddered each time she burned alive, guilty at my sense of relief.

I felt guilt, too, at the way that south hallway pricked me with unease. There, I saw the mirror-sameness of my own confinement. The dense battle inside my mind between illness and intellect. Many nights, trenched by insomnia, I thought of the rooms next door. I wondered if some soul lay parallel, awake with me.

◇ ◇ ◇

In college, I read *Wide Sargasso Sea*, a postcolonial prequel to *Jane Eyre*, published in 1966. In those pages I found my latent scorn for Rochester—that spoiled, petulant colonist—burgeoning. Meanwhile, Jean Rhys's erotic rendering of Bertha, née Antoinette Cosway, stirred something between my legs. I loved her fierceness, her danger, even her instability. Her Jamaica, dripping with a ripe, hot power, blasted Jane out of me. I blushed my way through our class discussion of the book. As I carried it home, it smoldered like red coals in my bag.

Later that year, I lay warm with rum on a carpeted floor. It was south of midnight, electronic bass thick in the air. I stared up at M, who was kneeling over me. A woman with skin like my father's, dark hair tickling my cheek. She asked if she could kiss me. My body said *please*. My mind replied—*You can't do that to your family.* I gazed drunk-long at the path I wouldn't take, her arms soft in the light of a mute TV. Finally, I made a sad smile with my mouth, my shoulders an apology. *Oh.* She sat up, regretful and surprised.

I used the name of the man I didn't love, whom I would be faithful to and hide behind. The word *lie* did not occur to me. I was practiced in this turn—using language to erase, casting will against desire. Meanwhile, my flesh witnessed. Waited. Inscribed all I didn't say.

Occasionally, on the ward, I felt a stampede inside. A sudden animal desire to claw apart the eggy, faceless walls. I raced to the landline phone, with its too-short metal cord, and punched the numbers for C's cell. *Please, let me come home. Please.* I knew it was unfair to beg like this, but still I writhed and snarled. *I have to. I have to. I have to get out of here.*

My own intensity frightened me, but such outbursts were common in our sealed-off world. Often, another patient sat next to me on the second landline, sobbing some similar plea. But one afternoon my psychiatrist cut in midcall. In a long wool skirt, she stood over me, curls wagging like scolding heads. *You. Need. To. Calm. Down. There's no reason,* no reason, *for you to be this upset.*[3]

I hiccuped, nodding and rubbing my wet cheeks as I forced my shoulders back. I was desperate to project dignity to this woman, the head of my *care team*, arbiter of my privileges and, eventually, the date of my release. But it was increasingly difficult to tame the wildness surging in me. Its roar took my breath away. Something long silenced reaching for speech, groaning my whole body as it strived.

Still, I rebuked my tears, shame like hot mud in my throat. The doctor was right—there was *no reason* to act this way, to justify my pounding chest. *No reason. No reason,* I repeated internally. *You're fine. You're safe.* Waiting for the words to solidify, to overwrite my quaking chest. The doctor frowned, asked if I'd like an ice cube—a *distress tolerance tool.* Wanting to appear cooperative, I nodded. *Thank you.* She walked to the kitchen, returned with a cup, which she turned over in my hand. The frozen hunk was shaped like a small grenade. She nodded and walked away. For a long time, I sat there under harsh hall lights, cold water dripping down my arm.

◇ ◇ ◇

I lived in the outside world—outside the tunnels, that is—for twenty years, unable to breathe no matter how I tried, like a man who is drowning. But I did not die. I wanted to get free but could not; I was a prisoner unable to escape. But I did remain unchained. How often I yelled at those about me, "Please, everyone! I groan at the burden of the great secret I bear on my shoulders! Please help me!" But all that came from beneath my mustache was a meowing sound, like that of a cat.

These, favorite lines from my favorite book, came often to mind. A strange little volume published by Emile Habibi, a Palestinian author born in 1922 Haifa, titled *The Secret Life of Saeed the Ill-Fated Pessoptimist.* Part science fiction, part political satire, called by critics *bewildering, unsolvable, bizarre.* When I stumbled onto its pages at the age of twenty, it struck me as the best map of the world I had ever seen.

In group sessions, we named our neuroses or had them pointed out. Therapists in pilling sweaters made lists on a whiteboard that never fully erased. *Exercise Compulsion, Body Checking, Restricting, Purging, Counting, Weighing, Compensating.* In the early weeks I found something refreshing in our discussions, which brought both tears and giddy morbid jokes. A kinship built of shared hells and humility, of hidden things made plain.

But as time passed, the curriculum cycled back to its start. We met at the same whiteboard-palimpsest, green marker scrawled over brown. Asked again to peel back our scabs, to bare our festering places, hanging our heads over the blood. We were not asked who had cut us or why the injuries went uncleaned. A few gripes about *diet culture* aside, no one spoke of the carnage the world could be. No suggestion that outside these four walls, society itself might be diseased. Anorexia, our arid planet. Like Amreeka, a land without history.[4]

◇ ◇ ◇

She loves you very much, habibti, my father reminded me in phone calls through my adolescence and early adulthood. *She always prays for you.* Somehow, my grandmother had become this—a tender figment. Love channeled from a distance. Disembodied, secondhand.

On a Tuesday, I broke, halfway through a buttered bagel.

For weeks, I had been chewing through larger and larger meals. Mostly, I vacated my senses, returning thirty minutes later as I stared at a scraped plate. But that morning, biting a stale cinnamon raisin, I knew with sudden, utter certainty that I could not carry on. I watched my hand slip my bread under a napkin in a flash.

Around me, the noise of breakfast vanished under the booming of my heart. Then the napkin was balled up with the bagel, thrust deep inside my pocket. I glanced up. Every pair of eyes appeared to be elsewhere. My limbs went limp, my cheeks flushed with blood. I suppressed a smile. For weeks I had ducked around the ward, bowed like a fearful child, jumping to obey. Now, I tingled, drunk on petty rebellion.

The supervising nurse waited until the end of the meal before turning to me. She spoke in a low voice. *Stay right there.* She moved to the door and called to the manager down the hall. I froze, swept with bewilderment at my stupidity. *Half a bagel? What the fuck? What was I thinking?* The other patients were dismissed, a few casting sympathetic glances at me. I'd been in their place several times, as others were caught hiding food. Each time, I was baffled at their audacity. At the futility.

◊ ◊ ◊

To live with anorexia is to live in a fascist state of being, one ruled by a cruel and illogical board of Kafkaesque tyrants . . . a rule inexplicably coalesces from nothingness and turns into gospel in a matter of milliseconds, writes Kelsey Osgood in *How to Disappear Completely.* Here enters the dark genius of anorexia, the logic of its insanity. The tyrant's strength can be captivating. First, it allures with an illusion of control, seizing familiar myths: sex appeal as panacea, self-discipline as ultimate ideal. Inchoate emotions—fear, emptiness, anxiety—funneled into a clear morality. A body on the way to becoming *better,* consuming only what is *good.* In a world wide with chaos, a narrow offer of purity.

The first *no* is electrifying. Self-denial is a power that feels limitless and clean. After, to repeat this false euphoria, deprivation must be stretched further. Further again. A sandwich is halved, then becomes a crust. One mile run becomes four, then eight. And so the disease sprawls, colonizing time and energy. Eventually, unchecked, sickness engulfs even the most sacred things. Relationships and work. Commitment. Honesty. These losses barely register because tyranny, at this point, feels like benevolence. Relief as life's ambiguity succumbs to oppressive certitude. Days gone quiet, gray. Senses constricted to their narrowest point, trapped in a closed compulsive loop.

At its most ruinous, it kills language completely. Thought severed from form, an exile most profound. *The tenacity of anorexia comes from its discursive construction*, write Andrew Lock, David Epston, and Richard Maisel in "Countering That Which Is Called Anorexia": *[It] confines and silences those inside it, so severely does it limit and usurp the ways and means they have of storying their experience.* This is the warmth that overtakes the frostbitten sleeper just before her snowy death. The seduction, nearly complete. I nestled into the cold. Silence had become my only dream.[5]

◇ ◇ ◇

When my grandmother died, I was startled by the size of the nothing that I felt. I grieved for my father, but told none of my friends she passed. I was ashamed to realize they had never heard me speak her name.

They buried her in Jeddah, Saudi Arabia. *Jeddah*—the transliteration of جدة, Arabic for *grandmother*. On the shore of the Red Sea, a city nicknamed *Mermaid* and *Ocean's Bride*. Her final refuge, a home we'd shared for half my childhood. I did not make it to the funeral— Muslim burials are immediate, make no time for transatlantic flights. It felt as if, for my arid grief, I had been both spurned and spared. Instead, inside a buttoned coat, I wandered Philly streets named after trees. Silent, waiting for a window to open inside of me.

The last time I saw her, I kissed her and saw both our smiles strain. By then I'd regained my Arabic, but there was little I could say. A freshman at a prestigious university, I was fulfilling the family dream and felt bewitched by a life in bloom. She seemed to have fallen out of time. In a dim Jeddah apartment, she lay too still on a sleeping mat, TV beams playing on her sunken cheeks.

There had been no single moment of abandonment. Mine was a betrayal of degrees. Somewhere, I had begun to discipline my love, had taken in language about value that did not include her kind. My body, too, was long since honed into all that was not-her. Its memories of our enmeshment, the soft shelter of her lap, locked inside my bones. That last day—or was it night?—we murmured rote blessings in dim light. Well-worn words. An ancient choreography and an echo of the first salaams she had laid on me. Soon, a second bout of cancer would take her. She might have known this; I did not. Around her, the air was thick with unspoken things.

I don't know what came over me, I said in a post-bagel summit with my care team. *It just happened, like something outside of me.* I could barely hear my own words over the roar of self-loathing and disbelief. But when I looked up, I was surprised to see smiles and nods. *Exactly. Are you starting to see now how severely ill you are?* My doctor's eyebrows arched at his patient's breakthrough. Once again, I listened to the official version of me: a woman shattered by her monomania, the desire to be thin. Tragic insanity, malignant narcissism. *You hid that bagel because your obsession with losing weight is* that *strong.*

She sent me out of session with the assignment to complete pages in a body image workbook, but I faltered at the writing prompts. I could neither *list my least favorite body parts* nor *name three things to celebrate about my looks.* These were impossible not because I loathed my body but because I had no idea how to enter it at all. Though I knew other patients spent hours agonizing over mirrors and scales, I had always avoided both. I realized I could not remember a time when I had not felt this way—vaporous, a fugitive from my own flesh.

Staring at the useless pages, something in me began to tear. In these humiliating weeks, I had taken the doctors' story of me as my own. But now, the faint beginnings of a rift. It was true—*I was sick*—but this affliction was more than a revulsion of body fat. My bizarre behavior, the starved limbs, the hordes of shame—these were the groanings of an alien language. A muffled, fevered semaphore. In my next session, I looked up at my doctor's face and read condescending boredom. In an instant, I accepted that I would not heal inside those walls. The staff, which worked deftly to restore my flesh, could not see what stalked my blood.

A resigned obedience overtook me then. Good behavior to hasten my release. At meals, I kept my eyes lowered, finishing with time to spare. I complied with the sit-and-never-stand rule during our free hour. I helped clean up after our Friday Yahtzee game. I continued to avoid mirrors but smiled back at the nurses who told me I was *gaining on schedule*. Trying to believe the inching number on the scale could be a simple victory. Attempting daydreams in which my fleshy body felt free. But when my mind turned to the future, I always found it blank. I remained a diffuse collection of impressions, absent the gravity of desire or intent. Beneath the empty canvas of my mind, that red murmur persisted. I sensed it was only biding time.

PROGRESS REPORT PT *** *******

Over the past months the patient consistently
and convincingly **denied SI** and she was very
engaged in **enhancing her coping skills** should her
level of distress rise again in the future. At
the time of discharge she reported an overall
positive mood, a **hopeful outlook** and + **enjoyment**
from activities on the unit.

◇ ◇ ◇

One of the first Arabic words I learned was *sunny*. A morsel of sounds I loved to munch on, filling my mouth with honey gold. مشمس, *mush-miss*, I savored under my breath. So like مشمش: *mish-mish*, *apricot*, one of my favorite fruits. Summer nights, my grandmother cut one after another, feeding me small velvet suns. In winter, we ate mish-mish as leathery morsels, or as translucent jam smudged inside pita. For years, I could not remember the English words for these two things. *Sunny, apricot*—why would I use these paler, colder words when I possessed their truest form?

Besides, mish-mish was something we ate in Arabic. Before we moved to Saudi Arabia, mish-mish came from the *Middle Eastern* grocery store we drove long Illinois miles to reach. There, I trailed my father, whose banter with the store clerk began before his foot was through the door. I stared into barrels brimming with pistachios, bulgur, rice. I admired the plastic bins full of brine and floating cheese, pickles of vivid yellow, purple, pink. Inhaling amid loose herbs and spices, I felt the tingle of unconsummated memory hover just beneath my brain. And I laughed in amazement as the grocer inevitably plied my hand with treats. Dates, rosewater nougat, sesame biskut. No other store I knew gave things away for free.

In the hospital, every breakfast arrived with a yogurt cup. The fruit-on-the-bottom type, individual packs. It was the kind of decadence I dreamed of as a child, when our fridge held only buckets of fat-free plain. On our trays, the fruit flavors came at random, in predictable varieties. *Cherry, Strawberry, Blueberry*. One morning, I was surprised by an orange-colored top. *Apricot*. Something reared up in my chest. *Mish-mish*, I whispered to myself as I pulled the first bite to my lips. Artificial sweetener gummed my teeth. The flavor was like light.

I felt the faint twitch of instinct stir in my fingers. A loosening in my abdomen. For the space of a yogurt cup, I gobbled. There was delight in the swift dips of my spoon, the press of jam and sweet cream against my tongue. As I licked, my mind's ear stirred, filled with sudden words. صحتين وعافية حبيبتي. يخليكي الله Dormant, familiar blessings, sung in my grandmother's voice.

The utterances should have come as a shock; it was years since she had died, and her memory seldom rose to mind. But as the rhythmic benedictions continued, my body softened, rocking gently to their beat. الله يحبب الناس فيكي. كُلي حبيبتي An old-young peace spread like ink, released from my deepest cells. I finished the food on my tray, silently answering. تِسلم إيديكي يا ستو. *May Allah bless your hands.* For an instant I was sure that if I turned around, I would see my grandmother there.

The rest of my stay, I arrived each morning hoping for more mish-mish. None came. When I asked fellow patients if they'd ever received an apricot yogurt, they all said that they had not.[6]

Though I maintained a flawless record at meals from that point on, the staff often admonished me that my chances of recovery were not good. *Only one-third fully make it,* they told me. Mine was a longstanding illness—fifteen years with minimal treatment, pushing me to the far, wrong end of the bell curve. The week before my discharge, my psychiatrist told me she wouldn't be surprised if I came back. When I fumed to C about this later on, he was quick to dismiss her words. *That's not going to happen.* But at night, my fear beat its wings against the windowpane. I could not tell whether it was trying to fly out or in.

My social worker told me to wait a few months before trying to resume work. She prescribed a seven-hour-daily outpatient program for me to attend the first twelve weeks. *There's no way you're ready to return to normal life.* I flinched, then caught myself. To the suggestion of three more months of forgone income and autonomy, I returned a smile. *Oh no, of course not,* I agreed.

In my discharge papers, she made a note in a column marked Patient Weaknesses:

Patient is over-eager to please her care team.

In my head, I counted: 144 hours to my release.

On my final day, the staff exchanged their warnings for distant smiles, lukewarm congratulations. My file had closed. They gave me a pass to eat breakfast at a diner down the street, supervised by a nurse of my choosing. I took Patty, a proud *Jersey gal* who had a naked crush on C. *Girl, stay straight out there, okay?* She repeated her familiar warning to me as we sat down: *You don't want to go die and leave your man behind for some other woman!*

I laughed, surveying the huge, laminated menu. My stomach sparked with adrenaline. I ordered pancakes, thrilled at my breezy tone, the server's cursory nod. *Just two women out for a bite*, I thought, starstruck at my ability to be so ordinary. I pictured myself devouring the food with the gusto I had once envied in the undiseased. The stack came quickly, the cakes flopping over the side of my plate. *Well, these are too big, obviously*, I thought, spreading the butter paper thin, carefully eating half. Patty had been the one to report me for hiding the half bagel. Now, she winked. *Don't worry about it. This is your day.* I left the rest behind, my carafe of syrup still full.

When I returned to the ward, the other patients thrust notes into my hand: *Today your real life begins!—You can do this!—Never look back!!* Behind me, the metallic slam of the two front doors. I turned and saw C. The nurses burst into cheers of *Congratulations!* but he seemed not to hear. His eyes latched to mine, his face so naked in its joy that I turned briefly into stone. *Turn back*, the thought flapped in my chest. Nothing this pure and breakable belonged anywhere near me.

But I pushed my way back into the moment, hungry to make it mine. My social worker stood and gave me a first and final hug. *Be very careful out there.* I tried to mirror her solemnity, but all I could think about was the door. Outside, a gray, grainy rain misted us as we ran-walked to the curb. C hoisted my suitcase a few inches from the concrete, too excited to wait on dragging wheels. My hair went horizontal in the humidity. We slid into a taxi, its worn seats smelling of sweat and cigarettes.

As the driver pulled away, C snapped a selfie, our faces shining with condensation and relief. He sent the photo off to B and family, the group text filling with crying emojis and hearts. *You both look so happy!* In the frame, my smile is almost too wide, eyes blazing with fear or hope.

Part II

لسان
Language

غربة

Ghourba

Every Arabic word bears a secret.

Each one blooms from a root of two or three letters (on rare occasions, four).

The seed always appears, on its surface, simple:

to write: ك - ت - ب

to build: ب - ن - ي

to trust: ص - د - ق

But inside the kernel sleeps chapters of meaning, volumes of possibility. The letters unfurl, move around on a vast web of forms, swelling with added letters or chiseled by diacritics. The sounds bend and stretch to reveal hidden inflections. Concepts become causative, reflexive, transitive. Patterns emerge, letters constellating into clouds of meaning, an exuberance of nuance.

From م - ل - ع—*to know*—grows علّم, *to teach*. Later, تعلّم, *to learn*. Later still: استعلم, *to inquire*. Individual characters foresting into a story.

Grasp of these grammar systems opens centuries of significance, a world of thought and speech—but true fluency cannot be taught. Language desires not mastery but surrender. A life immersed in the world to which the words belong. Only then will the entire body become an ear, fine tuned to the time and silence that quivers around speech. Deeper still, discover that some words require initiation all their own. Their meanings are like one-way glass, a view only some will know.

غربة is one such word.

No Arabic speaker I've met can define it in a sentence, or even five. Its truth is an aura, an aperture. Nevertheless, I will spell some of it for you here.

It comes from the three letters غ ر ب—a root that means both *strange* and *West*.

غربة is a state of being derived from both these terms. It is the word used by Arabic speakers to describe the experience of being *abroad*, but the meaning evoked is not one of holiday or adventure—it is closer to *away*. As in *away from home*. *Absence* as a place.

It can be used anytime home is left but is most frequent, and most pronounced, when the speaker has gone beyond the Arab world. It evokes an alienation that is reflexive, radiating from a displaced, unsettled core. Exile as a fugue, a self dislodged from self.

The place that one leaves is بيت, بلد, *home*. This means not only land but شعب, أهل, *people*. And in the Arab sensibility—I'm tempted to say the human sensibility—a self is inextricable from these two. Each غربة, in this way, is utterly unique. Contours shaped around particular losses, names and bodies yearned for, and out of reach.

The *strangeness* of being *away* and *westward*, then, is an estrangement from oneself; surrounded by غرباء, strangers, one becomes, too, غريب.*

---

* A stranger.

❖ ❖ ❖

Occasionally, when we were small, our father spoke to us of geography.

Daddy is from a place called Palestine, he said in a lesson captured by my mother on the family's camcorder. In the footage, my father sits in a small rocking chair, brown eyes intent, a little shy. My younger brother and sister are absorbed by the array of blocks on the floor, but I am close to my father's feet, fluffy blond head thrown back, mouth pink and agape. He holds up a globe, his fingers sliding toward a sliver of brown and green. He tilts it toward me to reveal cramped lettering: *Israel/Palestine*.

I hop up to look, my nose nearly skimming the painted plastic as I squint at the hair-thin ink. I am vaguely aware of a thing called *countries*, loosely grasping that these are places full of people that are like—but unlike—me. There is no mention, today or any day that I can recall up to that point, of the first half of that forward-slashed name, that thing called *Israel*. There are no tales of shed blood, no wistful tributes to a lost homeland. My father simply hops his fingers, jumping decades and tragedies.[7] Due south, he points to an orange oblong slab of land. *That's Saudi Arabia. That's where Sittoo lives.* My father uses the فلاحي word *sittoo—honored lady*—our dialect's term for *grandmother*. I squint again, trying to see her.

My grandmother, like these countries, feels important and vague. It would be one year until she came to live with us and two years until we uprooted and moved to Jeddah, her adopted city by the sea. In our lesson, my father did not linger, did not try to bridge the difference between *Jeddah* and *Palestine*. Instead, the video shows him smiling, rolling the world to my left. He lands on a green sprawl labeled *The United States.* His finger taps another dot, *Chicago,* which clings to a lake shaped like a tear.

And here is where we live, my father concludes, his voice a flourish. Impressed by the blue distance between *there* and *here,* I blurt, *Whoooooa. Those are . . . those are two faraway places!* My father looks up at the camera, his face twitching with repressed laughter. *That's right, habibti,* he replies, trying to match my seriousness. The lesson ends here, gaps passed over, dismissed. I have enjoyed the attention of my father, playing with this ball called *The World.* But after this lesson, I remain just as bewildered by a pair of photos hanging down the hall.

At the far end of a row of family portraits, these two were smaller than the rest. Daily, I passed by them, trying in vain to avert my eyes. Each time, I failed, back of my neck pricking as I raised my head to stare. The first photo is small, its frame a cheap imitation gold. Inside floats a black-and-white image of a barefoot little boy. He squints in long-gone sunshine, a crease in the photo cutting a furry line above his brow. His resemblance to my brother is striking, yet the somber child feels sealed off.

It was my mother who informed me that this boy was my father, standing in a place called *Gaza.* A name with serrated edges, a word I'd not hear again until years later, buzzing on angry TVs. Her explanation ended there, and I felt with strange certainty that I was not meant to ask more. Instead, I studied the images—the sand and debris at the boy's feet. Jagged, harsh shadows suggesting noise and heat. The whole scene left me feeling both lonely and alarmed.

The second photo was better preserved, and more ominous to me. A black-and-white portrait of the same small boy with his mother, posed unsmiling side by side. The woman only vaguely resembled the grandmother I would come to know. Still in her thirties, her cheekbones were full and smooth, her thick black hair tied in a loose ponytail. She unnerved me with her dead-forward stare, the grim line of her mouth. The boy tilted toward her, regarding the camera skeptically, as if ready to defend. Chaos seemed to quiver just outside the camera's gaze.

These photos jarred with the others on the wall. The rest were poised, inviting, blooming from sepia to color. Shots of my mother's childhood: a blond girl in bobby socks. A picture of her own mother, a woman with coiffed hair, hands on a glossy harp. Bright photos of our young family, taken in a Kmart studio against a blue-cloud wall. I memorized all these pictures, imagining myself into their worlds. But I passed my eyes over the corner that held my father and his mother. Looking at them directly left me cold, swimming in something I couldn't name.

◇ ◇ ◇

The day of my discharge, C and I rush up the stairs of our third-story walk-up, noticing but not remarking at the way my legs ride the stairs easily. In the weeks before my hospitalization, C had carried me, fireman-style, up to our door. Now we stand together at the threshold, cheeks close as C reaches from behind me to turn the key. The lock clicks once, twice. I crash inside, dropping my backpack as the apartment surges toward me. It looks smaller than I recalled, tidy, with traces of dust that betray disuse. For the last four months, C has commuted uptown to visit me each night after work, riding the train nearly two hours home afterward, arriving only to crash in bed.

On our table, three bouquets of flowers are backlit by a window slurred with rain—one from C, another from his parents, a third from my family. I run to the bedroom to scoop up our startled cat, Mowgli, and turn to the sound of a loud pop. C grins, brandishing a bottle of Veuve Clicquot, sweet vapor wafting from its uncorked neck. He forgot to put it in the fridge so we sip it warm, smacking our lips before reaching for each other's.

The first kiss floods me with microfamiliarities. The soft, urgent bottom lip. The faint, warm scent of his neck. Dormant sensations—pleasure, safety, relief—stir, whirling in the dark barrel of me. Our tongues search, accelerate. His hand grasps the meat of my arm, and my head swarms with conversations from the hospital. How often the women agonized about intimacy—fearing their *restored* flesh would disgust their men. *We're keeping the lights off. Forever.*

Unlike them, I do not fear C's disgust. Even when I was my most skeletal, he called me *beautiful*, his conviction calling from somewhere beyond the literal. Then, though my sickness was invisible to me, I saw others flinch at what I became, their distance widening. Still, I saw him see me lovely. At our engagement party, a lifelong friend of his pulled me aside. Informed me, *C doesn't love easily. But when he does, he gives it everything.* She leveled sea-colored eyes at me and held a few long beats. The party ruckus fell from my ears as I submitted to her search. I was relieved when she clinked my glass, the jingle of ice cubes waving me on.

So far, her words have proved true. C's love is a green tree, bursting in my living room.

Still, raising my head, I struggle to meet his gaze. A man of fewer words than me, his eyes are a multitude. Now I see a hopeful hunger. Joy, unafraid. And it is not my body that constricts as we strip but the space inside my chest. I look away from his eagerness, chuckle, say, *Okay, easy there.* It is a running joke between us—my persistent shyness, even after several years.

I did not flinch this way with other men. Their eyes always seemed to look just past me or else glazed over with fantasy. I was eleven when the first boy taught me how to please him—he was fourteen, the older brother of a playmate, pulling me around the corner from my house. He started calling me his *girlfriend*, and I learned myself as character. Growing up, I would find stories like this one everywhere, in the press of others' words or lips. Their pleasure, a reward I had not sought but then felt beholden to achieve.

I was primed for this sort of love, the kind shaped around another's want. As a child, my parents' smiles lit me gold from toe to throat. Too often, the air around them seemed to pucker, sagging with a load I did not understand. I lived to be the brief break in their clouds, to conjure the Daughter They Deserved. Her form shifting across the years, but always cheerful, hardworking, and weightless. When She brought them delight, I stood back, half-warmed by the glow. A stranger grateful just to be in the room.

And a stranger I would remain. Occasionally a man would make my body run hot, but mostly, I moved inside romance like a good tenant. Sojourning in others' stories, I learned the dialects of their affection, of their need. The men were mostly kind, and I called my gratitude *love*. *Perhaps this could be me*—I tried to believe, as my lines shifted with each one. And when I left those men—over and over, I left—I told myself it was not because I was cruel. I claimed to be a *free spirit*, but the greater truth was I feared the shelters I built for myself. In the end, what I loved most was the door.

But C confounds me. The self he offers feels light on artifice, directs me to no supporting role. He startles me with his breezy ease, anchored somehow with solidity. Against him, champagne-kissed in our apartment, I feel translucent, vaporous. Though my trust of him is deep, I still fight a squirm at the sense of being seen.[8] I hold his gaze to the count of five, then lean into his lips. Relief in closed eyelids. Gently, we begin to move again.

A faint plop as my sweater hits the floor. The sudden brush of air on my arms. I see shock, reverence in C's eyes at the sight of healthy flesh. *You were dead, Sarah. You were dead.* A little shock in me, too, to find that this time I do not flinch. *Stay with him*, I exhort myself as he pulls me in.

The first difference is the lack of pain—before, despite C's meticulous care, sex often left me wincing, even bruised. Now, I have enough flesh to be clasped, to keep me from shivering when bare. Still, we are soft with each other, quiet like the morning's rain. I close my eyes to taste his touch. Starved, I had lacked most sensation. Then, I relied on mechanics, my pleasure mostly feigned. Now, I feel my skin respond, pulse and color where once was gray.

Here is where our story should melt into new, indefinite happiness. Instead, an essential distance persists, wedged between the moment and me. I toggle in and out of myself, my perspective shifting, roaming around the room. While my body moves toward climax, I waver, left behind.

◇ ◇ ◇

I used to joke I had Bedouin in my blood, desert in my bones. I said this to deflect accusations of flightiness, making light of my refusal to root. I dwelled in my life like a series of tents, eyeing the stakes each night. Along with boyfriends, places were things I loved despite, and because, I knew I would leave. And perhaps some part of the Bedouin quip was true. Origins insist themselves, whisper in cells and dreams.

My earliest coordinates were desert-set: due west of Mecca, on the lip of the Red Sea. I was conceived in the swelter of a Saudi summer, my parents' bodies pressed together in a room half-packed for their divorce. They had been married five years when they decided to separate, unable to reconcile their religions and their love. She, a born-again Christian, and he, the son of a long Sunni line. Just one of the many differences they had tried to contain, first with silence, then with words.

Their marriage was a leap of faith, a heart-wish overriding the improbability of their affair. They met on New Year's Eve, 1983, at a house party in a rich Chicago neighborhood. My mother's friend, an ESL teacher, was the host. My father, her student, crossed snowy streets to attend. A few months into his first midwestern winter, the cold still took his breath away. But his blood glowed in those days, something electric and newly loose in his limbs, seven thousand miles from home. The first week at his graduate program he had called his parents in Jeddah, tears of homesickness on his face. But his father refused to pay for a return ticket before Ziyad completed his degree. Theirs was not a family that could afford to look back.

From then on, Ziyad's hunger was a gift that multiplied, his days eager inhalations of the new. By New Year's Eve, he had spent four months in this land with sprawled horizons, thin air that filled his lungs but never full. For a semester, he sat in a class of fellow strangers—Colombian, Sudanese, Chinese—rehearsing the motions of success. Practicing the letter *p*, the difference between *gone* and *went*. *Hi, how are you?* he murmured to himself, alone. *How do you do, sir? The pleasure, the pleasure is all mine.*

He would not have called his past *unhappy*—happiness was not the primary unit he used to measure the world. A twice-refugee by second grade, his was a world of full-time surviving, delight and violence living side by side. His earliest memories blink awake in Deir al-Balah, a refugee camp in Gaza where he was born to my grandmother in 1960. He was seven when war displaced him to Jordan, then to Jeddah, where his family lived in Little Palestine, a large ghetto made of kin.

It was there he met his father, Musa, who had left Gaza for work in the Gulf before Ziyad's birth. It would not be easy to love this man, whose sun-scorched face clouded often. Ziyad would never see his father as he had been before his displacement, before the wars. Once, he'd been a farmer proud of his crops, singing blessings to his wife as she approached him in the field, their lunch hoisted on her head.

The life they rebuilt as refugees in Jeddah was narrow, pinned in the seam between hunger and enough. *Together* meant endless shifts at Ziyad's father's corner store, bellies full but with expired cheese, apricot jam gone brown. Instead of Gaza's silver sea, there were empty lots where boys named after villages played with homemade balls. He and his mother wept separately, their private griefs a weight each hoped the other would be spared. Burying the memory of the beach, Ziyad learned to love football, and, when Saudi boys mocked Falasteen,* discovered how to throw a fist.

Then, in his seventh-grade English class, came a visit by American emissaries.† He giggled with nerves at their blond hair, then gaped as their film reel projected the wonder of the United States.‡ In the dark classroom, bright families sashayed down leafy roads, flanked

---

* فلسطين, Palestine.

† "The Near East is of great strategic, political, and economic importance to the free world. The area contains the greatest petroleum resources in the world, essential locations for strategic military bases in any world conflict against communism, the Suez Canal, and natural defensive barriers . . . current conditions and trends in the Near East are inimical to Western interests . . . the nations of the Near East are determined to assert their independence and are suspicious of outside interest in their affairs . . . distrust and hatred [have replaced] the former colonial subservience . . .

"The United States should . . . win the Arab states to a belief that we sympathize with their legitimate aspirations and respect their interests . . . and seek to guide the revolutionary and nationalistic pressures throughout the area into orderly channels not antagonistic to the West."
    —National Security Council, "Statement of Policy by the National Security Council: United States Objectives and Policies with Respect to the Near East," July 23, 1954

‡ "The tools used included financial assistance, pamphlets and posters, news manipulation, magazines, radio broadcasts, books, libraries, music, movies, cartoons, educational activities, person-to-person exchanges, and, of great significance for the Middle East, religion . . . 'Psychological' plans included providing history and social science textbooks to schools to 'influence their curricula in directions favorable to the United States, in order to counteract the Communist trend in many education institutions in the area.'"
    —"U.S. Propaganda in the Middle East: The Early Cold War Version," *National Security Archive Electronic Briefing Book No. 78,* edited by Joyce Battle, December 13, 2002

by happy dogs. *The streets,* he marveled from his desk. *The streets are so clean, so straight.* This detail, talismanic. In a young boy's mind, a myth was planted, bloomed. Amreeka: where earth lay smoothed and silent, a land built for superior lives. Ten years later, his American university registered him as *Egyptian,* telling him *Palestine* was not a country,[9] not a choice. But as he crossed green campus lawns, he felt his feet might lead him anywhere.

He arrived at the New Year's party alone. On his way, his mind turned over his usual pep talk: *Hold your head high, look them in the eye. Don't be embarrassed by your mistakes. You are just as clever as them.* Though he was a good student, in the presence of Real Americans, his English often fell crooked from his mouth. Some smiled, leaving Ziyad to later wonder whether the grins were kind or amused. Other times, he noticed women scanning his dark features, their faces closing, limbs tightening. But a new year was shuffling its wings. The warm house swam with Donna Summer, Michael Jackson, Prince. His teacher waved him over. She introduced him to her friend Kathy, a woman with blond curls who fought a blush.

They shook hands, made gentle small talk with the English words they shared. All she knew of Palestine was sung in Christmas hymns—*Nazareth, Bethlehem*—but they spoke of American things. Born and raised in Chicago, she was a newly minted music teacher and, like him, living far from home for the first time. Her new job had taken her to Queens, New York, where she lived in an attic apartment with a hot plate and single bed. After a lifetime as a sheltered Lutheran daughter, this was her year of strangeness too. Alone in New York City, she tried disco, improv, and wonton soup.

Now, she watched the man named Ziyad sign a guestbook in Arabic, the script delicate and slack. He translated: *I wish everyone a New Year of peace and love.* When he asked for her number, she surprised herself and wrote it down. In fresh, cold January, he called. She came to watch his pickup soccer team. On the pitch, he dashed with a dozen like him—men foreign, hungry, and whip smart. Later, she smelled magic as they spiced pots of rice in bachelor kitchens, dumped maqlouba onto the table, jostling shoulders and spoons.

◇ ◇ ◇

I open my eyes to the joyful shock of my bed. A happy yelp rises to my lips, but I swallow it to preserve the early calm. Beneath our creamy white covers, my limbs lie loose and still. Our bedroom floats in sunshine, gold leaking into the walls of brick. My First Day stretches before me like unblemished snow. Beautiful, and close to ruin.

C lies next to me, his eyes lidded and lips half-parted with breath. Dark hair, strong arms, a tall, muscled frame. He is a lifelong surfer and skater, his body a vigorous and sturdy fact that seems to mostly bring him joy. Now, I am astonished by the solid, the materiality of him. His presence, the clearest speech: he has chosen to stay. Each day, waking up inside a room, a story, he could leave.

I wonder whether, sleeping, I ever look this way: self-evident, at ease. A body parted from its language, at rest in time and space. If such serenity does touch me, it belongs to the hours I cannot reach. The softness of sleep recedes too quickly, a tide revealing the sharp bones of shore. In the silence, my skin grows tight, an eardrum stretched so taut even stillness booms.

The discomfort spurs me to my feet. In the early morning, our kitchen looks jagged and dark. On the table, glasses half-full of flattened champagne, lush bouquets gone opaque. I pause and wait for last night's euphoria to return. *I'm home! I'm home.* Instead, I am horrified by a flash of tears, the tremble of familiar grief. Inwardly, I reel, dart for the corners of myself. As if I might outrun, undo, the spoiling of this scene. Maybe I could even drop back into the instant of waking. Find myself gazing again at C's serenity, and discover it was shared.

After all, there were those glossy women who filled books and screens with stories of recovery bliss—*It's so worth it!* In photos, they accessorized their white smiles and trim bodies with boyfriends and ice cream. Implied: their battles were discrete, waged on narrow fronts of food and weight.* Victories were straightforward: an accumulation of correct behaviors, able bodies rightly arranged. The world itself was neutral territory, a mere backdrop for their return.

These sunny frames harmonized with the urgings of my hospital counselor. In contrast to the doctors' damning predictions of my relapse, she explained the future like a recipe. *Just stick to the discharge plan*, she repeated, listing my *recovery assets*: a viable job, a Good Man, my whole life ahead of me. I knew the list well, the outline of a life I had labored to draw myself. Yet beyond these borders, that old grief sprawled. There was a weight to its emptiness, an atmosphere all its own. In therapy, while my counselor and I made small *breakthroughs*, I heard its muffled roar.

When C wakes up, he finds me with a glass of water, gulping to drown the clawing thing inside my throat. His eyes shine, somehow even brighter than yesterday. I smile in return as he takes me into his arms.

Pressed against him, I feel a memory shift its weight, stir.

---

* "People with eating disorders typically have between one and four other psychiatric disorders ... Anorexia has the highest case mortality rate and second-highest crude mortality rate of any mental illness."
   —National Association of Anorexia Nervosa and Associated Disorders

Last summer, deathly thin, my pulse whisper-low. Zombie-walking down Eastern Parkway, a tree-lined promenade. Something abruptly loosening, like a balloon string cut free. My body, a silk thread dropping, forgotten, as I drifted to sunlit leaves. How natural it felt, as velvet darkness began to close. *Yes*, the thought wafted, *this life has been enough.* A relief, to release that faint thought. To feel the last wisps of me fade.*

And—then—how vaguely, how barely, I thought, *But . . . C?* How wearily I came back down.

It's so good to have you back, C says into my hair. I can only hum in reply.

---

* "'Sudden death' has been defined as the abrupt and unexpected occurrence of fatality for which no satisfactory explanation of the cause can be ascertained. It must be noted that the mechanism of death in EDs, particularly in anorexia nervosa, is poorly understood. In many cases, death is attributed to complications (which are not always well defined) and in cases of sudden deaths autopsies do not always clarify the main cause of death."
—Beatriz Jáuregui-Garrido and Ignacio Jáuregui-Lobera, "Sudden Death in Eating Disorders"

In the hopeful strangeness of our first morning, C and I reach for routine. Breakfast: I follow C's cue—pulling a bowl from the cabinet and shaking cereal from a box. He is quiet as I serve myself, as if afraid to disturb the miracle of me reaching for food. In a recent past I don't remember, I started the day with a pantomime of drinking juice. Now, we sit down at our small scuffed table. My muscles harden into armor, my breath beginning to thin.

In the hospital, I grew used to the regimen of meals, but never lost my dread. What menaces is not only the guilt that blares with each bite. It is the thickening of my senses with every shift in blood sugar, every morsel in my throat. Eating, I become material. An hourglass heavied with each grain, forced into the rush of time.

I lift my spoon with strain I try to disguise. I tell myself that this is freedom: milk and granola between my teeth. C and I sip coffee from a pair of mugs, handmade wedding gifts once wrapped and carried from Philly by a friend. I watch C's fingers curl around the ceramic, the steam rising from the burnished clay. We speak in hushed voices, awed by an ordinary instant after months of alien. Slowly, I drain my bowl and set it down with relief. The tremble in me softens, slightly. Perhaps it will be this simple. Perhaps I can slide back into my life, like a photo into a frame. Perhaps this time the frame will hold.

We do not have time to linger over our honeymoon mugs. For months, I've been living in an abstract film, suspended in no-plot. But life on the Outside is movement, built of narrative and arc. It must propel. I must prove. Move. C and I share a subway car, parting ways at Union Square. C rides uptown to work, and I follow my *discharge plan.* I must report at a for-profit treatment center for *partial hospitalization,* a seven-hour-a-day, five-day-a-week program mandated by my inpatient team.*

I enter a featureless lobby and ride an elevator ten floors. A receptionist behind thick glass asks for my ID, then buzzes me through the door. Inside, I am weighed and measured again, this time permitted my bra and pants. Next, I am screened by a shrink in an office strung with Christmas lights and Tibetan prayer flags. *How would you rate your satisfaction with your body right now? How often do you experience urges for compulsive exercise? For purging? Self-harm?* Next, she asks me if I want to try medication. It has been years since my stint on Prozac. I give the answer I hope will be true. *I think I'm doing okay on my own.*

I am shuffled to a third office, where a woman introduces herself as my primary therapist. She is roughly my age, southern, a self-described *blond.* Her hair is dark, so by *blond,* I think she means *spacey.* She laughs as she scrambles my paperwork. Today, she says, we will *just get to know each other.* As always, the first questions concern my mother—she asks me if my mother was fat, if my mother worried about her weight. The answers, now routine, arrive on my lips. I watch her trace me on a clipboard, nodding as I hit plot-points on cue. I have been told I am a *textbook case.*

PT is a high-functioning female in her 20s with a postgraduate degree, presenting with Anorexia Restricting Subtype. PT reports symptoms began in

------

* "Most eating disorder clinicians estimate that full healing from an eating disorder takes around two years of dedicated, uninterrupted care at a variety of levels of care . . . and would cost around $250,000." —Project HEAL

early puberty. PT's mother often worried about her weight and exhibited dieting behaviors at home.

She stops short when I mention that I moved to Saudi Arabia at age eight. *Wait—what? You?* I explain my father's origins—*Palestine.* A blank stare. *Arab.* She startles. *Oh!*

What follows is a familiar routine: a scrunching brow, eyes unashamedly plowing my body and my face. Registered: green eyes, blond hair, skin a color Clinique labels *Neutral.* My observer notes my native English, other details they consider anathema to my ethnicity: perhaps I hold a cocktail in hand or stand before them in short sleeves. Perhaps we were just flirting, the conversation greased by their assumptions of our similarity. Now, their brain jams over the sudden arrival of my Arabness.

Years of practice have taught me ways to abbreviate this exchange. Usually, I shrink my body into a joke—*I know, you'd never guess I'm Arab. I'm so cleverly disguised!* Most begin by shaking their heads—*so hard for women over there!* Next, they revisit my phenotype. *Ah yes, I see it now. / That's why your eyes are so big. / That's why your eyebrows are so dark.* Once, *Yes, you have Arab teeth.* Some end with a joke of their own, throwing hands up in mock fear: *Uh-oh, don't blow me up!*

Then comes the final coup: *What is your mother?* they ask. *What,* not *who*—we are speaking, now, of *things.*

*American,** I say.

---

* Later in life I began to clarify *white American,* although for these listeners the two have always meant the same.

The moment of catharsis arrives, their anxiety vanishing. The world makes sense again, its borders rehardening. *Aha! American! You must take after her.*[10]

No one who truly knows me would call me my mother's daughter. Yet I know what they mean.[11]

The wedding nearly swallowed my Muslim father in its swell of Caucasian Christian splendor. The ceremony was held at a Chicago church lined with my mother's family, her bridesmaids draped in lavender. The presiding pastor was her cousin, one of many reverends in her clan. The groomsmen were her brothers, with the addition of my father's Arab classmate—the lone fellow foreigner. At the center, my father beamed, his slender frame cut against stained glass. Twenty-five and Nasser-handsome: a prominent, chiseled nose, hair blacker than his rented tux.

Guests brought their Midwestern Nice to the chapel, pushing smiles across stiff faces. Her parents, dismay tucked inside their Sunday best, gazed at their only daughter's strangest choice. She, their church piano player, graduate of sixteen years of Lutheran schooling for which they'd scrimped and saved. They had protested the union at first, speaking through the voice of Saint Paul: *Do not be unequally yoked with an unbeliever.*

She'd matched them verse for verse. Couldn't it be, she asked them, that this man was a sheep soon to join the fold? *Aren't all things possible with God?* My father, for his part, did see in her something like salvation. He'd fallen not only for this Princess Di look-alike but for the way her country made him feel. Like a man cut loose from history, a pioneer on the cusp of home.

His family, thousands of miles away and unaware of their union, would have been finishing al-ʿisha' prayer as my parents made their vows. Earlier that day, he had faced them for his own salat, bowing his dizzy head to the east. His thoughts flew to his mother, guilt clanging in his gut. He was her favorite, her most loyal son. Until now, his life had the shape of necessity, forged in the narrow spaces of collective circumstance. But his two years on the Great Plains had been a strange, spacious dream. Here, men spoke like fate was a thing to make, control. He used American words to steady himself: this woman, Kathy, made him *happy*. His mother would forgive.

There was no dancing at their wedding. No alcohol. No sex before their vows. Their piety met in common negations, agreements to withhold. But their love was warm, eager; in the photos, their eyes meet again and again. In these instants locked forever, neither shows any doubt.

First, they shared a tiny house on the edge of his Urbana campus, furnished with a queen-size waterbed and a TV with no remote. My mother learned to cook lasagna. They took walks on snowy streets. *Back to the Future* was the movie of the year. When the mood struck, they danced in disco clubs. She filled Arabic workbooks with words she'd never speak. He finished his classes, hid knives of homesickness in his throat. On the phone, his mother tried to disguise how bleak her missing was. Then, a family shock: Ziyad's father had taken a new wife, and had forced my grandmother to move out.

So Kathy learned how far *duty* could span. Her husband flew to his mother's side. Kathy got her first passport and, to her parents' great dismay, boarded an eastbound plane. Ziyad had asked her to try Jeddah for *just two years*, and she learned she was unafraid to change her life. She arrived in a white skirt and blazer, stark amid the hajj pilgrims and their ihram robes. My father awaited her, beaming, a crowd of in-laws at his side. Their bodies were a shifting atmosphere, names lost in a haze of jet lag and foreign sounds. But my grandmother was unmistakable, distinct. My mother would always remember, as I would, that first clasp of those arms, the blessings rained onto her head.

My father drove his mother and his bride home. He had rented them a small apartment on the edge of town. In the morning, goats muttered and honked outside their window, shepherds herding them to graze. My mother tried to acclimate—to the heat, the absence of a phone, the cockroaches that fled the construction across the street to invade the walls and floors. My father worked a split shift, and in his absence, Kathy was alone with the older woman's tears.

Returning home, Ziyad sat long hours by his mother's side, their pain a private room. Outside their language, Kathy's loneliness was frightening. She still knew only the slimmest outlines of her husband's history. The snowy ground where they met had felt like an unspoiled field. But there was something decades deep in the way my sittoo cried and her son consoled. Perhaps Kathy began to feel it then. How survivorship is a country of its own, one she would never know.

And Ziyad could never know how much the transatlantic move had dislodged his wife. From girlhood, her sky had always tilted one way, her imagination grown to match. He'd been born estranged from homeland; she'd been planted in the heart of God's favorite country on earth. Ziyad, a *resident alien* since age seven, did not consider how it would jar Kathy to be a first-time foreigner at twenty-five. Nor did he realize how little her life had prepared her to understand his world. For Ziyad, it had never been possible to not-know about hers.[12]

Neither could he guess how oceanic, how inscrutable his language seemed. The English alphabet had circled him all his life, from the labels on humanitarian rations to his marriage certificate. Even when he fumbled in its grammar, English did not hit his body as a shock. But Kathy was still petrified by Arabic beyond a few memorized words. Among guests, she bobbed in the sea of others' voices, trying to float on her smile. And Ziyad, grown in thronging spaces, never guessed that rooms packed with family might feel to her like a crowd. How even as she learned to eat with her hands, her body hungered for home.

But Kathy's heart was not one that reached for bitterness. For the next five years, she built a busy life, one that she could love. She took on private piano students and directed choir at the American school. At their concerts, my father beamed, mystified by his wife's talent to fill a hall with sweet sound. In his own work, he labored up the ranks. With his increased salary, the three of them moved farther into the city, to an apartment with a telephone. When one of his brothers entered a tumultuous divorce, Ziyad asked Kathy if they could take in one of his two nieces for a time. My mother insisted they foster both.

For a season, their household was three generations thick, joys and worries nested inside the container of their days. Between Kathy and her mother-in-law grew a warm language of gestures, a silence filled with ease. She learned that the older woman cherished the chance to be of use. Kathy, never attached to the domestic, easily surrendered to Sittoo's deft hands. With her touch, the rooms stayed spotless, modest meals made a feast. Between her tasks, she lay down to rest. Kathy caught small sighs followed by soft snores—flesh remembering, then releasing, itself.

The newlyweds found a rhythm, their young love sustaining one year, then the next. Still, their differences accreted—expectations unspoken, unmet. Missed understandings, disappointment clouded in silence and bided time. Exhausted patience pressed against their pact to ignore. Time, once abstract and abundant, grew starker as months ebbed. The question of Future loomed.

It was over beliefs that they finally argued, their faiths clashing, sorrowing. She could not surrender Jesus-as-God; he could not forfeit tawhid to Trinity. After months of tears and prayers, their theology remained a chasm they could not cross. Like the father of both their faiths, they heard the call to sacrifice. Two hearts prepared for the altar, bleeding as they agreed to separate.

But *belief*, in the end, is a word entwined with love. From a West Germanic root meaning *to hold dear, to desire. Love,* the landscape their theologies could not tame. At the last moment, their belongings already divided, they abandoned doctrine for instinct. Their romance, like most, had been built of little things, peculiarities clutched like portents, strung together to feel like fate. *This party. That song.* It was this they chose to trust as they abandoned their goodbye. *It felt meant to be.*

America would be the gospel they could share. Its promise so familiar it scarcely took any faith: to exorcise history and difference, making all strangers belong. Those straight streets, each opening toward a *destiny* anyone was free to claim. They imagined their future child as a private melting pot. *Half-and-half,* they'd call her, an alloy bridging what they could not. The positive pregnancy test came in a Jordanian hotel room. Their future grew gauzy, sunlight caught in window drapes.

America preempted them, sweeping toward the Gulf with war. My mother left first, fleeing the gathering clouds. Her parents celebrated her return—to reason, to home. Her mother watched Kathy's belly rise, scandalized each day my foreign father did not appear. Across the ocean, Ziyad shuttled between work and relatives, stealing days of normalcy. Facing west, he watched the Red Sea drink the sun. From that horizon came the planes, U.S. army aircraft bearing half a million militarized bodies that would make Saudi Arabia their base.*

Perhaps the roar of these killing ships shot Ziyad to the past. In his bones still lived the rattle of Israeli planes, the rip of hull and wing diving just above his head. On television, he watched Iraq scorched

---

* "We have before us the opportunity to forge for ourselves and for future generations a new world order—a world where the rule of law, not the law of the jungle, governs the conduct of nations."
       —George H. W. Bush, address to the nation on the
           invasion of Iraq, January 16, 1991

"Muslims burn with anger at America. For its own good, America should leave [Saudi Arabia]."
  —Osama bin Laden, "Declaration of War Against the Americans Who
    Occupy the Land of the Two Holy Mosques," August 23, 1996

by American fire. He heard dead civilians named *collateral** in English, but the grieving mothers spoke his tongue, his history. For the first time, Ziyad doubted Amreeka's dream for him.

In this storm of irreconcilables, the fact of his fatherhood was absolute. In Illinois, my mother's body arced toward opening. Still, he was slow to speak of his planned departure to his mother, delaying her heartbreak and his own. Only after canceling two flight reservations did he force a confession from his lips. She was inconsolable. He implored her to trust God, murmuring about return. In his last days, he begged promises from his brothers to be the good sons she deserved. He rode one of the last commercial planes out of the Gulf, landing less than a week before my birth. But I had loitered, too, stalling past my due date, covering for him.

Uninsured, my parents left the hospital with an eight-pound American citizen and a $10,000 debt. Our first home was a small apartment furnished with an old piano and shared with three Saudi-born rescue cats. Bathing me in the kitchen sink, my parents marveled at my pink limbs, a body pure enough to absolve sin. Their smiles were hours long. They tried out their new names—*mother*, *father*. Words big enough, perhaps, for a past to be lost inside.

---

* "It never occurred to us that it was a place where civilians went to take shelter—we thought of it as a military bunker in which command and control facilities resided . . . Civilian casualties happened, this was a legitimate military target, it was hit precisely, it was destroyed and put out of business—and there was very little collateral damage."
—General Merrill McPeak on the bombing of a shelter in Amiriyah, Iraq, on February 13, 1991, which killed over four hundred civilians

Ziyad was unsure, at first, how to hold parenthood. For the first five years of his life, his own father was absent, a figment made of words. Like hundreds of thousands of other dispossessed Palestinians, my grandfather had been forced to look for work beyond Palestine.* Like me, Ziyad had been conceived in Jeddah, on one of his mother's rare visits, but she'd returned to Gaza for his birth. There, Ziyad toddled in a world of women, ran from his street into the sea. In first grade, he snuck swims on his walk home from school. Thinking himself clever, he left his clothes on the shore. When he arrived home with salt behind his ears, his unfooled mother scolded him for risking his small life in waves. Her fear slid off him. His mind, unlike hers, was still untouched by death. To him, the sea was endless love.

In Deir al-Balah, their three-room, unfurnished home was host to frequent visitors. Some were returning from hajj, a journey that always passed through Jeddah's Little Palestine. They came bearing news of Ziyad's father. Over tea, the guests told of how Musa toiled on Gaza Street. How he lived alongside fellow refugees, their dialects and grapevines replicating village ties. Before leaving, they passed my grand-mother a wad of Egyptian pounds, its thickness hinting at how her husband fared. The money vanished quickly as she rushed to repay debts.

A few months before his sixth birthday, she took Ziyad on his first trip outside the camp. She left her other sons in the care of family, gripping

* "Between 750,000 and 900,000 Palestinians (making up 55 to 65 percent of the total Palestinian population at the time) were forcibly displaced between the end of 1947 and early 1949, half of which were displaced before the unilateral declaration of the state of Israel which triggered the 1948 Arab-Israeli War. Ultimately, 85 percent of the population living in Palestine at the time were displaced from the territory that became the state of Israel." —*Survey of Palestinian Refugees and Internally Displaced Persons*, BADIL Resource Center for Palestinian Residency and Refugee Rights

her youngest as their two-day journey stretched from shared taxis to trains. Out of Egypt, they rode steerage in the belly of a barge. وَاطِي, my father would describe it. *We were low, so low.* Water sloshed their legs as the ship pitched into the Red Sea. Everyone down below grew sick, but a kind man briefly snuck my father to the deck. Fifty years later he would still recall the jeweling water, the breath of salt and space.

After docking, they met a stranger on a large and noisy street. Young Ziyad was appalled as he watched the man's hand caress his mother. He launched himself at his father with fists and shrieks to *get away from her.* He stayed defensive, arched back unsoftened by their words: *Baba, Abook.*

In the strange home where they stayed, Ziyad grabbed a fire iron, swinging at the man's crossed legs. He refused his parents' coaxing, Musa's proffered coins. It was not until their final days that something inside him switched. Maybe it was his mother's ease around the man; perhaps the son's flesh recognized its own. But the thing called *Baba* grew sudden arms and legs. *Ibnu,* a son held a little tighter to the earth. تعلقت به. *I became attached, a branch of him.* At back of the westbound barge, the boy stood and wailed. He watched his father shrink with the shore, losing him for the first time.

On the boat, his mother wrapped herself around him. In her lap, her son felt the first tremors of a fate she had hoped to delay. The throb of answerless questions, a splintered history. Perhaps her throat welled with an apology that was not hers to give. Perhaps her heart shut its eyes, or maybe she searched the ship's slimed ceiling for Allah. Her hand rubbed his little shoulders, stroked his narrow back. On the heaving sea, her touch built a small silence inside the storm.

❖ ❖ ❖

In a room with long, colorless couches, roughly thirty eyes follow my hunt for a seat. I sit in a corner, hear the end of a talk on *coping with uncertainty*. I watch neuroses clash—there's the leg shaker and the woman who reports this as *triggering*. An outspoken ex-Orthodox queer woman draws glares from an observant adolescent in tights and a skirt. In the brief periods between sessions, a few teens ask me about my lowest weight, and whether I'm on Instagram.

I demur and retreat to the bathroom, where a sparrow woman in her sixties makes a cold clasp around my hand. Eyes wide inside wobbly liner, she tells me to *recover now. Eat pizza before it's too late.* At lunch, I am handed a paper plate already limp beneath a baffling *Thursday Quiche*. I sit across from a high schooler who deftly hides food, next to two women in their upper fifties eating only fruit.

I am submerged in a matrix of new jargon and policies—daily homework, scheduled mindfulness, dress codes, acronyms. A dietitian hands me a complex chart of *exchange requirements*, letters and numbers stacked in columns labeled PROTEIN, DAIRY, FATS, and STARCH. *You'll be on Meal Plan C.* I am tasked with calculating the values of each component of my meals, turning in a full record twice a week. Again, I feel myself disappear behind a grid, a system both simple and arcane. My blood flashes with apprehension, the red murmur darkening. I had expected little of this program yet now feel danger in its impotence. A tremor in me asking, *Is this it?*

We are dismissed at 3:00 p.m., encouraged to take a snack as we go. I dart past the apples and granola bars. By the elevator, a watercolor poster intones: *YOU ARE THE POINT.*

I pass through revolving glass doors, letting the rush of bodies sweep me two blocks before I realize I have no route in mind. For a moment I stand immobilized. Everywhere, the tea-toned glint of high-rise windows, elephantine blocks of stone and cement. The gray sky is diffuse, dimensionless. In my brain, synapses fire useless sparks, each flare swallowed in small oblivions. Memory evaporates. I am nowhere. I have no name.

Predictably, the first fact I recall is my phone. I slip my hand inside my pocket to discover its soothing weight. Pulling it out, I tap my passcode gently as a prayer. A reflexive comfort hits as icons light my screen. I open a navigation app, which autofills my home address. Relief ripples again as I see the name of my street, eight letters that somehow endured the brief obliteration of time and space. A blue dot quivers at one end of a route snaking from Manhattan to Crown Heights. Gratefully, I fall in line.

For the first few weeks after my discharge, I see the sun only once. The days are wet and the shortest of the year; by the time I leave my program, the night's cold breath is on my neck. Dreading solitude, I haunt coffee shops and clothing stores. Buying nothing, touching nothing, the hours a hall of doors I pray will stay shut. In the evenings, C cooks us dinner. I fill my plate with shaky hands. At the table, we make conversation like acquaintances, feigning nonchalance as I labor through my bites.

Clearing up, we loosen to a cautious silliness, lobbing soft jokes, brushing each other with our fingertips. When his back is turned, my smile drops. I am glancing at our ceiling, at our walls. Shelves, books I have read but cannot remember. Shoes in the foyer, a small infantry of absent feet. A front door where any moment a woman will arrive to claim her rightful place in this life. She will be beautiful and furious, and I will run.

When C and I married, we created our own ceremony, a splice of his Jewish roots and my own hybridity. Under a chuppah wrapped in olive leaves, we heard recitations from the Torah, Bible, and Qur'an. In addition, before our vows, I asked B to read Mary Oliver's "Wild Geese." I preferred poetry over liturgy, and these verses vibrated with something like holiness. The first lines like a benediction:

You do not have to be good . . .
You only have to let the soft animal of your body love what it loves.

Simple lines, perhaps veering into cliché, but I hoped the words could be an offering for our guests, for C, for me. The gentle notes of *let, soft animal, body.* The release of tender flesh to lead. *To love what it loves.* As if it were as simple as that—to trust and dignify the organism of me. I repeated these lines often to myself, trying to coax softness into the hard lines I'd become. By then, I had been starving and otherwise harming myself off and on for fifteen years. Cutting and cutting at the creaturely parts of me. Wishing and wishing that these small murders did not feel like the only way. *Less, less,* the only relief I knew.

Once, I was a soft sister. A hot-blooded animal thing. Cinched inside too-big shorts, I clambered in and out of trees, clapped against existence with pink lips and scabby knees. I fell in love with a blade of grass and popped it in my mouth. I belonged only to myself, stretched flat across the carpet to cool on summer nights, caressing the warmth of my sunbaked arm.

Now, in bed, I ask C to clasp my wrist as we drift off to sleep. In the darkness, this pressed flesh is the only part of me that is real.

❖ ❖ ❖

My grandmother, still a young woman in Gaza, woke often with a thudding chest, the night tangled in her hair. With young Ziyad in tow, she sought solace from neighborhood women. One read meaning in coffee dregs, peering into small porcelain oracles. Another, Sheikha Amna, offered prayers and protective charms to secure the younger woman's fate. These women offered my grandmother story in the chaos of exile, reason and agency inside loss. But later she ceased searching for such solace. قدر الله—in matters of fate, it was best to contend quietly. The blue plumes of her bakhoor wafting wordless, heavenward.

My father inherited this reticence. All his life he has refused to repeat, or even ponder, his dreams. He fears these nocturnal breaches, the wild logic of their shapes. Their carnivals of forbidden feelings, or worse, their subtlety—the visions of the everyday, tedious until they're not. Bullet-speed comes the rupture, monster, loss. All this, too close to life's true fickleness, reminding the body it is soft and full of fragile love. Too much, too, in the warm swath of American fatherhood, to admit where his nights carried him. How he ferried back to Jeddah. To Falasteen.[13]

My mother stopped speaking. Her eyes had gone wiggly and off-white, her cheeks an unnerving pink. Next to her, my father started saying words. The skin of his face somehow tighter, tinged with a grayish light. Eight years old, my stomach filled with sparks. I tried to shake the electricity from my fingers by tickling my sister's ribs. On the carpet, we poked each other, squealing, our bodies rolling, flopping from side to side. My five-year-old brother squeaked along, dimples dancing on his cheeks. Trying to dispel our parents' strangeness, we laughed double hard.

Their words hovered above us, baffling. *Moving, country, leave.* Still, I understood what they needed when they said *It will be great, right?* I kept my eyes averted, sticking out my silly tongue, nodding and chirping *Yeah.* I felt the air shift with this word, the lines of my parents loosening. Soon, they dismissed us, and we tumbled back to play. Around me, the world appeared unchanged. But I was unnerved by a new sense of dishonesty, how both my parents and I had wedged language between us, trying to displace unspoken fear. What happened to the danger no one named?

Our world emptied quickly. My father disappeared first. In Jeddah, my grandfather Musa was now deathly ill. My father rushed ahead to be with him, leaving my mother in Illinois to sell our home. She vanished, too, lost to us in her mad rush of packing, yard sales, and calls to the Saudi consulate. The oldest, I tried to entertain my jittery siblings, swallowing my own ache at the rapid, baffling change. When I explained to friends that I was *moving to Saudi Arabia,* they nodded with blank faces. Adults, by contrast, were grave. My mother's friends looked at us with tragic faces, murmuring about *safety* and *the girls*.[14]

On the morning of our departure, adult legs hustled around me, lifting the last boxes off a carpet raked with footprints. I watched my mother, skin iridescent in the rainy dawn, her blond ponytail hopping as she dragged luggage down the drive. When she called me to the car, I picked up my knapsack, a treasured possession purchased at a recent garage sale. Inside, I'd packed my diary, a few Nancy Drew novels, and the half-used sleeve of Lisa Frank stickers gifted to me by a neighbor. I glanced back at the house, its drawn curtains like shut eyes. My stomach went cold. Already, the building looked distant, impenetrable. No longer related to me at all.

Across the dingy arrival hall, my father reappeared. Five foot ten in his well-worn jeans, a shock of familiarity after two dazed days in transit. Rushing toward him, I registered a new potency in his smile, a vigor and assurance to his stance. As if the sight of us on Arab soil relieved him of some unspoken ache. After a spree of delirious hugs, we tumbled behind him into the steamy night. The ride home was a smear of bright, bleary wonder. A used Crown Victoria—*a new car!* Warm orange juice boxes waiting in the back seat. Maniacally bright Pepsi billboards sailing the desert sky.

The next day we were amazed to discover our bodies had slept senseless past 3:00 p.m. We raced each other into our new reality, squealing as we lost ourselves between four bedrooms, two sitting rooms, and balcony. *We live in a mansion!** Outside, our small compound was a riot of tropical landscaping—date palms, frangipani, lantana, and bougainvillea making a lush, shady maze. For years after, I'd wander long hours among them, smitten by pastel and incandescent blooms. My favorite time was dusk, when even my skin turned rose and adhans laced the sky.

A few days after our arrival, our home still mostly bare tiles, the doorbell began to ring. In what seemed like an instant, the house

---

* "A Saudi model of company town [compound] goes back to the first Aramco-built version in the 1930s, with high-amenity housing for US and British oil company employees."   —Harvey Molotch and Davide Ponzini, "Enacting Exclusion in Contemporary Gulf Cities" teemed. Dressed formally in thobes and oxfords, smelling of hair gel and strong perfume—these laughing, embracing strangers were introduced as family. My cousin Selwa, her deep dimples printed on each of her children's cheeks. My عمو Ahmed, hands cracked and stained with auto grease—mischievous and loud. Men sprawled on furniture and floors as women drifted into the kitchen, dodging the scramble of children already playing tag.

I entered their throng, shy but enticed. At the center of the main room, next to my father, my grandmother sat cross-legged and grinning. Her hands flew, wagging fingers in jest, then grasping her son's knee as she laughed. The sight of her startled me; it had been a year since she left Illinois. In the months we'd shared a home, I'd begun and ended my days with her, the hours nested in her soft attention, our laughter conjoined. And then—after days of weeping I did not understand—she had disappeared.

As she sat before me, every inch of her was familiar—her firm arms stretching the thin fabric of her thobe. Her wiry gray hair in its loose ponytail. Her prominent, faintly hooked nose, which echoed on my father's face. That voice, both musical and hoarse. Yet the still-unfathomable newness of the setting rendered her surreal. She fit perfectly here, while my own neck grew hot with the sense of trespassing.

My father waved me toward her—سلمي على ستّك. The room turned their eyes on me. I moved, yearning yet slow, across the room. She pulled me to her fragrant chest, but as her blessings poured I realized I was struggling to follow her Arabic. Inside this strangeness, the language seemed to scatter in the air, meaning splintering, half-grasped. Dazed, I was passed from arm to arm, each new relative covering my cheeks with kisses, returning my salaams, cooing over my American beauty—*shugra! blond, fair!* I blushed, sensing that, in this room, I was both loved and peculiar.

The ritual greeting was the only part of the interaction that was scripted; at its end, I was lost. I stood halfway between the living room and the hall, torn between my reflex to retreat from the strangers and my attraction to their mirth. The conversation carried on in rapid, overlapping Arabic, the air thickening and bright with banter, a warmth I could not grasp. Hidden, I stood for a long while at the threshold, trying to soak in their glow.

◇ ◇ ◇

I wake in our Brooklyn apartment at 6:30 and do the light yoga routine my treatment team has approved. A few stretches, some downward dogs, all slow and *restorative*. I must step off the mat after twenty minutes, resisting the urge for push-ups, for lunges, for any movement that will break a sweat. As for any newly sober addict, my life has become a private gauntlet, riddled with traps visible only to me.

My sobriety depends on preventing caloric deficit. A hard workout, a delayed meal, the onset of emptiness—any ebb of nutrients is a trip wire. It takes only a lick of hunger for the net to begin to close. Corrupted neural pathways, decades deep, begin to sing. Where others would grow irritable, I find a sick calm. Before long, I am entranced again, hunger a spell I never want to break. With it, the seductive pull of compulsion—to transmute hours and days from ambiguity to certitude. Life orchestrated into a single purpose—emptiness.

Peeling myself off my mat, I shower, then walk dripping to the small closet in our bedroom. Each day, I eye my old clothing— odd and ugly pieces, purchased as my devastated frame began to defy normal sizes. In those sharp-boned days, I swaddled myself in layers—tunics and baggy tees, pants I cinched and then discarded when even my belts failed. I am afraid to touch these articles now, as if their dimensions might make real what my eyes have, so far, denied: the forty, or fifty, more pounds of me. A number, a body, I do not know how to grasp.[15]

In the hospital, I blunted this reality with avoidance, smothering my changing form in comically oversize sweaters, cheap and stretchy tights. Such was the common uniform for the patients on the ward, tenting ourselves in fabric as we chewed our way to discharge. Now, dressing, I move delicately, afraid to jostle a breast or feel the wiggle in my thighs. Such whispers of womanliness swarm me with a disgust I am not ready to confront. I am grateful for winter, the excuse to hide inside sacks of crocheted cotton and wool. Passing mirrors and windows, I glance away or skim only above my neck.

At the day program, I follow the schedule written in lopsided marker on a whiteboard in the back hall. Often, the staff are too busy to write an update, obsolete lists lingering for days. It makes no difference to me. In the cramped space I move like a shuttle in a loom, careful not to snag as I count down minutes, hours. Unlike in the hospital, it is easy to win approval here. Most of the clients fuss through meals, then slump, sullen and silent, through group therapy. I chew my food quietly, portion my voice across the day, *participating* with guarded words. Hiding in plain sight.

These hollow gestures seem to persuade. The attention of the staff grazes me, then moves on. Each time, I feel a shudder of apprehension, and relief. After four months in a panopticon, I am desperate to avoid being patronized, probed. Yet in spite of myself, the words of my social worker circle in my inner ear. *One of the worst cases I've ever seen.* I search the faces of the staff again, desperate to share their credulity.

Here, too, are patients who joke they are *lifers*, veterans comparing notes on residential programs in Florida, Philly, California. But my Medicaid insurance is tenuous, coverage dispensing only a few days at a time. At the end of each week, my caseworker logs into a portal, punching in my PROBLEM CODE. Beneath, on a form, she marks SOME PROGRESS, reports CONTINUED NEED and requests further funds. My CARE PLAN: increments of time and sickness for two companies to trade.

In the afternoons, I begin to frequent a coffee shop near Flatiron and sit at a small table near the door. I loiter, avoiding home and its perilous silence until C returns from work. I drink my Americano alone; I have not yet reached out to friends. I still blaze with humiliation when I imagine facing those who watched my grotesque decline. In my bag, there is homework from therapy to complete— *feeling logs*, short articles, charts to record my every bite. As always, I also carry my journal and a book or two. Each day, I place one of these objects in front of me as alibi.

Laptops and elbows crowd the tables around me. In chinos, skirts, and suits, companions lean together to be heard above music and hissing steam. A long, quick queue cycles past, customers glancing up from fast-typing thumbs to order lattes and cold brews. When someone grabs a pastry, I feel a voyeuristic thrill. I try to imagine myself that way—busy, confident, blithely munching a sugary snack as I rush back, full of purpose, into the fray.

Outside, the sidewalk is its own conveyor belt as bodies stream uptown and down. I recall how I moved to New York for this—to mingle with a crowd so dense and swift that it seemed sure to lead somewhere. A woman still young enough to enjoy the strange halo they called *potential*. Now, I realize the days that passed so slowly in the hospital have been surging ahead out here. Whatever I'd managed to achieve in my three New York years means nothing in this churn. The city has poured itself into the gap my body left. It did not miss me.

We visited New York City once as a family, but the memories are blurred by overstimulation and my parents' ambient stress. For a few days, the six of us walked ourselves ragged to avoid the cost of taxis and the pre-smartphone ordeal of the subway. Twelve years old and exhausted from helping watch my younger siblings, I dragged my tired legs behind my father. I tossed frequent glances between him, marching ahead of us, and my mother in the rear. They unnerved me with their odd expressions—both vigilant and dazed. Against the sharp lines of Manhattan, I saw my parents were small.

But their tension lifted as we stepped from the ferry at the feet of Lady Liberty.[16] The statue cut a shadow out of the late morning sun, and in its shade my parents' faces went smooth. Perhaps my mother took my father's hand—such were the moments that sparked their shy affection. As if soothed by the display of American majesty, the sublime rock upon which their shaky marriage had been built. *Only in America!* my mother chuckled as my father sprinkled za'atar over Thanksgiving leftovers. *Only in America!* they sang as we celebrated Christmas and Eid with a single pile of cookies, some shaped like wreaths, others cut into crescent moons.

Yet I sensed there was a reason my American grandparents *forgot*, over and over, that my father did not eat pork. I felt their eyes on me at holiday dinners as I dutifully passed on the main course. My siblings followed suit, while my mother silently speared a hunk of the pink meat, her cheeks matching its hue. After, my stomach unsatisfied, I listened to my grandmother gripe about *too many leftovers.*

Later, she turned on Fox News, bathed us in its trumpeting sounds. Sometimes, she'd goad my father using words I did not yet understand—*Islamists, security threats, Jews.* My parents resembled one another in these moments, both sitting politely, hands folded in front of them. My father, trying to respect his mother-in-law, preserving her honor as she degraded his. My mother, quiet at his side, face continuing to flush.

You're lucky you live in a free country, my American grandmother said to my father, to me. Above her head, the paneled wall danced with the colored light cast by the screen—tones of ketchup, blue jay, milk. To her, our move to the Middle East in 1999 was a mistake bordering on sin. Each summer, we visited for a month, sleeping on her basement floor and hearing her daily reprieve. *You must be so happy to be back!* Her voice somehow the opposite of glad as she preached. *Isn't it awful there? Especially for women. Aren't you so happy you're American?*

Always, *America* invoked alongside demands for ambiguous gratitude. In truth, I loved my life in the so-called *Arab world*, where I rarely felt deprived of more than Cap'n Crunch. Still, in her living room, I nodded. Half-obedient, half-convinced. Then, I marveled at the odds of my blessed fate. On my grandmother's TV, I saw how many people—virtually the entire planet—had been born to inferior lands. My stomach squirmed just as it did when I heard my grandparents' pastor proclaim *Jesus is the only way.* How could most of the world be damned?

◊ ◊ ◊

On the other side of the Atlantic the news invaded us too. In Jeddah, we rotated our weekends between hosting and visiting the apartments of uncles, cousins, and Sittoo. The television was a frequent backdrop, soccer and commercials buzzing beneath rowdy conversations and card games. But on certain days, the screen tuned to a jagged, smoldering place I knew was Palestine.

An Arabic chyron galloped beneath reporters in flak jackets, frames of exploding sky. On these days, our crowded room held a single breath. The news cut to dust-drenched children, their necks and arms flopping, too limp. Women dressed like my grandmother, wailing in shattered streets. On our side of the screen, the room broke into a clatter of clicking tongues, then muttered refrains— وحوش, حيوانات.* From there, the conversation would rocket beyond my understanding.

After, my father's face held heavy clouds. The black-and-white photographs from our hall had disappeared during our move, but in these moments, I felt the small Gazan boy in the room. A maternal urge welling up in my ten-year-old chest, I fought the impulse to

---

* "While the rivalry between Hamas and the PLO played a role in this escalation, the Israeli forces' massive use of live ammunition against unarmed demonstrators from the outset [of the second Intifada] (they fired 1.3 million bullets in 'the first few days' of the uprising) was a crucial factor, causing a shocking number of casualties. This mayhem eventually provoked some Palestinians . . . to take up arms and explosives. It seemed to perceptive observers that the Israeli military was well prepared to escalate and may have intended to trigger just such a development. Predictably, Israel turned to heavy weapons, including helicopters, tanks, and artillery."
—Rashid Khalidi, *The Hundred Years' War on Palestine*

cradle my father's head. I trembled as I asked him, *Is Palestine going to be okay?* Sometimes, he only clicked his tongue. For years, his most common answer was, simply, *Pray for Palestine, habibti.* In the silence after, I felt his parent-heart add, *Thank God you're not there.*

Coming to and from our Brooklyn apartment, I slouch, dart, zigzag around familiar streets to avoid being seen. I am unready to be recognized, unsure how I will address the friends who last saw me as a corpse. Now, I ache with embarrassment at my past oblivion, my grotesque performance of normalcy. Suddenly, I can recall the vague pain on friends' faces. The way their gazes jumped, looking anywhere but my body as I made small talk, smiling my pinched smile, ignoring my food. But it is not only this mortification that has me scuttling through my neighborhood, half-disguised in hats and hoods. As I rush past my old coffee shop, I realize: I want to stay a stranger. The radical loneliness of the past months has been a warped kind of relief.

As I duck toward the subway, the memory returns. The shift I felt in those last months, my life imploding room by room. My physical limitations defied denial, cloistering me from friendships, whittling my work. I felt guilt as I shrank from the world, but beneath this thrummed a subtle, illicit thrill. An alien lightness. Release from a strain I had not known was there.

Now, my body recalls it—that murmur of panic, the press between my navel and neck. Gravity gathering, dragging, as I moved deeper into *happiness*. How bewildering, the misgiving that crawled me as the story solidified—a promising career, sweet husband, well-meaning American friends. So lucky, alhamdulilah, to receive all I imagined I should want. Yet inwardly, that shuddering sense of mistake. Compounding, thickening the grief that had no name. Until, in those hours of my deepest illness, my skin went quiet. Freed, however briefly, from the noise and motion of *belonging* to my life.

◇ ◇ ◇

Displacements are always multiple, wrote the Palestinian poet Mourid Barghouti, thirty years after the Israeli invasion of the West Bank threw him into exile. Here, he takes the noun غربة, *ghourba*—that ineffable experience of displacement, estrangement—and renders it into a throng, pluralizing it to غربات. The published English translation continues in second person: *Displacements collect around you and close the circle*. But the original Arabic is not so intimate—it is written in third person. Barghouti knew—those in غربات are already jettisoned, orbiting their experience from a bird's-eye view.

غربات تجتمع على صاحبها وتغلق عليه الدائرة. يركض والدائرة تطوقه. عند الوقوع فيها يغترب المرء «في» أماكنه و «عن» أماكنه. أقصد في نفس الوقت.

My rendering: *Displacements converge on the one who bears them, closing a circle around her.* She runs and the circle tightens. Falling into it, she is displaced* in *her places and from* her places—simultaneously.

---

* The pronoun in the original is masculine.

✧ ✧ ✧

When we moved from the Middle East to the Midwest in 2004, my mother called it *settling down*. By then, we had spent five years in Saudi Arabia, spanning my eighth through thirteen years. By then, *America* was a fun vacation, while the desert was my home. But a second Bush had launched another war[17] in the Middle East, and al-Qaeda, protesting Saudi cooperation with the U.S., began a campaign of anti-Western insurgency.[18]

Before long, we had grown accustomed to lockdowns and stories of kidnappings and raids. A French man was shot on our street. We began passing tanks on our way to school, their grim guns protruding from sandbags and barricades. One day, we'd watched smoke curdle above the nearby U.S. consulate. Guerrilla fighters had made it past the outer gates. Our TV flickered the story: automatic weapons, explosions, hostages. Nine killed, *none American, but still*. That night, my mother found my younger brother had carried his baseball bat with him to bed.

Again, my mother had urged for a move. Again, my father was torn. They debated—the U.S. offered *safety, a normal childhood, better schools*. But Saudi Arabia was where most of his family lived; by then my father was quietly supporting many of them. *Maybe*—he'd reprised the refugee's prayer—*maybe things would get better soon*. In the end, they struck another deal—my mother would move with us to Illinois, and he would stay. A separation they called *temporary*, though it would last eleven years.

Another ripple of diaspora, patchworking love and geography. Alone, my father threw himself into work. Like his own father,

Ziyad was relentless, each cent he earned a prayer for stability in a world that had always swayed. None of us thought twice when, as his goodbye, my father told thirteen-year-old me, *You'll be the second father now. Take care of them.*[19]

At his words, I felt my spine straighten. For years, my mother had recruited me into domestic duties—diapers, dishes, cooking—while announcing I'd *make a great mom some day!* I loved the soft intimacy of nurturing, but the mark of *mom* stirred only a sense of dread. The meaning of this word, it seemed, was *sacrifice*, a life turned indoors, subjugated to others' needs. *Father* felt like a call not to self-effacement but bravery, strength. I pictured myself standing, shoulders squared, between my siblings, mother, and the world.

On my first day back in the United States, I woke to a house full of boxes, a mother who looked like dread. I slipped out the front door and walked a grid of tan cement and sprinkled lawns. Vans glided by, their bumpers announcing local football teams, prayers for troops and the unborn. When I found a main street, I stopped and waited to be seen. I had already learned that older boys liked to have my body in their hands. Perhaps now, some would pick me up. Maybe they would take me—anywhere, not-here. I stood for a few minutes before my mother's gentle face filled my mind. My father's admonition boomed. *Look after them.* Pained by my selfishness, I turned back toward my new address. I began to learn the art of stifling, of trying to stay.

I tried many anchors. I built fences out of duty, tied tethers of love and guilt. Yet for the rest of my life, I continued slipping through doors, wandering out, away. I have walked for hours in soaking shoes and snowed-over streets. I have walked across foreign cities, into woods and through ravines. I have walked farther and longer than is decent, but I have always returned.

Until, the year before my hospitalization, something in me knocked loose. My meandering walks grew malignant, metastasized into compulsions that frightened me. For hours each day, my brittle body drew helpless mazes, pounded Rorschach routes of city blocks.[20] I walked until my bones seemed to weep, past coffee shops full of laptops, schoolyards with swinging swings. This world of nouns had become bewildering—how did each object know its place?

It was on a hot afternoon walk, quaking from one nowhere to the next, when that balloon string cut and I drifted out of my skin. Bird's-eye, above Eastern Parkway, an amniotic, amnesiac peace. It was not *home*, exactly, but the end of a yearslong chase. Dissolution feels like salvation after so many fruitless steps. Body, history, becoming vapor, escaping me. *Me* a thought I could abandon at last. The thrill of a sudden answer: to exhale everything.

Except one small, hard catch in my throat.

C found me a few hours later, curled up on our bed. I heard the door open, watched his feet approach. I looked up at him, his face scraped with its usual weary grief. *Hey, are you okay?* I nodded. On the dull plain of my mind, a thought stirred, a few grains of sand brushed by the breeze. *I came back for you.*

Though I tried hard to forget this day, I could never be the same. Now, the instant of death lives in me, beastly and beautiful. It is a memory that alters. The murmur in my blood, coursing in my fingertips, drumming behind my ears. *Suicide* is not a term I heard in treatment. My near demise is addressed like a dodged bullet, *thank God you're safe* the final word. Yet it is no simple rescue when captor and prey share a name.

Perhaps there is something innocent, even natural, at the heart of this death-drive. A body, exhausted with what it carries, homes itself toward void. The swimming warmth of booze, the anesthetic of sex or sleep—oblivion as a crude coherence. Bodily impulses indicating desires our minds dare not speak—for a lost purity of being, a child's self-forgetful sense of home.

In this way, our displacements teach us the shape of what was lost. غربة resists indifference. It stirs the instinct to return, a longing that can sustain or break a soul. With all those aimless miles, I was spelling something true. That my lucky life sat inside separation. My body, scratching for the exit. Clawing at the closed loop of my language for the Elsewhere, the Someone, I might be.

Exile, wrote Edward Said, is *like death but without death's ultimate mercy.*

> *Even if we find ourselves decently in new places, the old ones loom behind us as tangible and unreal as . . . absent causes for our present state. Sometimes the poignancy of resettlement stands out like bold script imposed on faint pencil traces. The fit between body and new setting is not good. The angles are wrong . . . We perch on chairs uncertain whether to address or evade our interlocutor.*

❖ ❖ ❖

The first dream is a vague visitation. I wake as if surfacing in water, fragments of memory frothing at the edges of my brain. The presence of another's arms, sagging and sinewy at once; that particular scent of rose water and sweat, cardamom and cooking steam. It is the third week after my return from the hospital, but for a few floating moments I am in 1998, buoyed by her warm chest.

Reality breaks slowly. I am startled to find a grown body beneath me, long legs and soft breasts. My warm, dream-hugged muscles stiffen. A cold spot blooms on my back—the familiar, permanent chill I have felt since childhood. Stamped there on some forgotten day, when I decided that the world is capricious, and there is no one to keep me safe. This patch, where my body senses its own exposure, the absence of guarding eyes.

I squint my way to the stove, flick a burner beneath our red teapot. I wait for the morning to sharpen into focus, for language to come. Where have I just been? Who was with me? A sense of knowing licks the corners of my brain, then recedes. Bubbles murmur in the belly of the pot, steam escaping the open spout. I watch the moisture flutter and fade, the water spending itself in the dark. When I hear C begin to stir, I cut off the flame. I slip into the shower, filling our tiny bathroom with fog.

C and I linger in tentative triumph as I try to let life woo me back. My birthday comes two weeks after my discharge, and we plan a sushi date. Snow is falling outside as I enter the bathroom to get dressed. I apply makeup for the first time in months. My routine has always been rudimentary, which I euphemize as *less is more*. I cover any dark circles, sometimes lengthening my lashes with mascara, perhaps applying blush. Friends have given me halfhearted tutorials in the secrets of contouring, shadow, lip—lessons we both know will go unused.

Yet on this birthday eve, I am experimenting. Thinking, perhaps it is not healthy to reach for translucency every time. Perhaps it would cure something if I painted myself bold. After all, recovery slogans urge me to unghost—*Live out loud! Dare to be yourself!* Exhortations that speak in terms of courage, of a simple, if radical, choice to release withheld truth. Yet so far, *treatment* has felt only like subtraction—of symptoms, of ego parts. A dismantling that reveals no substance, only the size of my falsehoods.

Be yourself! Perhaps it should be this simple. Staring in the mirror, I feel the bud of a brand-new shame. Late twenties and lost—an overgrown cliché. I open the mini makeup kit C's mother gifted me in the hospital on Christmas Eve. I make two imperfect marks along my lashes. I discover a tiny matte red lipstick and slide a velvet coat onto my lips. I dab half away, smudging a piece of paper with what looks like blood. I emerge and grin at C, feigning the appetite I hope will come. *Let's eat!*

At a candlelit counter, we splurge on omakase, each sushi bite placed before us one by one. After months of hospital meals and Ensures, I am still startled by *real food*, its depth and delicacy. I feel full, ready to leave, by the fourth piece. But I am also in love with the dim, warm huddle of me and C. We make gentle jokes, make a list of favorite things. *The Indian Ocean. Carmenère. That time on the roof.*

I swirl in the soft shadows and sake buzz. Around me, stylish couples lean together, their smooth skin and tinkling voices suggesting ordered, sexy worlds. I caress myself with the thought that I might enter such a story too. That tonight, I might be the woman laughing on the sidewalk, loud in lipstick and new boots. Breathless, elegant, heels clacking home, into a future made of bright sturdy wood. Waking tomorrow to see my smile has survived.

Mourid Barghouti was displaced by the same war that ejected my young father from Gaza in 1967. Barghouti was in Egypt taking an English exam the day he learned Israel had occupied the rest of Palestine. Emerging from his classroom, he stumbled into his new state, announced on a stranger's car radio: he had become an exile, غريب.

It would be two decades until he was permitted to visit the town that, when he left, was home. Forty years later he looked back on the life that rippled from, and remained forever in, that moment:

لكني أعرف أن الغريب لا يعود أبدا إلى حالاته الأولى. حتى لو عاد، خَلَصْ، يصاب المرء بالغربة كما يصاب بالربو، ولا علاج للاثنين.

But I do know that the غريب *can never go back to what he was. Even if he returns. It is over. A person is stricken with* غربة *the way he is stricken with asthma—there is no cure for either.*

My father has both.

The pockets of all his jeans bear the hollow shape of his inhaler.

◇ ◇ ◇

On a Friday, I break the first rule.

It begins with a subway stop. On my way home from the outpatient program, I should have descended at Madison Square to catch the R train at 4:00 p.m. I should switch to the A after crossing the East River. By 4:40, I should be in the stream of bodies rising at Nostrand Avenue. Instead, at 3:55, I let my body drift past the yellow stairs leading underground. Now, my feet carry me downtown. *I'm just stretching my legs*, I reason, quickening. *Just a little fresh air.*

Promising myself to catch the R at the next station, I think careful, innocent thoughts. *What a nice day. What a nice park.* In my head, the hospital's chief nurse looms, forever frowning in her bifocals, T. J. Eckleburg with bangs. I shudder as her thick German accent once again intrudes, repeating her last words to me on the ward. *I think we'll see you again.*

I reach the next subway stop and breeze onward. I continue to the tip of Manhattan, taking in the cold but lively sidewalks of Chinatown. I have completed a two-mile power walk by the time I descend to the train. The car rattles toward Brooklyn, and I stand frozen and thudding by the door. Soon I'll feel the first gentle tugs of hunger, the ebb of blood sugar dulling the edges of my brain. With this, waves of old euphoria. A familiar, lukewarm tide.

After this, I begin getting off the subway earlier and earlier each morning, extending what should be a four-minute walk to fifteen, then twenty. I arrive at my outpatient program flushed and calm, drunk with sudden relief. In the afternoons, I use errands to excuse a second, meandering stroll, and by dinner I am serving myself a little less than I should.

Hunger, accreting slowly, sheathes me from my dread. As its buzz rises in my ear, I feel the wobble of desire. I want to relent, to dissolve. Of course, it pains me to tell C so many silent lies. His trust is a small animal caught in my slow, cruel squeeze. But, I reason, this may be a necessary bargain: to find the edge of emptiness. A measure of absence that will sustain but not destroy me, senses dulled just enough to make living feel humane.

Still, my body registers rising danger. My heart pounds when, as a patient at my program throws a fit, a staff member rolls her eyes to me. This conspiratorial grin, confirming I am succeeding at a game I need to lose. Even after my therapist walks me through a trauma diagnostic that scores me as *moderate to high*, the look she gives is not concerned but humoring. *Maybe you'd like to check out a trauma group?* she offers, like a book club I might enjoy. She then tells me that she's promoting me ahead of schedule—up to the *Reintegration Track*, one step before *Discharge*.

Though I fear this false confidence, I cannot stop exploiting it. One day, I am seized by the desire to throw my lunch away. I am startled to find it is easy. The trusting staff rarely checks on me amid the chaos of mealtime. I stride straight to the trash bin, its black bag already greased with rejected food. I begin to do this frequently, each time hoping and fearing I'll be caught.

My weight begins dropping immediately. I quietly plan ahead. I'm weighed only biweekly now—a good-behavior privilege. On those mornings, I fill my belly with liquid and slide small, heavy objects inside my bra—tricks I'd often heard others describe. I tell myself that, of course, I will not lose indefinitely. I only need to disappear a bit. *No big deal.* I tuck a string of thick glass beads under one breast. I chug a bottle of water, then a third. *There's no need to worry them.*

رؤية
Vision

What does it mean to see a thing? In Arabic, the answer comes in multitudes.

ر - ظ - ن: a basic three-letter root. Here, the word overlaps most simply with *to see*—as in *eyesight, to glance, to view*. But even here, the language knows the eye is no neutral organ. نظر is also a thinking word, meaning not only *look* but *consider, contemplate*. The mind, ponderous on its side of the glass, insistent or inquiring. From here, the word may elongate—نظرية, *theory*, existence as curiosity and change. Or the three letters may harden, a shift in syntax making نظر *opinion*—reflection replaced by a static frame.

ر - ص - ب: another common word for *vision*, this word carries a halo of the unseen. بصر: not only to glimpse or gaze but also to *perceive, discern, grasp*. An acknowledgment that sight is collaboration, interpretation, a mind touched by what it sees. One of Allah's ninety-nine names grows here: الْبَصِير. Divinity as the *One Who Beholds All*. The word is seen 148 times in the Qur'an, in ten different forms. *We have seen. They see. All vision. Your sight.* And once: يُبَصَّرُونَهُمْ. A single compound word that says *they will be made to see each other, themselves.*

ر - ا - ق - ب: this word is a one-way mirror. Here, *looking* grows narrow, needles toward its mark. The observer seeks not to comprehend but to *supervise* and *surveil.* The root slants to give us رقيب, مراقب—*watchman, inspector, guard.* The observer, presuming authority, reduces the observed to surfaces. There is no direct contact between the two, but the effects may cut to the bone. Looking becomes control, رقابة, *censorship.* Uneasy flesh reflexes with رِقبة—*wariness, vigilance.*

ر - أ - ى tempts us to lose all distinction between the eyes and the mind. In its simpler forms, it means *regard, notice,* and *behold.* Already, the word suggests a body, a subjective, conscious gaze. From here, it forks. On one side, it veers with judgment: رأي, *opinion,* يرى أن, *to express a belief or view.* On the other, it goes feral, corkscrewing into fantasy: رؤية, as in *vision [for the future].* Seeing as soul-scope, as possibility and play. Next door blooms رؤيا: *imagination, aspiration, dream.*

This root gives us مرآة, *mirror,* too—as well as راية, *banner, flag.* Here, the root touches a nerve. It reminds us of the entanglement between the selves we think we see and what story we salute. Vision as proxy for belief, or the power we can lose.

◇ ◇ ◇

I have the sense of C's eyes trailing me, gazing silent and betrayed each morning as I sneak out. My furtive walks have surged to long fugitive runs. Hours before dawn, stomach scalded with black coffee, I curse the creaking stairs as I slink down three stories to the street. I stuff my ears with airpods, slip into the watchful dark. I almost, almost, almost think so many things. But all thought is disarticulated as I jerk forward, the pavement a hammer on my bones. I accelerate, stoking my blood to a gallop. Soon, I will lose language completely, become nothing but burning breath. But in the moments I still have a body, I feel cold wet trace my cheeks. A groan—not so much uttered but overheard. One word nearly forming on my lips. *Please.*[21]

❖ ❖ ❖

Bodegas begin rationing Purell. On the subway, eyes quiz each other above slowly multiplying masks. Some friends begin *working from home*, a transition they describe as novel and *only temporary*. We are in the dregs of February, still unclear whether something like a *pandemic*—a word we associate with other places and decades— can actually touch us. An acquaintance several income brackets above us tells C to *watch the market*—we'll know the world is ending if the stocks begin to plunge. In the meantime, says this millionaire, *there's nothing to worry about.*

I want to be convinced. I want the sickening comfort my father chased for decades on my behalf. That American middle-class hubris, imagining I am safe from crude threats like war and plague. Still, the news tells me the virus is threading its way across the earth. I cannot imagine that New York City, a global hub, will be spared. It is even harder to imagine that the American health care system will handle any outbreak well. The winter air crawls inside my clothes. I suggest to C that perhaps we should stop commuting too. Maybe I should end my outpatient treatment early—*just to be safe.*

We hesitate, weigh the risks of infection against the danger of relapse. We lack the capacity to imagine either reality, but we dutifully attempt. *This virus sounds serious*, I say, hunched with my laptop on the couch. *But how are you feeling about treatment?* C asks, standing in the bedroom door. We look at each other. Our joy breathes nearby, soft and still scabbed with recent wounds. I feel there is only one answer we can bear. I tell him *I think I'm doing okay.*

Later, in the middle of the night, I open my my phone and type slurry, half-conscious notes. *What is the word for saying something that sounds so right when you're saying it, like something you'd hear someone else say, and you're both in love with how right it sounds, and afraid . . . afraid of how much you want to mean it, and how unsure you are that you do? Or that you even can?*

Some mornings, I force myself to sit with C for breakfast. I hold my mostly hollow bowl to my chest, hiding its emptiness. I look him in the eye, resisting the urge to ogle his cereal-plump spoon. I fidget, get up over and over again—water for myself, then for him, then to refill my tea. A chain of needless motion, to seek distraction from my hunger and deflect C's attention from my meal. As I drain another cup of sencha, I reach over and stroke his hand.

One day, while C is out, I lock myself in the bathroom and get on the scale. With my bra unstuffed and bladder empty, I see the truth: I have dropped twelve pounds in less than a month. Doctors had warned me that I would still be in *hypermetabolism* after discharge. My body is a roaring furnace performing unseen, in-depth repair. Even small shortfalls in calories will peel flesh off me, zap those painstaking hospital meals.

What are you doing?! I stare in the mirror, my chest pounding, head surging with the certainty that *I need more help*. The face in the glass blurs. In my mind's eye I watch myself, over and over, leaving the ward that final day. Hand in hand with a *Good Man*, his cheeks painted with pride. I want to get lost there—in the moment of potential, the future still untainted by my touch.

I try to imagine what *more help* might mean. The tightening loop of my *care team*. C forced into the role of surveillance, scrutinizing the scale and my meals. I see the humiliation of failure. And worse—I see myself anchored in my body. Locked inside a life I want to love but cannot understand.

I fall asleep a few hours later. I stand on a green hill, dense grass blued with dusk. The air is balmy, with a soft salt thickness that hints at a nearby sea. Something about the gold undertones of the sky tells me I am east of the Atlantic, that I just missed the wail of the maghrib adhan. A small figure sits not far off, a slice of white in loose robes. She is facing away from me. I want to call her name, but I find I cannot speak.

I recall no prologue to my grandmother's appearance in our American home. My siblings and I were still small enough, perhaps, for our parents to assume explanations were optional. Or perhaps they did inform us of her impending arrival and my child mind promptly forgot. Either way, our first encounter—that sudden sweep into her arms, her inaugurating tears in our embrace—was so abrupt that I awoke the next day with no memory she had come.

I rolled out of bed, strolled into the playroom, and dumped my blocks onto the floor. I played for what seemed like a long time, vaguely aware that the hour for breakfast had passed. Normally, I relished late meals as an excuse for more Lego time, but when my stomach growled, I looked up. The sunlight had thickened to an almost noon-bright glare.

I registered a clamor in the kitchen below and hopped up to investigate. Rounding the staircase, I glimpsed a strange sight framed by the arching kitchen door. It was a domain my father rarely broached, but that morning he squatted, smiling, on its bright tiled floor. My grandmother sat cross-legged beside him, rolling up the sleeves of her pink thobe. Though I had met her as a baby and briefly greeted her the night before, this was the first time I would remember fully seeing her.

I watched my father watch his mother, her face focused and serene as she arrayed her arsenal: a bowl of soaking vegetables, a carton of eggs, a towel spread with herbs. Between them stood a small, flaming propane stove. The air hung heavy with bold scents I'd soon learn to discern: garlic, زعتر, onions, مريمية, and the bright pungency of frying olive oil.

The kitchen I saw was not my own. I was peering into a portal, a telescope of time and space. My father, in this frame, was transformed. He hugged one knee to his chest, his head cocked toward his mother, eyes brimming with adoration. He looked impossibly young with the deferential bent of his neck, the hint of meekness in his shoulders that made the small woman appear, somehow, large. As they spoke, my grandmother rocked slowly back and forth on her thighs. The gesture had an incantatory rhythm, a quiet air of conjuring.

I do not live in a place, wrote Mourid Barghouti, *I live in time, in the components of my psyche, in a sensitivity special to me.* In that instant, they were alone, separate from place and year. A special shared compartment, a home that flickered between their familiar bodies, invoking past realities.

She murmured as she opened a Tupperware full of flour. With a coffee mug, she scooped a snowy pile into the bowl at her knees. My father cracked eggs into the fluffy mound, creating a faint plume of white dust with every plop. He worked his way through most of the carton before she signaled him to stop, lifting a drum of olive oil. The drum made mysterious metallic gurgles as it released its green-gold stream. Transfixed, I watched my grandmother whisk the mixture into a yellow goo. When she poured the batter into the heated pan, I felt a thrill at the hot hiss.

As a boy, my father often woke before his mother, fumbling in the dark for his school clothes. Each time, she implored him to lie still, but excitement shook his small body out of bed. Their new home in Jeddah made him uneasy, its two partial-basement rooms crowded by cockroaches and his father's sullen moods. He missed their home in Gaza, which they'd fled after the war in 1967. Since then, life had become inscrutable, his relatives and two of his brothers scattered from Egypt to Syria. Daily, his mother's face declared things he did not understand. The apartment was hot with held breath.

But school was a place where he could breathe, imagine, stretch. There, the small society of boys and books recalled his Gazan classroom, and new ideas made him feel rich. And so he'd sit impatiently as his mother made the morning meal, never allowing him to skimp. Tea, a boiled egg, grilled bread, and whatever canned cheese had expired at Musa's store. Sometimes there was jam— mish-mish was his favorite too. She eyed him as he ate, her pleasure tucked between firm lips.

As a girl, she had not been raised to see her life as a story starring her. Fate was forged by no individual but woven between souls. She took her first steps on ground her ancestors had plowed and grew up a stone's throw from their graves. Past and present, personal and collective—the delta of her early dreams. By the time she reached Jeddah at age forty, she carried two wars, a dead daughter, and twenty years of exile. Shocks that do not fade but pile, growing harder to name.

But Ziyad, barely seven, was still a garden she could tend. And so her fingers were prayers as she kneaded bread, fanned the scald off his tea. In the early light, she arranged his buttons, straightened the pants she had sewed by hand. She could help him look neat, remind him to bring his books. She could repeat *Allah yehmeek* and hope the Lord would hear. It was from his mother that Ziyad received his daily allowance of ten qirsh—four cents for bus fare each way, plus a little extra for a treat. He often skipped the snack. There was more pleasure in returning the coins to her.

Outside the threshold of their home, the family moved beneath a heavy gaze. The refugee, despite her private fortifications, remains both slight and scrutinized. The 1960s were a shuddering, shifting time in the Middle East, and the mukhbirin—government informants—were already in the streets. Throughout the region, colonial protectorates had cleaved into nation-states. The European retreat left vacuums competing factions scrambled to fill. Anti-imperialist movements collided with burgeoning oil states, Cold War jockeying, and an ascendent Israel.[22]

The Americans encroached. They were thirsty for oil and influence, distressed by the socialist movements emerging in some Arab societies. To counter Soviet influence, the U.S. backed the rise of monarchs in the Gulf and Iran. Once installed, these antidemocratic leaders feared domestic critics almost as much as outside threats. With American support, the anxious regimes built up their *national defense* and trained secret police to surveil.

Roughly two million Palestinian refugees resided in neighboring Arab states by 1967, and these masses, though mostly demure, unnerved their hosts. They troubled the neat lines of the nation-state, tangled simplistic notions of belonging and fealty. There was something disturbing about their liminality, the way fierce loss lit something hard and bright behind their eyes. Grief can give a body power, pare it down to recklessness. And there is something about life on the edges that allows a mind to cut both ways.[23]

And so, under these wary regimes, the walls grew eyes and ears. In Little Palestine, there were whispers of arrests and interrogations, of surprise betrayals. Even those who seemed to speak their dialect might be government spies. Once, a taxi driver prodded Ziyad's brother Ahmed. *Palestinian, yes? So what do your people think of the king?* When Ahmed launched into a list of grievances, his mother smacked him from the back seat.

So my father was raised in a world gridded with rules: *Carry your papers with you everywhere. Greet the police with courtesy. Let the teacher beat you if he must.* Still, Ziyad knew that he was lucky. His father had found him a place in a second-grade class, persisting in his search after the first few schools demanded bribes. At school, his best friend was Abdullah, a Saudi boy with one eye.

Ziyad only occasionally heard insults aimed at his nationality. *You sold your country to the Jews!* This, always the first jab, paired with the timeless reprieve—*Go back where you came from!* When these words and the fists that followed put a limp in Ziyad's step, his mother counseled him in their revenge. *Don't worry about hitting back*, she said, though he would learn to do this too. *Show them by making something of yourself.* Musa and Horea had long preached minority math: *You must be twice as good for half as much.*

And so, as a young man, Ziyad bought himself a Saudi thobe. At home, Falasteeni dialect still sang from his lips, but elsewhere his vowels hardened, inflected with the deeper gutturals of the Gulf. Each school report card drummed a boyish thrill up his spine. He carried his high marks home to parents' praise, but there was something larger he craved. Amreeka remained a hazy horizon, but a nearer vision tantalized. In his mind's eye, he saw himself as a doctor at a prestigious Saudi hospital. He imagined himself among native-born colleagues, accepted as one of their own. Credentials framed on the wall, he would be irrefutable. He would show them, make them see.

But for all those years, this is how each day began. The scene reprised in our Illinois kitchen, as I peeked: a small flame, a hot meal. A mother, her son, tender talk of small things. Their privacy a shelter built for two.[24]

Soon, I became enmeshed in this daily routine. I triangled between them on the kitchen floor, warm with morning light and boiling tea. My cells soaked in the scents of shakshuka and fatayer. Juicy cubes of tomato, onions dancing in oily steam. There was a deliciousness to our bodies, too—the primal comfort of my crossed legs against the ground, our fingers wet from rinsing vegetables or slicked with cooking oil.

English was scarce in these moments, but I barely noticed this. I did not yet know words could be partitioned like land. Arabic, like my grandmother, was a presence that seemed to both arrive and emerge. A gathering warm mist on my skin. Lumps of velvet and stone in my throat. Less language, more the laughter that followed, as my grandmother teased my father in her only tongue. Once, my father, his hair still licked with sleep, knelt by the propane stove wearing only pajama pants. His mother reached a finger to poke at the faint brown contour of his ribs. *Shu haadth? Shu haadth?* She clucked and dug against bone, making him jump. وين البطن؟! she asked him. *What is this? Where is your stomach? Where?!*

He was not thin, only young and lean, but I understood her joke. She wanted to fill him with her love until it could be read on his surfaces. I saw that flesh could be evidence of what we are given, what we take. That was before I learned bodies could tell the wrong stories too. Before I was told that my own would need to be small as a hyphen, strong as a bridge.

Look here. She clapped both hands on her belly. *Haadtha butin! Haaaadtha butin!* She thumped a second time, then grabbed and squeezed, jiggling her smooth, round rolls. *Now* this *is a belly!* All three of us jiggled now, the moment gooey with laughs and steam.

I couldn't wait to eat.

❖ ❖ ❖

At home, C appears innocent of the corners I cut around my plate, trusting me to follow my prescribed plan. Skipping snacks and skimping portions, I tell myself the nutritionists' orders are exaggerated. They would like me to have dessert at every meal, butter on all my bread. *They know it's unrealistic,* I tell myself as I serve half a scoop of rice, *that's why they overshoot.* Throughout the day, I carry creeping, secret pain—shin splints, stabs in the chest, the whimper of rattled bones. Still, each morning, I run. Heaving toward a violent euphoria, the brief loss of everything in a blaze of lungs and blood.

Returning, ears ringing and skin lathered in sweat, I pray C is still asleep. I tip-toe to the shower, turn the spigot to cold. Draped in water, I savor the last licks of oblivion. To the murmur of better judgment, I recite my empty line: *Tomorrow I'll take a break.* Later, I watch C emerge from the bedroom. My sternum kicks with the thought of what I missed—eyes opening beside him, all soft words and rested limbs. I look C in the eye less and less.

You can't see yourself, the hospital staff often repeated to me. And to some extent, I know this is true. To the bewilderment of others, I have never seen a thin woman when I look in the mirror. And contrary to stereotype, I don't see a fat one either. Different from body dysmorphia, mine was selective sightlessness, yielding only vague impressions of my face and clothes. A brain-imaging study published in the journal *Neuropsychologia* asked a group of anorexia patients to look at a series of photos. They displayed normal neural activity when asked to look at photos of others, but *when the women looked at pictures of themselves, their visual cortex went completely blank. It was as if they literally did not see themselves.*

These optical lacunae are cast as part of the *lack of insight* attributed to the disorder as a whole. Most assume anorexics are lost inside delusions, impervious to the havoc they wreak with their bizarre extremes. Yet I have watched many mourn their illness, even as they cling to it. In group therapy, we raged at the way anorexia bent us to betray our loved ones, our values, our own organs and bones. Writing in the *Journal of Psychiatric Practice*, researchers argued that more than half of anorexia patients actually do recognize their illness as defined by others' terms. *A future without the disorder* was the thing they could not see.

I know I am hitting every relapse cliché: *resumption of symptoms; weight loss; increased anxiety.* And I have heard what this might cost—*heart failure, brain damage, death.* In the hospital, my social worker added to the list of medical risks with personal admonishment. *C might be loyal now, but don't test him. Relapse often leads to divorce.* It is a litany of possible losses that should strike me with repentant fear. Even so, a confounding cleavage lies between my knowledge and belief. These horrors feel abstract compared to the whisper in my skin.

It began in girlhood—the crawl of an imagined appraising stare. This alien observer had no discernible shape, no name, but its presence pulsed with disapproval. Under its watch, I fumbled, triple-guessing even the most private, mundane things. *Is this right?* I asked myself—about my toothbrush strokes, my handwriting, the outline my laugh made. I wandered to my mother late at night, in tears. *Did I do something bad today? Do I need to apologize?* She looked at me with veiled amusement, shaking her head. Back in my room, I hit myself with my own fists, then collapsed into troubled sleep.

Looking outward, I was bewildered. Others seemed to possess an unstudied ease, slotting into the world in a way that seemed ordained. I stole glances at them, searching for some secret cue they shared. I could never crack their code—instead, I developed an expat's expertise at mirroring. Of course, I was aware it was derivative to build a self from so much watching and response. Below my sternum lived a phantom sense of loss, of mistake. And sometimes I could almost glimpse her—the girl who had no master, performed for no violent gaze. Yet an inexplicable fear held me, trapped in orbit, surveilling myself across airless space.

In this way, the cruelty of anorexia did not deter but inspired trust. Its endless punitive commands felt appropriate, even comforting, in the midst of formless shame. Regimen as pseudo-self, a form to deflect the faint, persistent protest of my unlived life. When its stir threatened to undo me, I fixed my eyes on the hard surface of my striving. And I glimpsed it in others' faces—how innocuous, how useful, I managed to appear.

Now, *recovery* has stripped me of every compulsive structure, all contrived righteousness. Inside my too-empty hours, the weight of the old scorn gathers. Now, I snatch only the slimmest shards of punishment, of relief. The fleeting piety of a brutal run. The vindictive *no* spiking, subtracting, my meals.

I cannot tell if C feels it—the pocket of silence pillowing between us. How carefully I move around him, brittle with guilt. At the same time, I need him with an urgency I know is unfair. Inwardly, I am losing even my feigned belief I can escape this disease. It is only in C's eyes that I find a version of me capable of *making it*.

I try, in erratic bursts, to make this vision true. I fix us a candlelit dinner, eat a few extra bites. I ask him to meditate with me—then sneak peeks at his tranquil face, willing mine to match. I drag us to bars, where whiskey washes my nerves, blooming warmth behind my eyes. For an instant, I sink into my skin. Feel the swoon of heart swinging back to chest. Hitting it like water, a hot pink spreading beneath my ribs. One beat, two beats, to pretend that this can last.

❖ ❖ ❖

You've lost weight, the dietitian tells me during our weekly check-in. A faint, innocent sound drifts from my throat. I will my forehead smooth, halt a clench in my jaw. But the woman is still turned away, showing me her back, draped with a shiny black braid. Her keyboard clacks. *Just a few pounds. This sometimes happens.* The difference on her charts is not the truth. I have been deft in manipulating my weight, but now too much has vanished for these tricks to suffice. *We're just going to put you back on Plan C.* She moves her mouse to a single click.

Take the warning, I tell myself the next morning, pausing before I slither out of bed. *Ask for help.* Ten minutes later my veins gulp endorphins, qualms melting in rising heat. To my shock, these runs have become an addiction more compelling than hunger. There is just a lick of pleasure in this cruelty. I was young when I discovered the peaking, electric thrill of pushing my muscles to their brink. As a preteen, I played baseball with older boys, earned grudging respect for my swift legs and mean defense. Playing first base, I dove hard after the ball, smacking my body in red sand, proud to mingle my blood with the dust. I fell asleep counting scabs.

I began to bury that tomboy the year I made starting lineup on the fast-pitch team. I was twelve, triumphant, and hungry. After practice one night in our Jeddah villa, my mother found me proudly composing a stack of sandwiches. My appetite alarmed her. She warned, *Better watch how much you eat. The season's almost over, you might start getting chubby.*[25] Her tone was casual, helpful, certain that she was only offering common sense. Jarred, then ashamed, from that day I began chasing hunger over strength. My early, clumsy lessons in starvation coincided with the year I quashed my first conscious crush on a girl. She was petite, freckled, and a fellow lover of books. We called ourselves bosom buddies, à la Anne of Green Gables, but when my feelings for her went off script, I moved reflexively to erase them.

These self-subtractions felt like reflex, though they moved against my instinct. The baseball field was the last place I felt permission to be fierce—in all other things, I was acquiescent, nervously jumping into the frames others laid. And so doubt did not occur to me when my would-be crush's brother—whom I envied as the second-best pitcher in our league—claimed me as his.

My friend group celebrated the triumph of landing a *boyfriend*, yet this victory felt hollow compared to the glory of a good game. But my baseball days were numbered. We moved back to the United States, where, as a female, I was offered only *softball* in a league so unserious and *girly*, it made the sport seem saccharine. I dropped out. My prized scabs healed. A solitary scar clung to my right knee, etching my skin in past tense.

Now, in the cold dawns of 2020, I discover something of my young fury in the way my legs tear the air. As the miles buff my mind to silence, my flesh merges with memories of its own. A whiff of my old athleticism, a brief visit by joy quickly overwhelmed by pain. Each day, a little louder—the sparks in my low back, needles in my left hip, my calves turning to lead. *Take the warning.* The thought flickers, but then my limbs are gripped, hardened by a separate will. From here, we are prisoner to compulsion, our brief communion cut as I pound on and on.

◇ ◇ ◇

More nights of dark waters and familiar, aching sky. Tides, my grandmother, her rose- and kitchen-scented arms. On these days, I wake with water in my ears. On these days, I move muffled in half silence, a sheath of near-memory. My cells rotate a quarter degree, briefly loosening from fear. A kindling hunger for her touch. I have no keepsakes of my grandmother's; this fact seems suddenly obscene.

In life, her belongings were few, a simplicity born of transience and poverty. She had a lavish practice of gifting—usually hauling one or two full suitcases of goods with her whenever she visited loved ones. But these gifts were mostly practical—herbs, teas, clothing, cookware—expendable materials of living, destined to disappear. Photos of her were scarce too. Most were taken later in her life, beginning when my father purchased his first point-and-shoot. An aspiring photographer, he roved, lens-first, inside his beloved, blossoming life. All my childhood, I witnessed his impulse to capture, memorialize, what he almost feared was a dream.

ما شاء الله، ما شاء الله.

I text my parents and ask them whether they have old photos to share, wincing at the abruptness of my contact. Lately, our usually close communication has retracted to a thin, careful rapport. During my hospital stay, I held them at a distance, exchanging meager emails and allowing them to visit only once. At first, this was an attempt to preserve, for us both, the myth of my resilience. Then, as *insight* slowly coalesced, anger swallowed me.

I recalled how visibly ill I had been throughout my teens and how diligently my parents had refused to see. In my memory, my mother attempted to intervene only twice—once with tentative concern, and once with panicked rage. I rebuffed her each time. After, we lapsed into a silence on the topic that would last the next fourteen years. At the time, I welcomed their denial, as it harmonized with my own. I feared my family's disappointment more than any illness. Our collective, feigned ignorance protected the reality I thought they needed, and that I wanted to believe. Then, on the ward, this abandonment fell open with a wail—*I was just a little girl . . . Why didn't they help me?*

I poured this lament on them in a family session arranged by my therapist over the phone. They listened, audibly stunned as I rewrote our history. *We're so sorry. But you seemed so determined, so strong?* After, I buzzed with a new outrage, but my guilt blocked the anger from its work. Within minutes, I wanted to call them back, to apologize and assure them of my love and gratitude. To prevent this premature catharsis, I cut them off. *Not forever. Just need some time*, I wrote in an email. *I love you both.*

Since the advent of the pandemic, we have begun checking in. Now, I soften the ice a little further with a text: *Hey, love you both. Hope you're doing okay . . . This is random, but I'm looking for pictures of Sittoo. Do you have any you could share?* A few hours later, I am squeezed on our small couch between Mowgli and C, fidgeting with postdinner hunger and reading a book on mindfulness. My phone chirps. *Hey sweetie. Good to hear from you. Here are some photos. Love you.* Thumbnails cascade down the screen. I jolt up and rush to the bedroom, closing the door behind me. I kneel in the dark, my hands cupped around the glowing screen.

In the first photo, I am two and a half, my face soft with baby curves, creamy with camera flash. My gold hair fountains atop my head, curly bangs framing raised brows. My mouth is open wide, pink and smiling, as if delivering a punch line. I stand tucked under my grandmother's right arm, her stout hand resting on my shoulder. The camera's angle gives a sense of stature to her short frame, which is squared toward the camera. Over her head is a loose white mandil.

We are both dressed in black thobes embroidered with traditional tatreez, newly arrived gifts from family in Jordan and Palestine. Now I know that, beneath that loose black cloth, her body hid a topography of pain—the undiagnosed spinal problems, the secret tumor in her kidney, the collapsed arches of her feet. Yet her brown eyes are steady, her lips brushed by a smile. Her lined face is bright, lit with love for the photographer—my father—and for me.

Hot sparks explode in my chest, prickling down my arms, welling in my throat. The details of the photograph—the lumpy faux-velvet couch, the rosebud wallpaper, the stuffed bird clutched against my chest—rise up and envelop me. I am both twenty-eight and two, my pores vibrating with the memory of that room. Yet the toddler also feels sealed off, opaque. At my back creeps a desolating sense of regarding the dead.

I look back at the protective wing of our grandmother draped across her shoulder, and feel again its weight. It occurs to me that among the dozens of photos that had decorated my hospital room, there was not a single one of her. No one thought to send me one, and I never missed her. Her absence a loss so entrenched I could not see it at all.

✧ ✧ ✧

It was a sunny morning, Sittoo rattling pots in the kitchen as I read on the couch. The doorbell rang, and a moment later, I heard Jill's voice. She was my mother's most fashionable friend, a *divorcée*, as I'd learned from the hushed voices of other women. I admired her, drawn by what might have been a protocrush, or simple conditioning. Too young to know about *sex appeal*, I understood some women were treated with favor, and this had something to do with being young, with looking smooth and neat.

I also sensed that most mothers were not thought to qualify. Their bodies, sapped and smudged, served as frequent punch lines, either in jokes they made themselves or set to canned laughter on TV. Secretly, I had begun to dread my gender, which I understood likely marked me for such a fate. But Jill was different, with her cropped hair, sharp lines, and fitted clothes. In her swagger, a hint that life might continue after motherhood.

I rose to say hello, meeting the two women at the corner where the hallway met the kitchen. I saw Jill stop in her tracks, their conversation dropping like a stone. Jill's pretty face puckered with shock and something like disgust. Her son Devon—a quiet, bowl-cut boy roughly my age—was at her side. His wide eyes followed hers, gluing to my grandmother on the kitchen floor. *Oh, wow,* Jill breathed.

Examining the source of their shock, I found a familiar scene. Sittoo sitting cross-legged, cotton thobe hiked up to her swollen knees, bare toes wiggling as her body gently rocked. Around her lay large bowls of zucchini flesh, raw beef, and onion stubs. Her deft fingers shone with grease as she pushed a pungent mixture of meat and rice into hollowed vegetables. She was preparing mahshi, a dish I knew to be succulent and labor intensive, but hardly remarkable. I saw no reason to stare.

Yet the moment gathered weight. Jill and Devon's silence was compounded by my mother's, her face pasted with a closed smile. No introduction was made; I assumed my mother was shy about her weak Arabic, but Sittoo had no English with which to extend her own greeting. Just a few feet from us, my grandmother seemed suddenly distant, confined to a language that, I now realized, sounded like gibberish to those outside.

Jill broke the spell at last, leaning over to Devon to whisper, *See honey, that's what people look like in other countries.* She spoke with a teacher's forced enthusiasm, as if trying to persuade a child that *math is* fun! The O of Devon's mouth broke into a question. *Why are her hands slimy?* His mother opened her own mouth, hesitated, then resumed staring without a word. I followed their gaze back to my grandmother.

My own vision shifted, taking in her details in a new and slanted light. I saw an old woman, her wiry hair tangled, her cheeks a filigree of wrinkles and age spots. She seemed both small and too large, her breasts straining the fabric of her thin cotton thobe. Noticing their stares, she lifted her mandil to loosely cover her hair, but the scarf slipped backward, exposing a bald spot at the crown of her head.

As the silence stretched, I felt my skin grow hot, prickling. I blurted, *She's cooking!* As if by naming that obvious fact, I could anchor Sittoo in context, banish their bafflement. Jill glanced at me, murmuring with grown-up politeness, *That's nice.* Then she turned to my mother, asking, *So she doesn't speak* any *English* at all?[26] Sittoo continued stuffing zucchini, her movements growing faintly rigid, her eyes fixed downward, toward her work. I stood, frozen and clenched, until, at last, my mother led Jill and Devon down the hall. I slunk away, alone.

I spent the rest of the day curled inside my parents' closet, feeling queasy and strange. With my cheek against the carpet, I inhaled the smell of my father's leather shoes, fingered the woolly sleeves of his jackets and my mother's faux-fur coat. Below, my grandmother's kitchen sounds continued, followed by the murmur of Egyptian movies.

My mother made no indication of noticing my distress. She did not come to find me, offered no comfort or apology. She did not explain that our guests' behavior was born of ignorance, a failure of manners that we might endure but not condone. Perhaps if she had, things might have gone a different way. Perhaps her explanation would have cooled the hot lead coiling in my gut, stalled this first imprint of shame.

My father, too, might have prepared me for this day. He could have relieved me, even a little, of the myth that we could exist in Amreeka seamlessly. He might have explained the small humiliations he swallowed, the wrongness others saw in him. Doing this would have cost us both some innocence, hardening the edges of his gauzy dreams. Cauterizing some of my soft, porous skin. But in exchange, I would have been girded with a sense of difference between myself and judgment cast from the outside.

Instead, in the closet full of hollow clothes, I soaked in a sense of confusing failure. What, *exactly*, had they recoiled from? Called to dinner hours later, I moved dazed and heavy down the stairs. Below, I found the air saturated with the smells of broth and beef, the table crowded with bowls, pots, and elbows. At the center, a steaming tray of mahshi gleamed, wafting meaty steam. A pot of molokhea also awaited beside a mound of rice. I slid into my seat, the familiar aromas loosening the knot in my gut.

But glancing at the kitchen, I felt my stomach reclench. There, framed again by the arching door, my father squatted by the propane stove. He was flipping pita with his bare hands, letting the orange flames lick the bread to produce the crispy char he preferred.* Sittoo sat beside him, drizzling tahini over salad. The scene swarmed me with sudden doubt. Their squatting, the loud talking—was this *weird*? We hadn't used the *normal* stove in months. Come to think of it, I didn't know another family who sat on the ground like us.

Meen aize khubz? My father waved a piece of steaming pita in the air, his Gazan accent ringing off the words. أنا! I chirped reflexively, noticing my hunger. He approached the table, tossing the hot bread back and forth between his hands, sending it sailing onto my plate. Tearing it into pieces, I relaxed again, each warm bite pulling me toward ease.

Yet as the meal continued, my vision began to toggle involuntarily, shifting from my internal point of view to a vantage just outside me.

---

* *I don't know why I like it burned,* he said to me one day. *Maybe it has to do with being Arab. You know? Sometimes when you think about what's happened to us, you just want to start something on fire.*

For the first time, I was not merely eating the meal but *watching* it. I watched Sittoo laugh and joke, watched the way she pulled the chicken apart with her hands, passing the tender parts to us and gnawing on the bones herself.

I registered each detail with a nervous curiosity. I recalled Jill's arms, clean and creamy against her blouse. All at once, I knew that she would have found my grandmother's manners repugnant. And I noticed how my mother opted for utensils, taking dainty bites, her chin free from grease. There was something vaguely moral in her detachment. As if she shared some secret knowledge with Jill and those other odorless, powder-dry women of the world. Some pact of purity and restraint that placed them above my grandmother, with her oily fingers and rippling skin.

I looked down at my own rice-flecked hands, the word *slimy* swimming to mind. A sense of panic swelled in me. How had I not seen?

After Jill's visit, I grew fretful, withdrawn. I asked my mother daily if we were expecting visitors, surveilling the front porch even when she answered *no*. Moving around our home, I saw evidence of our strangeness everywhere—a blanket of drying herbs on the floor, the prayer rug in the corner, the melodrama of mosalsalat on TV. Privately, these remained my favorite things, and for a brief time I believed that I could keep them, if only I kept them unseen.

Then the doorbell rang again. This time, my mother opened to find Katie, the neighbor girl who sometimes called me her Best Friend.

Blond, capricious, and a year and a half older than me, Katie was, I could only assume, *cool*. Our friendship was sporadic, consisting of her abrupt appearances, demanding access to snacks and our TV. It had been weeks since her last visit. She brushed past me into the house. I trotted behind, so flushed with shy excitement I forgot what waited inside.

I turned the corner to find her halted a few feet from Sittoo. This time, there were no bowls of gutted zucchini or foreign spices, only my grandmother's body planted cross-legged on the floor. She was an elder; it fell to us to greet her first. A handshake and kiss would have been proper, but I sensed she did not expect this from our American guest. I stepped into the space between them. *This is my grandmother,* I said to Katie, and turning to Sittoo, *This is my friend, her name is Katie.* I turned back to my companion, ready to proceed to the sandbox.

Katie's mouth hung open, shock staining her skin a mustard hue. *What are you saying?* she gasped. I froze, confused and mortified. But Katie was quick to parlay her shock into ridicule. She broke into a rough laugh as Sittoo welcomed her, سلام، اهلين. At this, my vision darkened, collapsed. From inside a tunnel, I saw only my feet, far below me, stumbling to the back door. I heard the wheeze of the door hinge and felt the clasp of cool fresh air.

Forcing myself to glance back, I saw her, still laughing, standing over Sittoo. My grandmother had cracked a smile, unspooling traditional prayers—*God bless you. God bless your family. God keep you safe.* Katie's guffaws grew dry and sharp, and I sensed she was now performing. *Come on,* I croaked, wobbling. Katie shrugged and ambled toward me. Outside, she mimicked our Arabic, scrambling noises that sounded somehow like both donkey and crow. *Dude, I can't believe* that *is your grandmother! What is she?*

After this, the hours were arranged by dread. By noon each day, my body was growing cold, clammy as the clock raced to three. This was the hour of Katie's arrival, which happened almost daily now. She was obsessed, endlessly amused by the old lady with the animal mouth. *Say something!* the girl barked at her, at us. Soon, my constant panic was transmuting into stomach pain. I begged my mother to turn Katie away from our door, watching through cracked blinds as my BFF trudged home. I exhaled. It was better to be friendless than watch my beloved Sittoo transmuted into a beast.[27]

Yet my grandmother saw no need to hide. I watched the bewildered looks of neighbors as she crawled onto the lawn to tend her mint bush. Murmuring to herself, the fabric of her thobe stretching as her hips and buttocks swung. I saw the same glances at my Little League games, where Sittoo sat beside the bleachers in her wheelchair, white hijab incandescent in the sun.

Later that summer, on a family trip to Wisconsin, we visited a petting zoo. My father wove my grandmother's wheelchair between pens of goats and horses, chatting in Arabic. I watched a khaki-clad family glance at her all-black abaya, then turn their heads again as she laughed loudly, baring a mouth of gaps and gold caps. I don't remember what she found so funny—perhaps I never knew. The memory remains only as a blur of heat. The shudder[28] in my body as hers was struck by all those staring American eyes.

❖ ❖ ❖

New York City postpones the Saint Patrick's Day Parade. There are over two hundred cases of coronavirus in the city, a number that confuses me. Two hundred souls seems small among eight million residents, but the world is using numbers in new ways. *Two hundred* cancels parades, reroutes CUNY classes online. It is a small but insurmountable breach in our dreamed immunity. C is told to stay home; I call the outpatient center to inform them I will not be returning.

In what feels like minutes, the entire city is submerged. The shuttered doors stretch for miles, dull metal splashed with ambulance red. From inside the sirened epicenter, I speak to loved ones in the Midwest. I explain lockdowns. The Clorox-wiped groceries, the DIY face masks, the empty lots turned to morgues. *Wow, they're taking this really seriously out there, huh?* I hear the sun shining on their end, the still-blue skies of denial.

On our feeds, a strange tapestry of hideous suffering braids with stories of *creative quarantines*. I read about corporate lawyers painting murals, watch a *pod* of children throw a pillow fight in the park. Endless photos of bread loaves prompt a visit to the grocery store. I find shelves plundered of flour.

On the radio, the CDC breaks from regular Covid programming to report, *As many as eighty-eight percent of people with a history of treatment for anxiety, depression, or post-traumatic stress syndrome said they had recent mental health symptoms,* and *overall, more than one in ten survey respondents said they had seriously considered suicide during the previous thirty days.*

As the world seizes in haphazard formations, C and I take walks. The global crisis knits a new, reverent tenderness between us. Beyond, we sense a vast loneliness taking millions of strange shapes. In this alien era, it feels miraculous to recognize anything at all. Our bond, the lean vessel we are riding from the past world toward the next. Our two bodies, soft and precarious, a shared inheritance.

For distraction, we forage each other's childhoods for new facts. We describe early obsessions—mine include Dostoyevsky, baseball, and endangered cats. He recounts how, when he was a young skater in Baghdad, *Transworld* and *Thrasher* were holy texts. At an abandoned basketball court, I watch him ollie and heelflip. His muscles fire with a lifetime of memory, but each landing brings a flush of fresh joy.

We replace Friday dates with a new at-home routine: each week, we pick a country—Egypt, Nigeria, Japan—and attempt a dish from that cuisine. We eat our handiwork while watching a film from the same country, squinting at subtitles, alive together for one more night. And each morning, C puts his hands and eyes on me. Repeating *I'm so thankful you survived.*

Each time, I fumble for a reply. *I love you too,* I say today. I watch the words cross from my lips to his ears. Each one, a shape I cannot seem to trace—the *I* is a stranger, *you* territory I cannot reach.

Love, the most maddening. Facing this word, I feel illiterate, left behind.

I hate Sittoo. Ugh!!

The words knife me as I read. It is another endless pandemic morning, and in a bout of anxious organizing, I have turned up a stack of old diaries. The earliest one now sits open on my lap. The pencil script, round and childlike, leaves a ringing in my ears. *She is so emberrasing in front of my frends!! She smells bad! I wish she didn't live here.* I slap the notebook shut. My limbs ooze down to my side.

Before reading this page, I had recalled fledgling shame. I had understood the encounters with Jill and Katie as deep, even disfiguring, wounds. Yet I had not remembered *hatred*. I had no inkling that I once wished my grandmother would disappear. But now, hit by these old frequencies, I feel their familiar pitch. These lines rhyme with the loathing I have long directed toward myself.

And I understand that what I read is more than a passing, mimicked rudeness. This anger is armor, the defensive snarl of a girl whose own flesh had become a site of fear. Because it was not just my grandmother's body Jill and Katie had rejected—it was mine too. Their revulsion trapped me inside a secret: that I, like Sittoo, felt most at home on the floor or squatting by the propane stove. That I relished filling my mouth with ورق عنب and wiggling to Fairouz. That I felt continuous with a body I had come to see as scorned.

Disorientation refers to the effect of racial encounters on racialized people, the whiplash of race that occurs while minding one's business, writes Ian Williams in *Disorientation: Being Black in the World*.

This awareness comes suddenly when one is unprepared to think of oneself in racial terms . . . These [somewhat violent] experiences recruit people into participating in the ordering system of whiteness, with or without their consent.

Williams describes these ruptures as endemic to racialized childhoods, writing particularly of what he calls *the Black epiphany.* In these moments, whiteness marks a young consciousness with its vindictive force, thrusting the body into awareness of its position in racial space. It is a revelation, says Williams, that *restructur[es] their understanding of the world.*

My epiphany was not a Black one, but Williams's words tremble me. What was that encounter with Jill if not an instant that restructured a child, a world? Watching Jill react, I was also caught unprepared, thrown into a new reality that ordered bodies in descending rank. That chill in my gut, the cold gust of an atmosphere I had been breathing unaware. The announcement of something awful, which I mistook as something awful about us.

It was easy to believe. Jill's stare loomed everywhere, its power confirmed by ubiquity. It beamed from TV ads, flickered on a neighbor's face. Fluorescent, its flash bleached every surface in its glare. Dazzled, I did not notice how much this gaze could not reach. Within me, a vast, private darkness, unburdened by shape or name.[29] But my eyes were turned outward, transfixed by that white woman who stood, purse forever clutched, at our kitchen door. Below her, hands wet with cooking, my grandmother's squatting frame. Me, caught, straddling the cold hallway and the warm, steam-soft room.

Williams writes that for the Black person, racialized encounters continue, compound. *I can no more stop the disorienting effects of [racist events] than I can opt out of weather or grammar*, he writes, drawing on the ideas of Christina Sharpe. *It's not that I find race in everything but that race finds me.* Though I had no language for it, I too lived beneath white rain. Yet while Williams's Blackness marked him for white exclusion, I sensed that I might be taken in. That my body could be bent to a narrow passage out of shame.

◇ ◇ ◇

My father pronounced the word *aah-sim-you-LATE*.* His tongue danced each beat into an ascending scale. The satisfaction of catching on, mouthing a strangers' language, moving in step with a crowd.

In Jeddah, nineteen and still stateless, Ziyad arrived to enroll in medical school. The registrar informed him there was no place for him, a Palestinian, despite his perfect transcript. To the student behind him, a Saudi who announced his C-average grades, the administrator offered a seat on the medical track—*or whatever course you like*. A final, unmistakable gesture, forcing Ziyad to see he would never be embraced by the country of his youth. The disappointment had the sting of love in it. Still, his mother's son, he refused victimhood. For the first but not final time, he cast his faith West. Enlisting the myth of Amreeka, where he would be judged by his hands and mind and not as *Palestinian* or *poor*. Amreeka, the benevolent meritocracy, the *colorblind melting pot*.

Except of course, it was not—not even in his mind. It had been *white* envoys from the U.S. embassy who dazzled my father's eighth-grade class, floating in with their blond hair, brochures shouting *Opportunity*. It was *white* Americans who starred in the films that stoked his immigrant dreams, who dominated the lecture halls

---

* "We should insist that if the immigrant who comes here in good faith becomes an American and assimilates himself to us, he shall be treated on an exact equality with everyone else . . . But this is predicated upon the person's becoming in every facet an American, and nothing but an American . . . Any man who says he is an American, but something else also, isn't an American at all."   —Theodore Roosevelt, 1907

when he made it there at twenty-three. *White* Americans who hired and managed him, who owned the nicest homes in every city he saw, who occupied the White House year in and out, commanding all those wars.

And so it was this white America that my father spoke to,[30] slicing his name to a single innocuous syllable. It was white America that he emulated, from the bill of his Cubs baseball cap down to ivory Reeboks. It was white America he saluted as he stood in the front yard, waving a garden hose over his lawn, a palm raised to neighbors with an unironic *Howdy!* And it was white America my devout father had in mind when he suggested, sotto voce, that I didn't need to wear a hijab—because *Americans might not understand.*

What I heard: that *American* must exclude so much of us, that their approval is how we know who to be.* A self, he seemed to say, could be reverse engineered. *Belonging* not inherent but achieved. And so my first grooves of self-rejection were carved by a hopeful blade. A few trims here. A chop, a prune. Eager, edging on disappearance, rest always-almost in sight.

---

* "I have heard that the United States of America does not consider the [Arabs] among white people or Caucasians, which is a condition for entry into their country. And the [Arabs] have set out to prove the error of the Americans."
　　　—*Al-Hilal,* leading Arab literary magazine published in Cairo, 1914

"Apart from the dark skin of the Arabs, it is well known that they are part of the Mohammedan world and that a wide gulf separates their culture from that of the predominantly Christian peoples of Europe. It cannot be expected that as a class they would readily . . . be assimilated into our civilization."　　　—U.S. District Court for the Eastern District of Michigan, *in re* Ahmed Hassan, 1942

Success, in this mode, was translucency. The slick sensation of causing no disruption. Gazes skimming over me, my presentation causing no pause. *Assimilation*, its oldest meaning from physiology: *absorb into and make part of the body.* My father and I, assimilating, racing to be consumed.

◇ ◇ ◇

I just want a normal family! I fumed in another journal entry, eight years old and still griping about Sittoo. I rode my bicycle up and down our street, imagining the worlds behind others' doors. I pictured gleaming foyers opening to lily-colored rooms. Hallways scented with vanilla, tables set with burgers, potatoes, pie. I began to see the darkness of my father's skin. I heard the oblong tilt of his English, noted the way *bismillah* stiffened our much-churched neighbors with alarm. Returning home, I was unsettled at the smell of garlic, newly disgusted by the aroma of my grandmother's مشاط الزهرة.

And I began to fear her fatness. The realization came to me in a flash—*Sittoo is fat.* Already, I knew *fat* to be fused with rejection and contempt. Now I could not unsee her soft flesh as a liability. I wondered about her bountiful meals, the lavish portions she pressed on me.

Everywhere else, I heard women moan when they failed to restrict, speaking of their full bellies with disgust. In this light, Sittoo appeared coarse, her jiggling stomach losing its charm. I did not yet fear my own belly—the battle against fatness still appeared to be an adult concern—but I understood Sittoo's was wrong. Her body, undisciplined. Too free.

This, my first antifat sentiment, seemed to come spontaneously. But it was whiteness, too, echoes of colonial imaginings. Racial ideologies have shaped Western standards of beauty and body size from at least the Renaissance. Then, increased visibility of Black people, due to European *expansion* in Africa and the African slave trade, destabilized dominant notions of the human physique. Early exoticizing interest in the Black body turned to denigration by the seventeenth century. The emerging field of *race science* burgeoned with attempts to define the differences between Europeans and those perceived as *foreign*, marked as inferior.

In this, women's bodies were of special importance, writes Sabrina Strings in *Fearing the Black Body: The Racial Origins of Fat Phobia.* Scrutiny of women heightened as *the racialized female body became legible, a form of "text" from which racial superiority and inferiority was read.*

Traders and so-called racial scientists composed treatises on Black bodies, sometimes describing them as weak but more often as gluttonous, undisciplined, and excessively large. These stereotypes were contrasted with the image of whites as slim, refined, and intellectual. *The slender ideal and fat phobia are not distinct developments,* writes Strings:

The fear of the imagined "fat black* woman" was created by racial and religious ideologies that have been used to both degrade black women and discipline white women . . . race [is] a double agent. It entails the synchronized repression of "savage" blackness and the generation of disciplined whiteness.

Those labeled *Asiatic, Semitic,* and *Turkic* were also described in terms of cultural and bodily inferiority—often due explicitly to their adjacency to *Africans.* An 1879 article in *Harper's,* entitled "The Fixed Facts of Beauty," cited Turks—a phrase also used to

---

* Lowercase *b* here reflects the choice of author in the original text.

refer to Arabs—alongside *African savages.* The writer described a Turkish harem in which a woman *stuffs herself till she is rolling in folds of fat.* Both these racialized groups, the article concludes, belong to *a lower order of beings.*

These ethnographic descriptions were used to both commend white women for their superiority and instruct them in its maintenance. White female readers were cautioned to strive toward thinness, lest they grow to resemble these lesser specimens. *Only in the uncivilized "Savage" world of Africa could a big girl be prized for beauty,* notes Strings, or, as another *Harper's* essay, "The Sorrows of the Fat," described, *that burning clime where women are, like pigs, valued at so much a pound.*

I hide my journals, sickened by the revelation of my scorn, my betrayal. My memories take on a new, uneasy hue. I recall the chill that grew between me and Sittoo. I eventually started to bring friends home again but no longer introduced them to my grandmother. For a while, she made a show of sitting up, craning toward us as we entered. Expecting, at least, the greeting that was her due. Conscious of my audience, I ignored her, and the ensuing gnaw of guilt.

I began holding myself apart from her in private too. I stepped around her as she cooked. I sat at the far end of the dinner tray, eyes cast to the side. Perhaps at first I reasoned, in my childlike way, that adults didn't suffer hurt feelings. Later, I imagined I was saving her embarrassment. Yet the truth was that my callousness frightened me. Already, I felt trapped somewhere apart, barred from return.

It is a joy to be hidden but a disaster not to be found, wrote psychoanalyst D. W. Winnicott in the mid-twentieth century. The quote would reach pop culture half a century later, making round after round. Less trendy is the body of work behind this phrase, his concept of the False Self. According to Winnicott, the False Self is a construction meant to protect the True Self in a hostile world. The False Self emerges early, when a child first feels misunderstood. It dawns on her that what matters most is not her internal truth but what she conveys, makes visible. This mismatch causes deep alarm, rupturing her personhood.

So the False Self appears. It sets itself as sentry, scanning the world for cues, tailoring its performance toward acceptance and safety.

This pattern can continue indefinitely, an artifice of postures and rules growing more elaborate with time. The more successful the False Self, the more likely the True Self will remain barricaded, silenced and unseen. The False Self becomes the only version she, or those around her, can know.

What my grandmother made of my betrayals, I never knew. But with time, she stopped calling me to join her for cards. She spoke to me less often, beginning to turn to my father to relay messages in English. Perhaps she began to see me, too, through the eyes of others: as the American I strove to be.

◇ ◇ ◇

The chair is in pieces on the floor. C stands over splintered wood and shakes. The air ripples in the wake of his brief, shouted plea. Tonight he will carry the broken wood to the curb, then stretch out in silence on our bed. I will lie rigid beside him, my skin all eyes split wide. I will listen to him breathe, aching to touch his hand. His words will run circles over me.

You can't do this again, Sarah. You. Can't. Do. This. Again.

After weeks of sneaked runs and skipped snacks, my body is whittled to sinew. Tonight, C pressed me to eat more, forcing me to refuse. Now, in C's blanched face, I read Newton's law. Actions, however secret, still echo in equal, opposite force. A chair raised above a head, then a chair no more. *Do you know what it's like to watch someone you love die? Do you know what that's like?*

His eyes punched in, brown irises inky beneath unshed tears. One brow kinked, so slightly—a fracture in his uncanny calm. This pucker, a flare of warning, flashing in the dark. I replay this instant again and again. I recall his hands. Moving in front of his chest, balled fists that looked not like violence but a child panicking. His limp, twisting wrists. *Sarah. Please.*

In Arabic, a popular expression of affection is عيوني, *my eyes*. There are two ways to deploy this phrase—as an offering, and as a name. *My eyes* may be given in response to a request—it means *I will do this for you, I would do anything for you, I would even give you my eyes.*

Alternatively, one might call a beloved *my eyes*, a reminder that what is most precious exceeds literal sight. عيوني, as in *my horizon is full of you.*

This is typical of our language, our passions bold and body-full. We say *I stand on my head for you. You are my soul, my breath.* We call loved ones not only *my eyes* but also *my heart, my life, the light by which our city sees.* Love and flesh mingle so tightly, we'd rather our bodies end before theirs do. We say تقبرني, *bury me.*

I see it now—how I might become our grave. *I'm with you to the end,* C said tonight, his arms dropping at last. *Whatever that is.* For the first time, I felt his promise sway. His gaze swerving, as if shifting its frame. Perhaps finally glimpsing the version of me that I fear: a vessel cracked too far to hold grace.

We stared at each other across the silence, and I saw his love again. Recognized its hands and feet. The flesh he has used for my survival, tucked with pain I have not seen. *Have you lost enough yet?* I have asked myself again and again, watching my life drain. Waiting to fear self-destruction more than I fear change.

Future love does not exist, wrote Tolstoy. *Love is a present activity only.* In bed, I try again to count the cost. I imagine a list of one word. His lungs move gently next to me.

Photos of me and my grandmother show my young body always leaning, pressing toward her. Her skin was perfect to me then, pillowing welcome against mine. In one snapshot, she is slicing a watermelon over a tray on the floor. A stout two-and-a-half-year-old, I lean against her, one leg up in the air, one hand thrusting fruit into my mouth. A sprawl of pink juice and tan limbs, open lips that might have been singing or laughing as I chewed. My eyes are grinning as I look straight into the camera's lens. I show no signs of shrinking back, no posture or pose.

Here, record that once, I was a single, beating flesh. Unlayered, no instants between the self who held and beheld. *Only the True Self can be creative and only the True Self can feel real*, wrote Winnicott. Perhaps only the True Self can love.

◇ ◇ ◇

I am planted in the grass, watching my grandmother pick through the na'na' she planted the spring she arrived with her suitcase of unknown smells. The garden would never be the same, the wild mint overtaking my mother's pansies, spiraling beneath tulips. The air lights with their bright smell as she stirs their leaves with her fingers. She smiles a private gap-toothed smile, her lips moving silently. A divot drops at the center of my chest.

My eyes open, and I am staring at the tangle of electric wires crisscrossed outside our window. They are mismatched, sagging, a fishnet washed up on silent shore. Already, the dark sky is beginning to milk with coming dawn. It is late for me, past when I should sneak out for my run. I close my eyes, turn and burrow into my pillow. Digging my way back to her.

نكبة

Nakba

Once the word نكبة meant nothing to us.

Today, it is the story we cannot outrun. نكبة—*Nakba*—is our address, our big bang. It numbers the particles in our universe, writes the borders of what can be. نكبة, all that is not, an arrested history. Dreams that become lies, and the lies we practice instead of dreaming.

نكبة. From the root ب - ك - ن, which originally meant *to turn away, deviate*, but also *to make someone unhappy*. An axis, a world pivoted a little farther from the sun.

Fascinatingly, a preeminent Arab linguist says to me, *the earliest meaning of "nakba" is "damage to the foot caused by a stone."*

A stone, a chip of earth fractured from its place.

David's prayer hardened to pierce Philistine brain.

A stone, like those flung against settler-soldiers,

answered with bullets and broken bones.*

A damaged foot. A limp. An involuntary bow.

Of course, adds the professor, نكبة *does indeed come to mean "disaster, misfortune, calamity, etc."*

Etc.: three letters that can spell anything.

One definition of *etc.*: The day Israel calls Independence. The world gone inside out, home becoming foe. 1948, half the Palestinian population—seven hundred thousand or more—driven from their homes. Bodies pushed underground. Villages razed to rumors, histories captured, a map remade.

Some call it *the Palestinian exodus*, with no perceptible irony.

Some families mark this event every May. Others, like mine, let the day pass quietly.

Etc. is easier to hold.

---

* "Israel's Parliament decided today not to investigate charges that former Defense Minister Yitzhak Rabin ordered soldiers to break the bones of Arab militants at the beginning of the Palestinian uprising . . .

"Mr. Rabin and senior military commanders have maintained that the beatings were allowed only while soldiers were trying to overpower and arrest Palestinians throwing rocks and firebombs . . . But his account has been contradicted . . . Mr. Rabin said, 'To the best of my memory, I never once said anywhere that bones should be broken.'

"There is no indication that the controversy over the beatings has harmed Mr. Rabin politically."
—"Israel Declines to Study Rabin Tie to Beatings,"
The New York Times, July 12, 1990

I slip out of bed and into our front room. Here, the air is a bruise, the gone chair a ghostly space. I sit on our love seat. Beneath me, its secondhand cushions sag, wilted by bodies I do not know. The corner of my eyes stick with sleep and the bright colors of my dreams. My body is rigid, half-coiled. Somehow, I am sure this empty room is crowded, thick with watching eyes. Yet this is not, for once, the generic watchfulness of inner hostility and shame. I sense that this host knows me, their gaze holding me like a name.

I fidget in my seat. I have long avoided such intimate recognition, revealing myself in forms and functions while remaining essentially unclaimed. It was easy to do in a life so full of leaving, origins smeared in rearview mirrors, horizons beckoning.

Yet for a moment, I am witnessed. Beheld, and holding. Still.

I cannot believe my eyes.

A trail of plain spaghetti noodles sprawls across my plate, flopping over its edge and trailing onto the polished wooden table. At my side, my hand dangles slick and warm from the fistful of fresh pasta I just flung. Each finger throbs, glossed with starch and guilt. I glance up and find C staring, his face painted calm. His serenity provokes me. In my ear, the buzz of shock ramps into a roar. I suck a ragged breath and scream. *I can't do this. I am telling you. C?! I CANNOT.*

Next to the plate of desecrated noodles are a series of carefully portioned toppings, set out in individual miniature bowls: shredded parmesan, chopped herbs, sliced chicken meat. Every detail a banner of care, thirty tender minutes of labor by C. My heart plummets to my heels, then keeps diving, disappearing through the floor.

I asked for this meal. For weeks, C and I orbited the absent chair. I was quiet, fearing to make promises I might break. Attempting to eat more, I found I mostly choked. When I tried to resist running, my will lasted halfway through the day. I began sneaking out in the afternoon, leaving C at his desk. Across our silence, I watched his body sag, the loose joints of trust abused.

In each instant, trying to resist a symptom, I chided myself with warnings of future consequence. Again, I googled anorexia relapse danger. I poured ominous vocabulary into my brain: osteoporosis, heart failure, death. Over and over, these prospective dangers failed to impute urgency. The present was a roar that subsumed all competing notions of time. *Now* is the obliterating and only tense of addiction. An endless emergency severing cause from effect. History had no hold on me; the future would never come. As time vanished, it felt not like murder, but relief.

On one run, heaving up a steep hill, an electric pain ripped my chest. I jerked backward, gasping for air. I placed my hand over the spot, just above my left breast. *Is this it?* I asked myself. A deep silence filled me, the pause between two breaths. A prayer rose to my lips, then died, swallowed in a sick sense of futility. The past could not be revoked. I had been sprinting toward this moment, creating it with all those tiny turns toward death. In what I thought were my leaving breaths, I found only four words. *I'm so sorry, C.*

The same month, C began waking with chest pains. Prevaccine and afraid of Covid-flooded hospitals, we waited two days, our home silent with alarm. He lay in bed, a hand on his heart, as I tiptoed, the cold spot on my back spreading, a branching freeze. When we got him tested, the results found nothing. But I knew: his affliction is love. Is me.

Real horror gripped me, at last, anew. A brief, diamond certainty: the violence of my illness has always been shared. Though it felt like suicide, I tried harder to make my compulsions obey. I anchored myself indoors. I found a nutritionist, letting her assign me a weight-gain plan I then failed to follow. *I need accountability*, I said to C finally, my heart stabbing itself with fear. His face flickered with gentle light. *Anything*, he said, a beautiful, terrible truth. Inside *Anything* was this—him, preparing lunch for me. *How's pasta today?*

he asked this morning, as I walked to the shower. I shuddered. *Sure. Thank you.*

But a few hours later, confronted by my plate, reality vaporized. C was no longer the beloved who saved and saved my life. There was only a pile of pasta that was clearly a triple portion. Rage engulfed me. C was playing tricks, trapping me in an absurdity of carbs. *This isn't the right amount*, I seethed. *Yes it is*, C responded, firm. *I measured everything exactly.*

A vicious panic took hold of me, neuropathways screaming *threat.* Without sight or thought, my hand swooped in, scooping roughly half the pasta back into the pot, spilling a few noodles along the way. Now we are both shouting—something we have never done before this year. My protest continues, though I have already realized he would never lie to me. This *must* be the meal my nutritionist prescribed. As I sob *This is too much*, what I'm really saying is *I can't.*

C can hear the real plea beneath my protest, and he answers it— first calmly, and now with shrieks. *YOU HAVE NO CHOICE.* Even in his distress, he calls me by his pet name for me. *You have no choice, S▓▓▓.* His tenderness is a room I almost crawl inside. *He would never harm you*, I think. Then I buckle onto the floor.[31]

But you'll be fine, right?

This was the question my father asked, ten minutes into his visit at the eating disorder ward. I was in my second week of inpatient treatment, still under ninety pounds. In the ward's library, my father's voice was pleading, small. I heard its familiar need. Sitting across from a corpse, he asked for permission not to see. He wanted my words to release him, to revise the ruined landscape of my body and all the history it spoke.

It was love that asked the question, a heart revolting at my pain. His love had asked so many questions like it throughout the years. Doubt disguised in declarations, naming *good girl, great life, better future.* Prayers camouflaged as fact. As if language alone could make true what he needed to believe: *The past has been lain to rest. You will escape my pain. I can keep you safe.* It was a generous sort of wishing, such a simple joy he sought. All he wanted was to see me thrive. It was the least I could do.

Six months before my father's question, at a dive bar where I let my gin and tonic melt, C broke our unspoken pact, addressing the bones in the room. *We need help, S▇▇▇*, he said, using his nickname for me again. For a moment, I wavered—or did the ground beneath me shift? A flicker of forbidden thought: I could place my hands in his, drop my head against his chest. I could cave to my exhaustion, let my sorrow roar. I could beg him to hold me as the earth beneath gave way.

I want to do this on my own, I said firmly, reflexes locking me upright.

I saw every part of him sink. I tried to revive him with words. *I know I said I'd eat more. It's just been so busy lately. I'll do better. I'll really try.* Always this dual gesture, enlisting imagined futures to abolish history. I finished my oath with a flourish, a feeble ornament for his concern. *Please don't worry. I'll be fine.* This was just shy of lying, or so I tried to believe—a falsehood deferred, and so, with it, my guilt. The ideal Sarah was always, possibly, waiting in some coming, new day. The *maybe* of perfection, cast backward over present decay.

◇ ◇ ◇

The ground is strangely cool on this smothering July day. The hard wood presses into my shoulder, elbow, left hip as I curl onto my side. *What are you doing?!* I cannot tell if this question comes from C or myself. I catch a faint whiff of chopped basil. The smell sings of soothing rain and green. A roaring shame closes over me. I crank my eyes shut, as if I might squeeze them hard enough to turn my skin inside out. As if I might drop into some other story, away from the wreckage I have made.

Not like this. The thought turns and turns. This is wrong, all wrong. I cannot, I *cannot* be this woman—creature—snarling, whipping her beloved's cooking off its plate. In active illness, I had only the vaguest awareness of my violations—how the disease bent me away from the most precious things, wrapping my hours around lies. The hidden half bagel in my pocket, the paperweight in my bra. Now, with clearer eyes, I confront a woman who throws spaghetti, screams. A woman still half in love with her murder, still pacing at the brink. I am terrified to behold her. Terrified to name her, me.

My eyes open and see a world tipped on its side. I roll my gaze upward. On his chair, C leans toward me, resting both elbows on his knees. His face is a palette of grim resolve. I imagine myself from C's point of view—a rabid tiger, pitiful, fur gnawed by my own teeth. The urge to hide is overwhelming. But the moment is a thud that will not end, and I must enter it. I claw myself up to the table, trying to talk myself down. *No reason, no reason*—I repeat the words the hospital doctor once used to scold me. *No reason to be so upset. Sarah. Calm down.*

But language keeps collapsing, a bridge that will not hold. At the table, I still struggle for breath, barely hearing C's gentle words. *You're safe, Sarah. You're safe.* Together, we try all the tricks we know. *Count five things you can see. Four things you can hear. Three things you can feel . . .* Together, we gather pasta back onto my plate. C pours olive oil over his own. With his gaze turned away from me, exhaustion surfaces, sagging his stubbled cheek. I catch a small, flat sigh. I lift my fork, and a roar rises in my ears. I plunge into the food.

The first bite opens a hatch in my panicked brain, releasing me to a muffled, weightless dark. A brief reprieve—in this dissociative cocoon, there is no buttery starch on my tongue, no warmth in my belly as it fills. But as the march of bites continues, my cells thicken, my brain sharpened by calories. I become particular, a single and specific skin. A torrent of half-formed thoughts returns, a pounding sense of rage cut with sudden plummets of grief. I barely have time to register humiliation—*what is wrong with you, pull yourself together*—before I vanish again into the storm.

For weeks, our life hurtles this way, from one hot crest to the next. The endless *now* of addiction clashing with the wild, extended moment of withdrawal. My body accretes ounce by ounce, each one aflame. Still under pandemic lockdown, I rattle against our brick walls, my lust for exercise a thirst I must not quench.

C attempts to soothe me with his fingers, kneading my foot, my neck, my hand. But the relief this brings is feeble, and I soon erupt back into tears.

I tell him refusing anorexia is *like having a superpower I can't use.* Like wearing ruby slippers I can't click, resisting my will to disappear.

The days stretch, stern and inscrutable, time a dilemma I cannot address. At the end of each, I am scabbed and out of breath, half surprised to have survived. But what am I enduring? I survey my hours and find only the barest traces—three meals chewed and swallowed. A shower. A pair of dishes washed. *Pathetic*, I think, then chastise myself. *Aren't you lucky to be alive?*

✧ ✧ ✧

It happens just like the first puberty: seemingly overnight. I step out of the shower and notice the wisps of returning breasts. Dread crosses my skin, a cold breeze tightening each pore. Fragments of memory bat their wings—sidewalks sticky with men's stares, the dark thump of a frat party, the hard meat of hands and jaws. The past I tried to petrify now throbbing, nourished by blood and flesh. With it, a lifetime of learned threat rattles back into noise. I begin to swaddle myself in loose layers before leaving home. Looking men in the eye now floods me with a familiar panic—but beneath it, a new, convulsing rage. Behind my downcast lids, I am volcanic. Sharp. I almost hope to be provoked.

A few weeks ago, during my phone therapy session, someone screamed. Eyes closed, I saw the darkness of my own throat, the vibrations of savage sound rising toward my teeth. In the silence after, I waited for embarrassment. *Yes, Sarah!* my therapist said on their end of the phone. *Let it out! Your anger is strength!* I winced at the cliché, then broke into sobs. I had only just begun telling them about Safi, a boss who sexually harassed me for my entire Fulbright year. He was not the most physically violent man I'd encountered— another man had raped me the same year, but Safi clung to me. For years, his memory has crawled me, filled me with loathing I swallowed, locked inside.

Until—eruption. Fury at Safi for his constant come-ons and public humiliations, all those trapped hours in his office, working beneath his gaze. And fury, too, at every man who preceded and followed, who taught me I was unsafe. A roaring force of compressed history geysering, barely articulate, until I had no breath. At the end of our session, I pooled, heavy on the floor. Feeling not relief but humiliation, regret.

How obvious the abuse appears now—not only Safi's treatment but a lifetime of words and touch. Rough and soft, all unwanted. Those mornings, waking with a brain scrambled by alcohol, body pulsing with a muddled sense of breach. How quickly I ducked away from the visceral sense of violation, choosing amnesia instead. How often I bore the misuse of men in hot, numb silence, or worse— downplayed it with a laugh. *What was I thinking? Why didn't I put up a fight? Why didn't I complain?*

You can feel stupid for not having seen things more clearly before, writes Sara Ahmed of her own reckoning with sexual violence, years after the fact. *Sometimes we are too fragile to do this work. Sometimes we cannot risk being shattered because we are not ready to put ourselves back together again. To get ready often means preparing to be undone.*

The only relief I find comes in releasing myself to sleep. Here, an exuberant darkness, a brief deliverance from who I am. Yet this realm, too, is thickening. Before, dreams brushed me softly, leaving only their scents. But now, the visions come clear, summer colors on a lake. I see my own form, always six or seven years old. A version of me before Jill, before lessons in shame and all my ensuing betrayal.

I run and climb through memory. One night, I revisit the lilac tree in our backyard in Illinois. The next, I am back in our sun-soaked kitchen, Sittoo stretching dough and singing rhymes. Even when I turn away from her, my grandmother surrounds. She is ambient, endless—and so is life itself. Here, there is no story buzzing the minutes, no sense of passage, of *never* or *next*. In this sense of total safety, I move with abandon, delight.

Waking, I spill like paint, colors bleeding to gray. Instantly, I miss my grandmother but push the thought away. Rising from my bed, I tell myself *these were only dreams* and heave into dim waking hours. I mention nothing to C, terrified these nocturnal trysts are proof of a cracking mind. Still, their hues cling to me. Sometimes I am sure I hear a small girl laughing in a voice like my own. Sometimes, amid the tumult of meals and mood swings, a silence falls in the apartment, and I feel someone arrive. For an instant, I am sure that if I turned my head, I would see my sittoo there. Her arms so close, I ache.

But I do not turn my head. Fears of insanity aside, my yearning for my grandmother feels undeserved. The words of my young diaries—*I hate Sittoo! Ugh!!*—still ink me with guilt. I cannot undo the years I spent obeying the dictates of that shame, pounding my days and body toward her opposite. I see myself now, pale and whittled, strung out on all the wrong concerns. *It is too late.*

Then, one morning in the shower, I split. The sound of my sobs brings C running in, stepping under the raining spout. Into his soaking shirt, we hear me say, *I miss her.*

After, my shoulders wet with dripping hair, I ask if he's ever heard me say her name.

◇ ◇ ◇

I become a scavenger, hunting for traces of her. I pore over the few photos I have, thumb through my journals again and again. Each memory is a room where I loiter so long I grow shy. Soon, I am stumbling at the edges of what I know. My fragments of the past are mostly from childhood, detail muted by the distance imposed by shame, then habit, then continents.

I flood my father with audio messages, imploring for what he knows.

What was her mother's name?
Which of her sons were born before the Nakba?
How did she end up alone?

It is only after I send a dozen that I wonder about his grief, whether the sound of her name will hurt.

The young Gazan boy speaks with a man's voice. His answers come in the form of recordings titled with my name. *ForSarah.m4a.* As always, he begins each by reciting the date, marking us in time:

> Hey, hey. Hey, how you doing, sweetie Sarah? Today is . . . this is April twenty-three, two thousand and . . . twenty twenty. It's shortly after one p.m. Okayyy . . . I have, uh, I looked at your questions, boy, so many of them I don't know wheeeere to start. Um . . . uh. Just maybe I think I'm going to jump back and forth and cover most of them or all of them, hopefully.

His voice is drenched in love, the pace searching, slow. Word by word, he offers himself, particles I have never known. Beneath his voice, I feel my cells settle, opening. My body, a doorway Time enters through.

◇ ◇ ◇

In the realm of maps and records, her trace has always been slight. Born without a birth certificate, her name was first written in 1955. A UN* worker made the inscription—once in English, once in French—and handed her the paper slip. Her name, a token traded for sugar and wheat, in languages she couldn't read. She would have been roughly thirty then. A refugee of seven years, mother to a daughter and three sons.

Before, in her Palestinian village of six hundred, names were kept by heart. She was *bint Mohammed al-Mukhtar, ibn Yousef.* Her lineage, a chain of masculine names, a tether to time and place. Her town, 'Ibdis, first appeared in Ottoman files in 1596, and may date to the Byzantine period between the third and sixth centuries, as *Abu Juway'id.*

The officials marked down thirty-five households that year, not bothering with names. Their interest was in dunum, the rich fields yielding wheat, barley, and honeybees. Later, the villagers added grapes and oranges alongside olives, chickens, and mish-mish. Hundreds of towns like 'Ibdis dotted the rolling countryside. Each

---

* "Following the 1948 War, UNRWA was established by United Nations General Assembly to carry out direct relief and works programmes for Palestine refugees. The Agency began operations on 1 May 1950. In the absence of a solution to the Palestine refugee problem, the General Assembly has repeatedly renewed UNRWA's mandate . . . When the Agency began operations in 1950, it was responding to the needs of about 750,000 Palestine refugees. Today, some 5.9 million Palestine refugees are eligible for UNRWA services."   —United Nations Relief and Works Agency for Palestine Refugees in the Near East, "Who We Are"

had its defining feature, preserved in stories and poetry. ʿIbdis's boast was its jamayza, the stately sycamore tree.

Horea was the name given to her when she was born. حورية, easy to mistake for حرية—*freedom*. Sometimes, I wish that was her name. The meaning of حورية is not fixed but hovers around *beautiful woman*. Sometimes translated as *nymph*, a word found centuries back in poetry and suggested in Qurʾanic verse. In English, it can also be rendered as *dark-eyed beauty*. Sometimes, *virgin of paradise*. Some hadith, hinting at colorism, describe a woman so gorgeous *her flesh glows translucently*.

Is this what makes an angel? Something desired and vanishing? She was translucent for me, too, for all those years. *Sittoo* lived inside the days and language that I knew. *Horea* was a vapor, a dream seldom told.

Yet her girlhood was a sturdy-bodied thing, her name double-known. She was daughter of the mukhtar—*chosen one*, a mayor of sorts, a man appointed to lead village affairs. For her, *mother* was multiple. Horea was raised by her father's several wives; then, after her father's death and mother's remarriage to a man on the Gazan coast, she was tended to by a sister-in-law. There, Horea's world was woven of half siblings, cousins, and the guests her brother Fawzi entertained.

Like most other village girls, she was never sent to school. Instead of holding pencils, her fingers grew deft at taboon dough, spark-quick as she flipped white-bellied bread over flame. As a young wife, she carried lunch daily to her husband in the field. Passing neighbors on the way, they embroidered greetings in the air. She set down the basket of bread at her husband Musa's feet. *May Allah give you strength.* Receiving, he returned *May God bless your hands.* After eating, she yoked her afternoon to his. Together, they sowed ancestor soil until evening called them in.

These were the days tucked inside her, hidden from my father and from me. Horea embalmed her childhood in silence, ʿIbdis shrouded in vague myth. My father would not glimpse this history until decades later, as Horea led him through its ruins, the past spelled in scattered stone. His timeline began in Deir al-Balah, a city in Gaza noted not for sycamore but for its date palms. He was born there in 1960, his birth registered by the Egyptians who, in 1948, replaced British occupiers after halting Israel's southern advance. On his birth certificate, ʿIbdis hovers in the white space around the words GAZA STRIP.

Horea welcomed Ziyad in a UN clinic, alone. Her husband was four years deep in ghourba, cobbling a meager living in the Gulf. She carried her newborn home on foot, her steps jaunty, jubilant. There would now be four of them sharing the two rooms Horea had built on an unused plot of land. This, a permanent makeshift shelter after months of waiting for NGO housing. The only furniture stood in the sand outside—an old table her second-born, Ibrahim, used as a desk. He was the family's brightest, with dreams of medical school. To its left, an area for kneading dough and a banana tree that refused fruit.

Like any child, my father was born to trust. Gaza was Falasteen was home was the world. Ziyad loved the small path his days carved, barefoot, between his mother's lap and the beach. Mornings, he woke to the coo of pigeons, a flock Horea raised and cooked on Friday after prayers. At these meals, he jostled his brothers for a double portion of meat. Above him, history webbed, conjured in the words of Horea and her guests. From time to time, he heard a moan slip from one, and caught a chill. He glanced up to see his mother's head shake, her shoulders slack. But these were only passing, distant clouds. ʿIbdis, war, and even *your father*—seldom spoken directly, these words had no bodies, no weight. With *before* locked away, he did not see his life as aftermath.

Silence may have many parents. There are kinds of love that stop language in its tracks. Perhaps she held back ʿIbdis's name to save it from the past tense. An absence spoken gathers mass, asking the body to bear it twice. Maybe her silence was a refusal, a declaration that grief should not be her sons' inheritance. In the end, survival is a language, a logic all its own.

Yet flesh may deny the omissions of the mind. ʿIbdis needed no speaking; it echoed in everything. It circled in the eyes of her cousins as they paced lost acres in their heads. Lived in the sturdy music of their dialect, consonants like hilltops, memory tucked inside تعبيرات. It hovered in the taste of bread, baked from UN-issued flour. The flat sameness of its texture recalled how the dough in ʿIbdis rippled, grainy with hand-milled gamah. Each bite a morsel of the months past—rain or dryness, farmers' worry, hands plucking, then grinding kernels of gold.

Even in quiet, Horea's body declared. Her blood and bones, surviving, refuting imperial plans. Before her birth, white hands had plotted futures to make hers impossible. These men believed history as forward march, *progress* measured by Europe's spread. Everywhere, they proclaimed the emptiness of savage babble, saw a blank slate in native land. One would-be author of Horea's history sat in London, an aging earl named Lord Arthur Balfour. As the British foreign secretary, he was lackluster, but in November 1917, he published a single sentence that would make him one of Palestine's lasting ghosts—

His Majesty's Government view with favour the establishment in Palestine of a national home for the Jewish people, and will use their best endeavours to facilitate the achievement of this object, it being clearly understood that nothing shall be done which may prejudice the civil and religious rights of existing non-Jewish communities in Palestine, or the rights and political status enjoyed by Jews in any other country.

The British were newcomers to Palestine, arriving by way of World War I as they battled Ottoman forces on Arab land. By November, they had claimed control over the territory. The war would not end for months, but they wasted no time writing new maps with their minds.

At the time of Balfour's declaration, the Jewish population comprised less than 10 percent of the inhabitants of Palestine. The British assertion—that Palestine should be transformed into a Jewish homeland—issued from a mixture of motivations. These ranged from the lobbying of European Jewish elite to the *romantic, religiously derived philo-Semitic wish to "return" the Hebrews to the land of the Bible* to *an anti-Semitic wish to reduce Jewish immigration to Britain,* writes Columbia professor Rashid Khalidi in *The Hundred Years' War on Palestine.* But however ambivalent his motivation, Balfour was definitive in what he chose to omit. *The overwhelming Arab majority of the population (around 94 percent at that time) went unmentioned by Balfour, except . . . in terms of what they were not.**

On the ground in Palestine, the Brits tried to stifle news of the declaration. They censored Arabic presses and silenced discussion of Balfour's words. They feared unrest among their Arab subjects, for whom the Great War had brought grueling violence, political suppression, and poverty. In the aftermath came not only British occupation, but the tremble of more coming change. Palestine was filling with foreign language, crowding with men's designs. Among the strange new words circulating was صهيونية. *Zionism:* the name of the European Jewish colonial movement that set its sights on Palestine.

Zionism, a murmur at first, grew louder as the Ottoman Empire collapsed. Its gears began to turn, settlers arriving to acquire land. Palestinians resisted, but not always uniformly. From Jerusalem to Damascus to Beirut, various factions attempted to organize, trying to guess at the severity of British, French, and Zionist threats. Some of them appealed to European courts; some of them smuggled weapons for defense. Their needs, desires, and beliefs were a wide chorus, full of difference, textured with unique configurations

---

* Emphasis in original.

of personal, family, and local history. They did not grasp danger equally. Most could not imagine their world might completely disappear.

Meanwhile, in the shaky decades between the *Great Wars*, the Zionists sped up their clocks. Their ranks were tight with a shared vision, the vicious simplicity of their designs. *I support compulsory [population] transfer. I do not see anything immoral in it,* wrote future prime minister of Israel David Ben-Gurion. *New settlement will not be possible without transferring the [Palestinian] Arab fellahin.**

Where the British had equivocated, occasionally trying to balance Arab and Jewish concerns, the Zionists sought no such compromise. There was a calculus to their taking, an antisilence, a capture made first with data, land apprehended with words. Preparing for a full-scale military assault, they built a covert inventory of every Palestinian town and settlement, called THE VILLAGE FILES.

To create these files, they recruited members of the Hebrew University cartography department, along with several of the world's top photographers. These teams used cutting-edge technology to gather aerial images, hiding small planes in barns. Others surveyed on foot, sometimes exploiting Arab hospitality as they entered homes for meals and took surreptitious notes—*number of households, number of livestock, number of men of fighting age.* And so the archive came for Palestine. Ravenous, arachnid. Its limbs reaching, weaving one silk strand and the next. There was nothing too meager to become prey.

----

* *Fellahin* refers to the agricultural, rural, or "peasant" class.

'Ibdis faced its first attack on February 17, 1948—exactly forty-three years before my birth. When the Zionist brigade arrived, well armed and British trained, the farmers of 'Ibdis resisted with the clumsy World War I weapons they'd smuggled in. The invaders had data, but the village had history, a long alliance with the soil. The trees and hills were familial, offering shelter, defense. Despite their many disadvantages, the villagers beat the soldiers back. 'Ibdis thanked Allah, unaware that three days before, the same army had massacred sixty civilians in the village of Sa'sa' to the north.

With the surrounding surviving towns, 'Ibdis hoped the squall had passed. The British Mandate was set to end that year, but it was unclear what this signified. Horea's village had survived at least two empires by now. Chatter of *partition* and self-government rumbled in the cities, but ideas of nation-states were nascent, as was Horea's firstborn son. She knew nothing of the competing maps the Europeans and Americans had drawn. She did not sense the fissures forming, the ground shivering under her feet. She made tea for her husband. She breastfed baby Mohammed. She prayed for their crops.

On March 10, 1948, Zionist political and military leaders, including Ben-Gurion, met in Tel Aviv. The village files were complete. Now, the architects of the soon-to-come Zionist state adopted Plan Dalet, a blueprint calling for the destruction of villages (setting fire to, blowing up, and planting mines in the debris), especially those population centers which are difficult to control

continuously...In the event of resistance, the
armed force must be destroyed and the population
must be expelled outside the borders of the
state.

'Ibdis fell in July. By then, the new nation had declared itself officially
Israel—but on many Arab lips, it would remain الكيان الصهيوني—
the Zionist entity. A foreign body, sterile and metallic, named only
for what it came to take.

Horea, Musa, and their newborn fled west. Halfway to Gaza City,
they sought shelter with Bedouins. For seven years they lived
like them, shifting tents and tribes. They were not far from the
scorched ground where Jaziya, Horea's favorite sister-in-law, had
been struck down. In this, Jaziya made history—she was one of
the first humans to be killed by a barrel bomb, a new technology
that made its debut when it was dropped from Zionist planes. The
same strike killed her two sons, as her husband ran toward them
across the field.

As refugees, Horea and Musa ate of hospitality first, then by
sharecropping in others' fields. Years passed. Horea birthed
two more sons, and their worry bloomed. Irregular work
meant frequent moves, but each time they loitered as close to
'Ibdis as they could. This despite ongoing skirmishes, repeated
massacres. Horea and Musa resisted following kin who had
scattered to Jordan and beyond. They held out on the prospect
of safer nights, of humanitarian aid. Better to sleep on borrowed

floors. Better with their fields almost in sight, their skin tasting familiar air. After all, the sojourn was only temporary. They would be going home soon.*

---

* "There can be no voluntary agreement between ourselves and the Palestine Arabs. Not now, nor in the prospective future . . . Except for those who were born blind, they realised long ago that it is utterly impossible to obtain the voluntary consent of the Palestine Arabs for converting 'Palestine' from an Arab country into a country with a Jewish majority.

"The native populations, civilised or uncivilised, have always stubbornly resisted the colonists . . . And it made no difference whatever whether the colonists behaved decently or not.

"This is equally true of the Arabs . . . Culturally they are five hundred years behind us, they have neither our endurance nor our determination . . . but they know what we want, as well as we know what they do not want. They feel at least the same instinctive jealous love of Palestine, as the old Aztecs felt for ancient Mexico, and their Sioux for their rolling Prairies. Zionist colonisation must either stop, or else proceed regardless of the native population."
                    —Ze'ev Jabotinsky, early Zionist leader, founder of the
                    Revisionist Zionist party, mentor to future Israeli prime
                    minister Menachem Begin, "The Iron Wall," 1923

The first quakes come quietly. My body, which weeks ago was pounding half marathons on little food, is coming suddenly apart. Headaches knife my skull sockets. One shoulder inches toward my ear, then locks. I ask C to rub my muscles, but his fingers find stone. I try ice packs on my forehead, Tylenol down my throat. The aches refuse to budge. Outside, New York City is still runny and gray, still frigid with virus fear. Once a week, I speak to my therapist. Most of the sounds I make are sobs.

Between this single weekly appointment, I build my own archive. I lose myself inside hours of transcribing my father's voice. Together, we stumble toward specificity, slowly recover details from his own memory or in the stories held by relatives we reach over WhatsApp. Uncles, great-aunts, Gazan cousins—they are surprised by the sudden deliberate inquiry. Histories shift inside skins, find their way to me in words—English, Arabic. *We grew* خوخ *,* مشمش*, almond. Lots of almond trees, I remember . . . All those different kinds of okra . . .*

I throw myself open, their language landing inside. I am captivated, devoted to all I have not known. I have only the vaguest notions of the present—grim meals I press through, a body I try to ignore. Meanwhile, each particle of history pulses me, vivid with texture and sound. This Palestine is different—more than fingers placed on globes, more than I found in the years I spent studying its history. Different, too, from the newsreels, the fractured landscape I have visited as an adult. This is the Palestine of my inheritance—brilliant, complicated, and sliding into loss. Full of bodies and limbs. I rush toward it, ravenous, headlong. Failing to notice the tremor as it builds.

Then one day, crossing our room, my back goes white hot. A violent cramp seizes me from hip to neck, jerking me backward as if by a savage unseen hand. It flings me to the couch, where C comes running to the sound of shrieks. The pain is unlike anything I have ever felt—as if my rib cage is zipping to itself, fusing with my spine. My muscles roar, an ache so raw I taste blood.

I call doctors and find them booked for months. I spend weeks waiting, tilted precariously to one side and weeping small cramped cries. My world is a collapsed room, a gauntlet of sudden obstacles. I can no longer bend to reach the water in the refrigerator. In the shower, my torso refuses to twist, and I must call C to wash my right shoulder, calves, and feet. After, I turn the faucet to its hottest point and place my back under the spray, feeling my blood rise, every capillary opening. I stay as long as I can stand it, asking forgiveness for the wasted water as I grow nauseous from the heat.

Yet no amount of steam will soften the hard shell of me. As the weeks drag on, my former life begins to feel like a dream. How strange, I think as I watch strangers walk by my window, striding on supple bones. How strange to think I once moved so carefree. But now—every motion terrifies me. The slightest tweak may trigger my muscles to wrench into a tighter choke. A primal fear drums through me, a body gone alien, unsafe.

Meanwhile, I watch my form thicken, spread. Moving, I feel its faint drag, mass passing through the air. I hear my feet tread the floor, the new meat of my thighs rippling faintly with each step. With each new sensation, my nervous system shrieks, demanding violent penance. Visions of savage workouts surge to mind. I shudder with the desire to run, to erase what I've become.

Yet now my physical limitations offer flecks of clarity. Pain, a fact cutting the storm of my compulsions, making them appear absurd. How foolishly I lashed my limbs. How wildly I wasted the health that is now so far from reach. I plow through meals with ringing ears, disgust slithering over me as I eat. Yet I persist, determined to offer my body what care I can. After, pinned to chairs and my bed, I swear my flesh whispers as it swells.

The night, too, turns on me. Once the domain of comfort, my sleepscape narrows, shifts. I am disembodied yet deadweight, panicked and glacial under a dark, closing sky. Behind me, something sprinting and silent. I wake with the aftertaste of a scream.

By day, my grandmother seems to halo, flicker in the corners of my eyes. I sense her haunt in my own body, feeble and hunched with pain. I recall the private horror that gripped me each time she struggled to move. I winced at her swollen ankles, the scrape of her legs as she pushed across the floor. I sensed those around me tensing, too, conversations wavering as their bodies turned toward hers. But when she declined help, their talk resumed, screening her groans with their words. Sometimes, under his breath, I heard the click of my father's tongue. *Poor Mama,* he murmured with a flat reverence. *Mashallah. So strong.*

Until now, I have used her memory as shelter, a lap for my rest. I made her mythic or mundane, but in both cases made her less. Seldom did I consider her body as lineage.[32] But her suffering had an origin, and it was not her state of birth. Inside her, she harbored decades. A childhood in which she tumbled, climbed, and ran. Years more in which she strode, harvested, made love. What relation did these selves bear to the form that I knew?[33] Did her history still stagger her, after all those years? Did she ever feel an urge to defy time, and run?

Between the Nakba and my father's birth, his parents lived years of slow defeat. On the road to ʿIbdis were settlers who shot to kill. Sharecropping for subsistence, Musa and Horea felt the future drain from their limbs. At last, my grandfather left for Jeddah, following thousands of fellow refugees who sought work in the Gulf.

Horea brought her three sons and baby daughter to Deir al-Balah, Gaza. Inside her, the dream of return to ʿIbdis became a quiet, unstirred pool. Outwardly, she shaped her life around her children's hunger, the question of a roof. Survival had changed its rules again—she was now a humanitarian subject, a unit of charity dangling from Western benevolence. Cousins showed her where to fetch water, where to stand in line for food. She negotiated shelter with one relative, then the next. On a warm day, she and her young family met the sea.

When her infant girl, Bahiya, caught measles and died, there was something different about this loss. Something about the tiny shroud lowered into borrowed earth. Seven years after the Nakba, it was becoming clear—some endings are cruel enough to take beginnings too.

◇ ◇ ◇

Ziyad, born after Horea's visit to her husband in 1960, was the youngest by eight years, and the last thing it was simple to love. She poured her care and need on him, filled her hours with concern. He was often sick, suffering from worms and stomachaches. She brought him to a local clinic where nurses poked his belly and gave pills to flush his bowels. When the parasites returned, Horea fortified science with faith. She worried Ziyad's beauty—his blond hair and blue eyes—had attracted the evil eye. She cuffed his pudgy wrists with red thread, walked him to Sheikha Amna. There, she watched the holy woman sprinkle him with blessed water, circle his neck with amulets.

To her, the world was always a mingle of diabolical and divine. As a young woman, she was once stricken senseless when the night sky split, a heavenly light over her. Like the Prophet, Horea had never learned to read but had pleaded that Allah would teach her the Qur'an anyway. In a flash, she received the fatiha. "The Opening," the first and most recited chapter, which she prayed each day to her death.

بِسْمِ اللهِ ٱلرَّحْمَٰنِ ٱلرَّحِيمِ ٱلرَّحْمَٰنِ ٱلرَّحِيمِ رَبِّ ٱلْعَٰلَمِينَ ٱلْحَمْدُ للهِ مَٰلِكِ يَوْمِ ٱلدِّينِ إِيَّاكَ نَعْبُدُ وَإِيَّاكَ نَسْتَعِينُ ٱهْدِنَا ٱلصِّرَٰطَ ٱلْمُسْتَقِيمَ صِرَٰطَ ٱلَّذِينَ أَنْعَمْتَ عَلَيْهِمْ غَيْرِ ٱلْمَغْضُوبِ عَلَيْهِمْ وَلَا ٱلضَّآلِّينَ

She taught her sons a devil-tricking dance to perform at the door: *One step out, one step back in.* Only blessing them afterward—*Go with God, and come back to me.* As an adult, my father—his baby blond gone black as crows—still obeyed her order to step out-in-out at the door. After, he'd turn around, amused, blowing her a kiss. She nodded at his laughing face, sober and satisfied.

But there are things no amount of prayers can stay. The next war came so quickly that my father, age six, did not understand why he was forbidden from the beach. He begged for the water, complaining of the heat. June in Gaza was blazing in 1967, but Horea kept her boys inside as armies approached. She and the neighbors had dug a trench, ready if the bombing came too near. Bored, little Ziyad crawled around the shaded hole. Looking up, he felt the static in the air but could not read his mother's eyes. A plane ripped the air above their heads. Eardrums splitting, he cannoned to his mother's lap.

Ibrahim, seventeen, begged his mother to let him fight. He'd heard some men—teens, fathers, retirees—had stored up arms somewhere. By the time she relented, he found only abandoned streets. A bystander approached. *Go home. The fight is already lost.* He added a bitter joke Ibrahim would repeat for fifty years. *We'll drink tea in Tel Aviv tonight.* What he meant was: *There is no more map of us.** Western historians named the conflict the Six-Day War, but for the Arab world it was النكسة. *The Setback.* Naksa, the long shadow of Nakba. The cruel younger brother of Catastrophe, reminding that there is always more to lose.†

---

* In seizing Gaza, the Sinai Peninsula, the West Bank, East Jerusalem, and the Golan Heights, Israel had tripled in size.

† In less than a week of fighting, an estimated 15,000 to 20,000 Arabs (Palestinians, Jordanians, Syrians, and Egyptians) and 776 Israelis were killed.

After three days of sheltering in place, they heard the loudspeakers for the first time. Scratchy electronic voices ordered households to hang white flags. It was Ibrahim, the would-be soldier, who hoisted his mother's snowy shawl over the door.

When the Zionists soldiers knocked, calling for all men above fourteen, Horea's two teenage sons emerged. At each door, the soldiers, young men themselves, shouted at the women to stay back. Blanched sons begged their mothers to comply. Husbands showed steeled backs to trembling daughters and wives. Ziyad slipped away, trailed his captive brothers with a cluster of little boys. In an empty square near the sea, he watched guns point, ordering the men's faces to the sand.

There are things that a body does not unlearn. There is a kind of fear that enters the blood, mingles where we cannot see. And there is pain that lives aloof from language, a deep-sea creature with no eyes. Beneath the skin, it keeps its own memory and time.

The soldiers were after not blood but gold that day. Each pocket was turned out, every wallet confiscated. The captives staggered away without their watches, bodies returned to them.

◇ ◇ ◇

Maybe you should slow down, C says of my archive making. His face is pitted with concern. I am half lying, half sitting in a chair. My left leg, recently and mysteriously immobilized, is hoisted on a stool. I lean diagonally to type. I shake my head, slow but sharp. Already, so much time has passed—decades, all those lifetimes, empires entire.[34] Now, I stumble over charred fields, kneeling to dig with bare hands. A penitent descendant. A hungry daughter. I want to rescue every fragment of us.[35]

But you'll be fine, right?

Before this year, my life was built as a *yes* to this question, my days articulated by its ever-pressing weight. *Resilience* as allegiance to a future divorced from present pain. Sometimes, this is a necessary time travel. There are years we survive only if we cheat. But our bodies are a bargain we break at our own risk.

The summer after college, as I was biking in West Philadelphia, my front wheel skidded, caught. An instant later, I was sprawled under my bike, legs limp, left arm pinned. I felt no pain but much embarrassment as a half dozen strangers moved toward me with alarm. I struggled to lift myself, flashing a wry grimace to my witnesses. *I'm okay, it's not that bad.* My left elbow, bent and studded with gravel, was already swelling to a mound of bloodied flesh.

The worried eyes remained, unsure. To disperse them, I used my good arm to push up to my knees. *See?* I stood, forcing a smile, and stole one last instant of normalcy. A second later, I began to sense what my body already knew. A sickening sense of slippage, somewhere deep within. My balance faltering, tilting, sinking me to the ground. One of the onlookers pushed himself to the front of the group. He was dressed in scrubs. *I'm a doctor,* he told me. His face frightened me with its tight certainty. *You need an ambulance. Now.*

In the ER, I waited delirious hours, electrified with pain. When the doctors arrived with my tests, their first words were *Do you have anorexia?* I froze, startled by the utterance of this forbidden word. They flicked on the light behind my X-rays, illuminating small cracked ghosts. My pelvis had shattered in several places, my elbow fractured cleanly in half. *People shouldn't break this way.* But after years of malnutrition, my bones were porous, thin. Unsafe.

As my head buzzed under midnight fluorescents, they brought waivers to sign. I grasped, only vaguely, that I was headed for surgery. The next two days exist only in my body—my mind, severed from all senses, locked in anesthetic silence. When I finally surfaced from the operating room, I learned my skeleton had been fixed with two metal plates, an internal brace, and four screws. Even so, the doctors cautioned I might not walk again. I replied that I had a Fulbright fellowship overseas and that I would be departing in eight weeks. The head surgeon snorted. I tucked determination into my jaw. *I'll show them.*

This was more than stubbornness. It was reflex. I had spent a lifetime living in reverse relationship with language; I used words not to describe but to control and deny. I said *I will get over this* instead of *I'm too afraid to break.* Three days later, I took my first, excruciating steps. At the news, my father cheered in an email— *You're a strong Palestinian! Just like your Sittoo.*

I heard these words often that summer as I lay suspended, adrift outside of time—on the trauma ward, back in the surgery theater, stretched across icy X-ray machines. Friends cycled in and out, suffusing my throbbing haze with vague reminders of earth. They showered me with flowers and cards, with words of encouragement. *You got this! You're inspiring! You are so strong.* I cried only twice. The first time when an ebb of morphine exploded me from the inside out, my teeth chattering with pain.

The second time was at the end of a long afternoon spent alone on the ward. By then, my friends were visiting less frequently, understandably occupied with their full, real lives. The gold light was dimming when a middle-aged woman poked into my room. *Hi. Would you like a visitor?* She held out a small chestnut pup. Its silky body warmed my skin, nestling between my broken arm and swollen ribs. My face, an instant river. I looked up and tried to laugh. *I don't know why I'm—* My voice was underwater. The woman nodded slowly, seeming to recognize something I did not.

◇ ◇ ◇

All summer, as I lay in the hospital, Gaza trembled and burned.

I almost never flipped on the television. Seldom looked at my phone or the news. But occasionally, I awoke to find the TV buzzing, clicked on by another patient or their visitors. I lay, my body a landscape of punctures and braces, and stared. Gaza as the cameras loved to show her: choking on smoke, caving beneath infernal skies.*

I made it to my Fulbright—much to my surgeon's dismay. I boarded the plane in a wheelchair. I arrived at my orientation in Jordan on crutches, waving concerned looks away.

---

* "Israel lost 6 civilians and 67 soldiers in the seven-week offensive it called Operation Protective Edge. Over 2,200 Gazans were killed and over 10,000 wounded, 10 percent of whom were permanently disabled. Half a million were internally displaced due to the partial or complete destruction of their homes."
    —United Nations Office for the Coordination of Humanitarian Affairs, Occupied Palestinian Territories, "Independent Commission of Inquiry on the 2014 Gaza Conflict."

◇ ◇ ◇

Spring is edging toward the summer of 2020 when I finally see a doctor. He is bewildered at my archipelago of pain—back, shoulders, hips, and feet. He sends me out for X-rays and MRIs, which return with no clues. I am referred to specialists; they offer confused squints and useless pills. Others tell me to *just give it time.* My symptoms cascade. I grow astounded by my anatomy, each part made vivid in its collapse. Absence, a presence most precise.

I am sent to hematology. There, a puzzled doctor performs an impromptu bone marrow biopsy. He lies me on my side and, without anesthesia, drills through my skin and muscle, puncturing my pelvic bone. I cry softly to myself: *I'm so sorry—it's okay, it's okay.* After, he shows me the harvest: a chip of ivory, a glob of quivering pink. I crane my neck to see the wound. A slit, a small eyelid dotted with red. He places a Band-Aid over it. I won't need stitches, he tells me—*it will heal on its own. Just give it time.*

No doctors could explain why my grandmother's knees gave way when she reached Saudi Arabia, her fourth and final country of refuge, in 1968. For thirteen years, separated from her husband, her small frame had been steel. Her arms had steadied worlds, her head bearing loads of water, nightmares, and wheat. It was not her own suffering but her sons' that prompted my grandmother to leave Gaza after ten grueling, lonely years.

The 1967 war ended in silence, white flags flapping above muzzled homes. Loudspeakers, the sole disturbance in stalled air, announced long curfews and brief reprieves. Rumors of raids circulated, the earth continuing to shift.

Gaza before the war had been a way station, ground for the quarter-million refugees who stoked village names like embers, their eyes warm with return. Now the lines around it hardened, cleaving futures and families, barring Horea's husband and oldest son. Beyond, parts of Palestine were declared *the West Bank*, while Arabs in Jerusalem were informed they now lived in Israel. The *displaced* had become *occupied*, and it seemed all oxygen had fled.

My father fell sick, uneating and unsleeping, after he glimpsed his teacher's corpse. On the eve of the invasion, the man who had taught him to read تجنن—lost his mind. Twenty years after his first displacement, the sight of Zionist armies was more than he could bear. Wild with loss and rage, he hurled from his front door. His last words, shouted over his begging family, were directed at the troops: *Get away, you swine!*

The Israelis forbade his burial. The teacher lay in the street for days while his family waited for the army to announce a brief break in the curfew. Even then, they were permitted only to throw shallow soil over the corpse. Days later, they unearthed him, bearing him to a proper grave. The young boy who is my father would never forget the smell.

Meanwhile, the occupiers urged the living bodies to move off the land. Trucks offered free rides to Jordan, where 350,000 new refugees had arrived in the Naksa's aftermath. Horea sent word to Musa—*Khalass. This is no place for our sons.* She put her name on another list. Leaving, she was asked to sign a set of papers she couldn't read. For a signature, they inked her thumb, and she pressed where they asked her to. Later this document would be used as evidence she had forfeited her right to return.

But returning, for now, was far from mind. Ahead of her, the road would take months. Her boys climbed into the truck, bent to give her their hands. They pulled away, their backs to the sea, the date palms, their two rooms in sand. Horea left her daughter's grave and the remains of their cat, Hamdan. A cat she rescued from bullying boys, arriving as a blur of black fur, sprinting like Ziyad for her lap. Did she have space to miss him too? Did her goodbyes form a rank, in descending order of their ache?

Does a body carry such separations as weight or empty space?

❖ ❖ ❖

In Jeddah, Horea reunited with Musa, loyal to him though she knew of his infidelities. When his labor left him bent-stiff, it was her shoulder that heaved him from room to room. Her hips, which hoisted his weak legs, then received him in their bed. In the tiny, roach-infested rooms they called home, she cleaned the floor twice a day, on hands and knees.

There is a word for this kind of woman—*samida*. A miracle of endurance, a body withstanding what it should not. In the 1960s, Palestinian resistance took her shape as symbol—a fellaha, a woman unmoving despite oppressive loss. Often, she is depicted as pregnant, her belly a moon beside an eternal olive tree. صمود*— a word rooted in *bulk, solidity, girth*. A body asked to be heavy, to anchor a shattered nation with her fortitude.

Perhaps the truth was telling itself, the day Horea found she could not move. After years of ongoing, legs buckling into flames.[36]

---

* Sumud.

❖ ❖ ❖

Ziyad [in English]: Hi, sweetie. It's Dad. So, just remembered this story. I never forget it. It's just really kind of like, Sittoo is kind of like way at the bottom . . .

[Pause]

I'm not sure I have kind of like, the——the, uh, what do you call it, um. I don't know what created that thing, but . . .

[Pause]

I remember after she came back from the doctor and she hated what she was told, probably about her knees, you know, no hope for that . . . this was in the seventies, maybe I was still in high school or something, or maybe, yeah.

[Pause]

[Sigh]

She was so upset, very very upset, she wasn't herself for a few days. One day, I remember, sweetie, she cooked us molokhea. And she brought it for us for lunch, and we tasted it.

[Breathes heavily]
. . . and it tasted awful. Not too much salt.
[Sharp inhale]

Unfortunately she put Tide in it instead of salt.

[Sobs]

She cried so much that day.

Kathy [in background]: Powdered Tide?

Ziyad: Yeah, powdered Tide. I remember that very clearly. Of course she took it to the kitchen, she threw it away. Then she went to the other room and kept crying.

[Cries]

She was way . . . at the bottom. And um, I gotta start digging down about that story, but it was so sad to see her, just blaming nobody but herself. Saying she's crazy, she doesn't deserve to be living, whatever, whatever, and uh, it was really tough day. A very tough time she had for a while.

[Pause]

[Sharp inhale]

Oh my God, I remember—— she wanted to kill herself a few times. She . . . she always thought about it. To burn herself.

Boy, those days . . . my goodness, those times . . . I don't want to remember those. I was so nervous and so scared for her. I mean, committing suicide . . . um. It was. Um. Anyways.

But, uh . . .

So, sweetie, just a story for you. Have a good weekend, sweetie.

❖ ❖ ❖

The next time I see my grandmother, I am awake. I am nestled beneath a blanket, under the watch of a European-trained therapist who, two hours ago, administered a large dose of medical-grade psilocybin. She is part of an underground therapeutic community offering evidence-based treatments not yet approved by the FDA.

I was referred to her by a friend—a Palestinian, a former political prisoner whose trauma left him on the cusp of suicide. I last saw him in 2018, in Oslo, where he lived as an asylee. Then, at a frigid bus stop, he pressed my bony hand. At the time, his urgency surprised me, but perhaps he saw the light ebbing from my eyes. He whispered to me of his psychedelic treatments—*It was the only thing that helped.*

In the muggy spring of 2020, I messaged him. It had been a year since I left my body on Eastern Parkway, then returned. But the memory of that weightless place still sirens, soft and red. *Recovery has not cured my lust for disappearance, only sharpened the pang as I stay. I know it may *get better someday*, but I am no longer certain I can last long enough to see. And so the text to Oslo: *I'm ready to try anything.*

On the couch in the blanket-dark, I look down and see her hands. Startled, I extend my arms, examining. The limbs are hers, age spots and gold bangles, sleeves pushed halfway up to cook. The wrists are soft and dimpled, fingertips scalded smooth by years of handling hot pans. I look to my right and left, glimpse shoulders round with muscle, double-strong after years of dragging weakened legs across floors. Looking up, I see my granddaughter wobbling toward me across the kitchen floor. My heart soars. I begin to clap, rising music in my throat.

She pauses on her toddler legs and begins, carefully, to sway. Her eyes, first narrowed with concentration, now gleam with awe as she discovers dance. My heart swells. In this moment, my body's noise—all that pain and memory—drops to a low hum. My arms move faster, pumping with defiant force. My song is a silly one, a children's rhyme—*noot ya batta, noot ya batta—jump, you duck, jump, ducky, jump!* For an instant, I am both the music and the dance. I was not young long, touched early by death, marriage, and sex. But once, I was a girl, a bird too.

Then the song drains out of me, and suddenly I can't breathe. A wall of wordless remembrance arrives, crashing into me. Crunching, compressing me into a smaller, smaller size. My spine contorts, my arms jamming into my stomach, legs forced against my chest. I can no longer see my granddaughter. I part my lips and begin to cry.

The cry startles my eyes open. In the darkness I look to see my arms are once again slim and young. Sittoo appears a little ways off, a body folded, fetal on the floor. Tears infuse the air. My heart pounds. I race toward her, urgently sure that I must move her elsewhere, somewhere safe. I hoist her on my back. As I lift her, I see that we are not alone—that on her own back is slung the body of my father, his limp form dangling. Beneath them both, I double over but keep the ground under my feet. I stagger forward.

Around me, images of my life appear. In a single instant, I am the small child who once rested in their arms. I am the woman who tried to climb the world without knowing what she bore. I am the flesh of their flesh. I am bits of brain and spirit, meat and minerals that remember what we have seen. Together, we are worlds, nearly two centuries of living held inside our frames. All our arms, so imperfect, trying to change what we cannot. All our words, the tender lies and soft faith we tried to use as steel. Our love, a tent we made and remade beneath the rain.

I lurch onward, coming to a set of stairs. Uneven, narrow, rising toward a dimming light. It is the entrance to our Brooklyn apartment. Quivering, I place one foot on the staircase and try to rise. And then—my legs turn to ghost. As I fold, I feel a new kind of remembering. As if I've known for a lifetime that this collapse would come. As if it has always been happening, my days letters that could only spell this end. Together, we make a heap, a pile of bodies halfway home.

Tears are in my eyes, but my lungs are still. In pieces, I find something that is almost rest. Here, a moment not of relief, but truth.

ذكر

Remember/Invoke

Arabic Lesson ٤#

In the Arabic language, memory is no quiet thing.

From the root ذ ك ر, the word *to remember* is inextricable from the acts of thought and speech. Its shape overlaps with a host of meanings that echo and compound. Strokes of significance thickening toward motion, toward communion, toward sound.

ذكر reaches wide arms, holding not only *to recall, recollect* but also *to bear in mind*. ذكر tells us all thought is an act of presence, of holding, harboring. To ذكر is *to mention* too. The incitement of naming. Flesh and voice as portal. Conjuring, carrying.

It is for this reason that ذكر is a pillar for the faithful, a practice in which a body remembers itself, spinning back into Soul. ذكر, in Sufi Islam, a ritualized recitation in a tempo of motion or breath. For others, prayer beads or counted fingers aid the remembrance of Allah. ذكر as a sacred puncture in routine. Words as reaching for, enacting, the unseen.

And so we see ذكر is a practice, worlds made by what we bear in mind or on lips. To remember is to reify; to name a thing is to bond.

ذكر, as a web of questions that might map a life:

What are you willing to admit you have seen?

Whose name is on your lips,
                    and
                                which do you answer to?

What did her mornings feel like? She must have had moments like mine—lingering, interstitial, reluctant to surrender the comfort of the dark. Perhaps, like me, she savored the sense of a body half-gone, adrift in liquid forgetfulness. How nice—fingertips a distant tingle. Toes lost in ocean sway. How delicious, the instant where this is all. Possibility, licking the edge of loss, lapping the lines of her.

Perhaps, in sleep, she found herself carried to 'Ibdis. Perhaps, sometimes, waking with lids still closed, she briefly knew she was there. That she might lift her head and see those dead beloveds, still pink with blood and breath. Maybe the smoke of last night's cooking lingered, particulate, in the air. Perhaps a new morning was dawning there, gray coalescing gold.

Would these dreams be a mercy—or their opposite?

Was it the whirring fan that surfaced her first, returning those two rooms stale with cigarettes, half-sunk under a Jeddah street? Which of her names did she remember first—*mother, wife, Palestinian, refugee*—?

How many times did she try to slip back into the dark?

◇ ◇ ◇

The first days following the psilocybin treatment are a quiet, cool hallway. I pace its eggshell floors, savoring the sudden calm. The air is soft and ribboned with a single sound. A note of recognition, ringing from the instant I perceived grandmother, father, me. In its thrall, I vibrate, body and mind merging in its pitch. We thrum across lifetimes and sound myself back to me—

—that quake, that crater. The clawing sense of wrongness, the pound of danger in my blood. The quiet suffocations in each bid to belong, the desperation to escape— These, history as fugitive, forced to roam through present denial. Fragments of a shattered birthright, lodging in dark corners, rimming bone and soul. Finding speech in my flesh, which is no respecter of lies.

I feel, for the first time, located—not in place, but as time. A convergence of years and memory, only some of them my own. Body as host, holding the privacies of others, secrets carried but not told. A slight rise in my spine, the gentle buoy of self-regard. The humiliations of my illness—*no reason, no reason*—softening. I am no longer bewildered by my collapse but by all we have survived.

◇ ◇ ◇

This new insight endures, even as the soft shell of *breakthrough* gives way. Now, there is some grace to draw on as I ride the jagged hours. Each day, a tiny, tenuous exercise, relearning to trust my mind. When a plate of rice feels like combat or an hour blazes with cryptic grief, I conjure lineage. Recalling disaster, our flawed feats of carrying on. How the dust of my own years still flies, coating nostril and lung. Those rough rooms, nights, years. Starvation itself, abuse. These stories themselves are not a balm. Yet they cool the fumes of my shame. Slowly, I am finding clearer breath.

But history, now invoked, exerts a will of its own. I sense it first on a warm morning, as my eyes open in bed. A disturbance, faint as an exhale coming from another room. I clench in every muscle, but it is too late. I felt it—a flicker of sensation in the hard clot of my core. I move quickly from my bed, climb the stairs to our unfinished roof. The sun bleaches my eyes, pulls me to the surface of my skin. I squint at the street below. Pigeons careen figure eights on the empty street. I try to ignore the shiver as it returns. Not bodily, but beneath it—a tremor, a thread of air, where stone silence should be.

Above me, the sky shifts, but I keep my eyes cast to the ground. I am not ready to name the changing light.

❖ ❖ ❖

I feel like a window that's stuck open, I tell C. What I don't say is *I feel like a broken window.* For days, I have camped on my own peripheries, throwing my attention into my limbs and head. Busied myself with cleaning, walking, talking, watching, reading—anything to keep me outside my rib cage, the punctured feeling growing there.

But the breach insists itself, stirring me with a cold air I recognize. I felt it first all those years ago in the hall, standing before the pictures of the Gazan boy and his mother. That hall, the darkest corridor in a home my parents hoped would be filled only with sun. As we grew, they faced us forward, toward windows of stubborn golden light. But in those two photographs, I found a slim seam opening to another time and place.

The first spring of Covid-19 has slid from sirened panic to molasses horror, a déjà vu of death and denial. Across this thing called a nation, lines of animosity are drawn and armed with a vehemence some people claim is new. Arundhati Roy publishes a letter describing Covid devastation in India, the U.S., and beyond. She declares *the pandemic is a portal,* a moment of ruin that might open to a new world. *The pandemic is a portal*—but only if we admit, and answer, the tragic weight of where we've been.

> *Our minds are still racing back and forth, longing for a return to "normality," trying to stitch our future to our past and refusing to acknowledge the rupture. But the rupture exists.*

Maybe every Palestinian home has such a portal, a rift where the wind of history may be felt wafting in. An aperture no amount of denial can close. Perhaps each of us must choose how close to approach. From a young age, I crept again and again toward that blue air. I caught the chill. The shiver never left me—some days, I kept it contained, that small patch of ice on my back. Other days, it crawled in the furthest parts of me, plunging to my fingertips, wrapping around my core. A private atmosphere.

For years, I have diligently disbelieved myself, flooding my mind with imagined suns. I listened to America proclaim endless summer, its emancipation from the past written in fluorescent heat. Four hundred years since Jamestown, the nation still insists that it is young.[37] Each day born as innocent, virgin land. Salvation in a white, white slate. A noisy kind of silence, a building over graves. *But the rupture exists.* Inside me, I feel it breathe.

✧ ✧ ✧

I heard you in the other room asking your mother, 'Mama, am I a Palestinian?' When she answered 'Yes' a heavy silence fell on the whole house, wrote Ghassan Kanafani in a letter to his five-year-old son Fayaz. Kanafani, a Palestinian revolutionary and writer who was assassinated by Israel in 1972, was born in 1936 in عكّا, an ancient city in northern Palestine perched proudly on the sea. The Nakba drove Kanafani, aged twelve, into exile with his family of ten. Years later, he and his Danish wife, Anni Høver, welcomed their two children in Beirut, in ghourba. Palestine was in their blood, but, like me and millions of others in the شتات, diaspora, they would learn Palestine as a wound.

"Mama, am I a Palestinian?"

When she answered "Yes" a heavy silence fell on the whole house. Kanafani listened to the sound of language succumbing to sudden truth. Then, the silence was broken by the sound of a young boy's sobs. *I heard you crying,* records Kanafani, who sat frozen in the other room. *It was as if a blessed scalpel was cutting up your chest and putting there the heart that belongs to you.*

Kanafani had met the same blade as a boy. A private rupture, as the Zionist army drove him and his family from their home. In the long procession of refugees, young Kanafani sneaked away from his family and glimpsed a scene of humiliation: the men of his community stripped of their arms by border guards, *so that they might enter the world of refuge—their hands empty.* Stunned, he stumbled back toward his mother, blue light spilling over him. Filled with distress, he writes, *I sens[ed] something I could not understand . . .*

218

Finding his mother, he reported the scene with alarm. *They are surrendering . . .* His statement was a question, innocence quivering under a knife. Kanafani writes to Fayaz nearly two decades later, *In the same way that your mother said "Yes" to you, so did mine then: "Yes," and there was silence as if something had fallen . . . I found myself weeping. I was born again then.*

For both Ghassan and Fayaz, their birth as Palestinians came through rupture, the knife-direct slice of that yes. A yes that must have pained the mothers who, uttering it, admitted their sons to a new, blue world. *Yes,* the moment Nakba becomes intimate, the word that names history as a space between your ribs. *Yes,* the threshold, the courage to hear, to answer, one's own name. It is a yes that touched me, too, though it took longer in my case, the blade blunted by distance and my father's instinct to protect us from pain.

Even when he brought us to Palestine, the year I turned eighteen, he insisted the experience would be soft, sheathed in American privilege. At the Jeddah airport, my father lined us up for our flight to Amman. He held out our passports. *You see these?* he said as we waited for our turn. Beneath a vicious-looking eagle, gilded script crowed *The United States of America.* On his face, the same satisfaction I saw each time he held those blue embossed booklets, slapping them down at immigration counters from Frankfurt to New Delhi. *These will protect you,* he told us, a pale glow on his cheeks. *With these, you can travel anywhere.*

But something was different when, the next day, we approached the border between Jordan and Israel. On the Jordanian side, we shuffled into a dusty departure hall. There, slender, dark-skinned men pulsed in corners, swathed in fatigues and strapped with guns. I watched my father's body approach them with carefully portioned swagger, deferential dips of his head. Here, the air smoked with memories of Jordan's battles—with Israel, and against the Palestine Liberation Organization (PLO) in the kingdom's civil war. Here, Jordanians policed Palestinians—sometimes as revenge, and always to appease the Israeli neighbors who would not forgive a breach. Still among Arabs, we were already losing grip on our fate.

After, on a bus sputtering toward the Jordan River, my father turned, sidelong, to us. In a hoarse whisper, he implored, *Remember what I said.* The night before, in Amman, he had instructed us to make ourselves smooth and small. *Don't speak to them unless they speak to you,* he said of the soldiers we would soon meet. *Be very polite to them. Remember, you have nothing to hide. Remember, you are American. They like Americans.**

The Israeli soldier looked bored as he flipped my passport to the first page. A moment later, a squint, a glance between my name and my suddenly not-so-Western face. I felt the hot wave of his

---

* "As two vibrant democracies, we recognize that the liberties and freedoms we cherish must be constantly nurtured . . . It's why we've increased co-operation between our militaries to unprecedented levels. It's why we're making our most advanced technologies available to our Israeli allies. It's why, despite tough fiscal times, we've increased foreign military financing to record levels. And that includes additional support—beyond regular military aid—for the Iron Dome anti-rocket system . . . So make no mistake, we will maintain Israel's qualitative military edge."
—Barack Obama, speech at the 2011 AIPAC Policy Conference, May 22, 2011

displeasure break over me. He pulled me aside, told me to wait, and disappeared with my passport in hand. Fifteen minutes later, three soldiers encircled me. Their questions came like spit: *What is your name? What is your purpose here? Where was your father born? What is your religion? Do you know anyone in Israel? Where are you going? Why? What is your occupation? Your name again? Where was your grandfather born? Why are you here? Where are you staying? Why?*

After, I returned on liquid legs and found my father gone. I saw him off against a wall, facing a soldier less than half his age. My father's body was taut, hands stuffed in his pockets, head tipped slightly toward the floor. *I am not a menace*, he seemed to spell. When he was finally returned to us, we answered his glum nod with our own. Together, we walked with forced slowness out of the arrival hall.

❖ ❖ ❖

The doctor enters in teal scrubs and a face mask. He gives me a Covid-era fist bump and a chipper *hey hey.* I am always unsure of how to take his breeziness; as he declares *it's great to see you!* I half expect him to call me *sport.* He seems close to my own age, yet I feel impelled to match his Uncle attitude, to play young and naive. In spite of myself, I shift into a higher voice and reduced vocabulary.

I am willing to do this because this man is the first and only doctor who has offered any relief from the chronic pain I now suffer from my unholy trinity of spine, muscle, and nerve issues. After straightforward tests and treatments failed, he remains the one practitioner who has not given up on me. I suspect his reason is both kindness and curiosity—he tells me he wants to *solve* my *case.*

This doctor has pressed his hands on nearly every part of me. He has watched my body transform, my weight drop and now steadily rise. He has punctured me with needles of various thickness, dispensing steroids into rogue tendons, anesthesia over screaming nerves. He has blotted my own blood off my skin, and he has heard me cry.

As he settles into his chair and opens my chart, I am prepared for flimsy small talk before we begin dissecting me. *How was your weekend?* he opens. I say, *Fine, and yours?*

Yeah, the trip was great.

You took a trip?

Ah, yeah—we went to Israel!

222

History charges through the wall, cracking on my bones.

Oh, how was it.

My voice is wet, but not in a way he will hear.

Oh, my God, just beautiful. We were just in Tel Aviv for four days, soaking it all in. We crossed over for one day into Jordan to see Petra. It was incredible.

Then he asks, *Have you been?*

❖ ❖ ❖

Outside the arrival hall, the light was bright and cold. My father
led us to a bus, the sound of Arabic emanating from its interior
like a warm extended hand. It soon rolled us away from the border,
passing under a gate emblazoned WELCOME TO ISRAEL. For the
next hour, we crossed a stretch of desert and met rolling, winter-
lush hills. Between towns and grazing grounds, olive groves
cascaded, flickering silver and freshly picked.

The terrain resembled the familiar landscape of Jordan, just a few
miles away. Yet there was ineffable difference too. It could have
been the double brightness in my father's eyes—lit once with
ravenous joy and once with shifting fear. It could have been the
way the faces around me wore entire lifetimes on their skin—layers
of weary determination, years of brazen survival, and so much
dimpled comedy. The textures of life made more visible, perhaps,
because of how near they stood to death.

This vividness was quickly muted, tucked behind blank stares when
armed Israeli soldiers boarded the bus. One stood at the front, two
hands on his gun, while another clomped down the aisle to check
papers. Standing over my father, he took our passports without a
word. He glanced from face to face while my father emptied his
gaze, eyes resting halfway to the floor. After, as the bus began to
move again, murmured conversations resumed. My father's silence
stayed.

As we approached Jerusalem, the signs of the occupation sharpened,
sprawled. It announced itself with the separation wall, its spine of
gray cement and razor wire punching up through grass and stone.

It glowered from the concrete watchtowers, manned or abandoned, rumbled in the battle between potholes and the road. And it was everywhere in the illegal settlements—white, suburban-style developments* spilling across hilltops, gnawing the green breasts of the land.

Even so, the overwhelming feeling of my first trip was quiet exuberance.[38] For two weeks my body was a map slowly filling, shapes learning, remembering, their names. Though my American clothes and imperfect Arabic still marked me as different, every hour beckoned some muted fragment in me to wake. A strange thrill to discover the Palestinian parts of my private life amplified on a public scale. But here, *Palestinian* was not a modifier, no exotic or alarming slippage from a narrow norm. To speak Arabic was to simply speak. *Palestinian dishes* were merely food.

Here, I was freed from the innumerable choreographies that usually moved me through the world. I had not known how exhausting they were—assimilative disciplines so internalized, they felt like instinct. A new feeling nudged to life: a fizzing, heady pride. A dawning depth of self, suddenly invoked, recognized. The discovery that the *from* in *from Palestine* was made of more than sound.

The Occupation has created generations without . . . a first place that belongs to them, that they can return to in their memories in their cobbled-together exiles, wrote Mourid Barghouti, who, exiled from Palestine, raised his son, Tamim, between Egypt and Europe. I had never

---

* "We should there [in Palestine] form a portion of a rampart of Europe against Asia, an outpost of civilization as opposed to barbarism."
   —Theodor Herzl, "the father of modern Zionism," in *The Jewish State*

thought to hunger for such a first place. Absence, improvisation, partiality—these features of my upbringing were so integral, I did not notice them.[39] And I had not grasped the extent to which all of us—from Illinois to Jeddah—were always compromised, enclosed. Minorities everywhere, we mostly carved quiet, tidy tracks through the world.

Our spaces were both monuments of makeshift belonging and testament to all that remained out of reach. In shabby Jeddah apartments, I played with snow globes, spilling glitter over the gleaming Dome of the Rock. My uncle Ibrahim's villa northwest of Amman perched on a hill high enough to glimpse the lights of Palestine. There, we sat for hours in a garden that bloomed with such ferocity that pruning was a constant, tender chore. Grape leaves dripped from a handmade trellis, figs and citrus swinging from pendulous limbs. Before, I could not appreciate the way this small plot invoked generations of harvest. How ancestral instinct spoke through my uncle's hands, the miracles he made of seed and earth.[40]

In Palestine, I glimpsed the whole of which my life had known only parts. Yet our spaces there, too, were riven with loss. Disrupted by soldiers and walls or the mental siege of knowing a day or body could be cut into at any time.[41] Nearly every Palestinian we spoke to had been in some way displaced, whether from their land, their livelihood, or their family. We reached across, and through, those losses. *Where are you from, Uncle, Sister? What family, what clan? How did you come to be here?* Here, there was no knowing another without questions of history, of horizons treasured, and robbed. *What is the earth that made you? What land does your body hold?*

❖ ❖ ❖

My father learned his losses backward, piecemeal.

When Horea and her sons left Gaza in 1967, Ziyad cried for weeks. The grief he felt was for the loss of his first place—its beloved beach, its world of familial arms. He missed the cousins, the schoolmates whose lives, in their symmetry to his, made reality feel whole. Of course, the word لاجئ had hovered over everything in Gaza, where the majority of residents were refugees. But this word, *refugee*, required memory, a knowledge of the world before.

Young, Ziyad had not yet experienced language as a form of traveling time. *Palestine* was the dust on his feet. It was Deir al-Balah, Khan Younis, Rafah—these he tasted with his body. It was these that he would miss. Ninety-nine percent of Palestine lay beyond the boundary of the Gaza Strip, still unreal to him. The closest he came to ʿIbdis was in the bodies of elders, survivors, their village tucked in remembering skin. To them, ʿIbdis was the hope their eyes met when they faced toward the east.

In Jeddah, the landscape shifted. On Gaza Street, Palestinians surrounded Ziyad, but this word, *Palestine*, began to mean different things. Here, neighbors held keys to homes from Nablus to Quds to Khalil. On the streets, accents and memories jostled amid differently textured pains. A new breadth of loss grew into view. This, too, was Palestine—blocks and bodies where violence shadowed joy, where every choice was a stone thrown against impossibility.

And so the blue light began to seep in, pooling questions that grew as he listened to his father talk politics. In these hours, *Falasteen* became a dialect Ziyad only half grasped. He caught a sense of distant armies—Syrians, Egyptians, Jordanians—who shared their struggle against an enemy who had twice humiliated them. Shame pricked as he wondered why it seemed the Arabs had known so much defeat. The name of ʿIbdis grew thin, thinner as Ziyad checked his schoolbooks and found no trace of it. There, Palestine was mentioned in past tense, drawn in the faintest lines.

By night, Ziyad fell asleep to the sound of Sowt Falasteen, the radio show transmitted by Palestinian revolutionaries out of Cairo, Baghdad, and Beirut. The dim room filled with strident notes of revolution, anthems of return. Songs to invoke a scattered people, casting glory on their cause. Marching voices, conjuring visions of power the day's hours had denied. Drowsing, Ziyad glimpsed his father's face, a strained pleasure around his mouth.

Stretched out beside them, Horea heard these bannered broadcasts but kept her thoughts to herself.[42] Perhaps their brazen promises sounded empty. Or, worse, perhaps they made her heart lift, the risk of naming hope. When Ziyad asked his mother about their adversaries, no curses touched her tongue. She explained the Jews had suffered badly. She said it was Palestine's misfortune that this suffering had been turned on them.

Each morning, after children and husbands dispersed, she and the neighborhood women traded visits, sharing breakfasts and tea. Their talk roamed between memories of Palestine and the latest gossip on their street. They talked maternal worries, fretted about the price of groceries, teased each other into hysteria. These, hours of ordinariness, the balm of the mundane. Arriving home from school, Ziyad often found her with these aunties, glimpsing a smile she seldom wore at home. In these moments, Palestine rested from the weight of rhetoric, withdrew from the demands of grief.

It was with his mother that Ziyad returned to Palestine. The Israelis, for reasons never given, had banned Musa for life. But by the time Ziyad reached sixteen, Horea was determined to visit home. As mother and son approached the border, she instructed him as he would one day instruct me: to be placid in the presence of soldiers. But when the border guard told him, *You're not Palestinian. You're Gazan,** Ziyad snapped back without a pause.

No, I'm Palestinian.

No, you're Gazan.

No . . .

Horea squeezed his shoulders. They crossed over with two bowed heads.

Nearly ten years had passed since Ziyad and Horea left Deir al-Balah, and their return reached my father like a flood. Tight joints softened in the familiar air, salt breeze a caress. Walking, their bodies traversed years, wavering between a gone time and what remained.[43] Ziyad thrilled at every overheard voice, the shape of the Gazawiya dialect filling the air. He felt an urge to follow every stranger, to press their arms and gush:

---

* "Is there a Palestinian history or culture? There is none . . . There is no such thing as a Palestinian people."
                              —Israeli finance minister Bezalel Smotrich

*إحنا أهل! أنا واحد منكم! بالله، تأخذ بيدي.

Their relatives greeted them with joyful shouts. Arms enwrapped their limbs and necks, kisses and du'a' like warm rain. Aunts clasped Ziyad's face, exclaiming at his growth. Children clucked and spun. The travelers dropped suitcases swollen with gifts, sank onto seat cushions, aching after three days journeying by land. Circled by her kin, Horea surged with life. She answered their clamor with laughter and reassurances that the two had arrived unharmed.

Beside her, a dazed Ziyad returned the chain of salaams, overwhelmed by the sight of faces at once intimate and strange.[44] Some were new to him, while others shimmered as half memories. But even the stranger's faces held some contour he recognized. In the coming weeks he would struggle to keep track of the dozens who now claimed him by name. But for the rest of his life, Ziyad would be in love with homecomings and live in terror of goodbyes.

Night after night, over pots of endless sweetened shay, history swam into him. His mother and her relatives turned for hours to reminiscing, trading long and layered tales of 'Ibdis, of a time before the wars. Sometimes, she startled Ziyad, flashing the smile of another age. Word by word, they raised a world inside him. There, new hunger grew.

The occupation had changed Gaza. Everywhere, the work of theft was plain. Illegal Jewish settlements appeared in both Gaza and

* *We're family! I'm one of you! Please, take my hand.*

230

the West Bank, bringing thousands of Zionists into their midst. But one strange blessing arrived with the occupation: because the Israelis declared all the land for themselves, Gaza became, briefly, relatively, porous. For a time, it became possible to travel from the Strip to the West Bank and even the territories lost in the Nakba— the territory called *Israel* by many, but which Palestinians referred to as *The Inside* or *1948*. A refusal: the *Zionist entity* was an actor, an idea—but the land still knew its name.

And so Ziyad found himself swept by relatives beyond the borders of his memory. Through their day trips outside the Strip, *Palestine* began to sprawl. In mere hours, he might find himself playing soccer in Hebron or swimming in Tel Aviv. Another strange intimacy: Palestine was far vaster than he'd ever seen, and yet all of it was so close. *The long Occupation has succeeded in changing us from children of Palestine to children of the idea of Palestine*, wrote Mourid Barghouti. *I have always believed that it is in the interests of an occupation, any occupation, that the homeland should be transformed in the memory of its people into a bouquet of "symbols."* That summer, Ziyad's homeland gathered, widened. It built itself in the sand behind his ears, the fried fish in his throat. The child of Gaza was growing, a son of Palestine.[45]

One day, in the weave of food, rest, and conversation, Horea's cousin made a suggestion: Why not drive the two visitors to ʿIbdis? Ziyad was eager. His mother quietly agreed. The drive took less than two hours. On the way, their eyes scanned for signs of the Israeli army, their bodies tensing with each blind turn and cresting hill. Even when obeying the law, the occupied body is still *trespasser*

and at any moment might be prey. Even so, the mood was lively, as memories unrolled with the road. Horea and her cousin conjured gone landmarks—*here was Beit 'Afa, that way was Julis.*

Then it was their own trees they saw. A crooked palm and broad sycamore watched, silent, as mother led son from the car. Where ninety-one houses once stood, they found crushed walls, dismembered rooms.* The ground was studded with broken stone, each one a frozen gesture, its meaning expelled. Amid the wreckage, Horea called to memory. *Down here was the diwan. That way was our field.* Her words stirred the hot, still air. A portal opened in her speech, past stepping through. Half-homes rose from their knees, the streets swept clean of debris. Horea rose, too, her back straightening with something like joy. An offering of pride.

Ziyad watched her with new eyes. All his years, he had grown in the penumbra of her grief. Its blue light washed his world, its rays cast, obliquely, from the rim of an eclipse. There were many sorrows he had names for—their departure from Gaza, his father's harshness, the cruel words thrown at Palestinians by sneering Saudi boys. But he had not understood that these were only shadows, the jagged, inverted silhouette of the life he might have lived. Dimness is only

---

* 'Ibdis was attacked by the Giv'ati Brigade's Third Battalion during the night of 8 July, resulting in a "long battle" . . . according to the account in the [Israeli-authored] *History of the War of Independence*. The Israeli forces "only finished cleaning the position by the hours of the morning." . . . This victory at the position of 'Ibdis was a turning point . . . from that victory onwards, the Brigade's forces did not withdraw from a Single position until the end of the war. —*The Interactive Encyclopedia of the Palestine Question*

half as dark without knowledge of the sun. For a few hours, he walked in the light of what almost, but never, was.

They stood a long time at the village cemetery. Before them, simple slabs of stone inscribed with Qur'anic ayat and family names. In their midst, a rough swath of destruction, crushed headstones left by the tread of bulldozer or tank. Grass crept around the rubble. There was no sign of construction or cultivation; this land had been razed to desecrate, to break the traces of Arab lineage and all suggestion of return.

The drive home was silence. Years collapsed into minutes, retracing catastrophe.

The state murders George Floyd in cold blood. In the streets, bodies and throats swell with too much memory, shaking cities with their roaring witness to the dead. On Flatbush Avenue in Brooklyn, the asphalt jars me through my shoes, shouts thundering on my skin. By the thousands, we sweat behind our masks, swig the water volunteers distribute alongside sanitizer and sunscreen.

There is a sense of recklessness in our thronging after months of quarantine. Yet our bodies must move, articulate what exceeds our words: horror, rage at the fresh, familiar violence inflicted on Black life. Unforgivably routine, in a country where my brown displaced father sought a safe place to plant my life. This history is mine too. The dissonance,[46] as always, makes me stagger, makes me wild. I dart and bob inside the tide, hoisting my cardboard sign.

C jerks and jogs to keep up with me, his tall frame taut with nerves. We return home dust-coated and vibrating. In our kitchen, I turn and find C's face an ashy green. His eyes are strange, glassy and two shades darker than usual. I feel a bottom drop out under me. He blurts, *We can't do that again.* His voice is pleading, scratched with hurt. I am bewildered. Our first connection came through activism, and we have attended protests together for years.

What? We have to!

We can't. Please, S███.

C! They're fucking murdering people!

He halts. I watch him try to stretch his heart around one more fear. In an instant, I recognize this as the shape of us. Me, with all my needing. All my dependencies and demands. And him, a rope tethered only to himself.

But now, his eyes dart, his tall body quivering small. *Seeing you in that crowd . . . I was so scared, Sarah.* He is blubbering. *What if someone hurt you? What if something happened?* There is so much I still have not grasped—how my body has been the porcelain cross on his back. *Every subway platform,* he says. *Every time you were out of sight.* Reels of imagined horror. *What if you collapsed? What if you fell?* He is growing frenzied. His arms pinwheeling from his forehead to his sides, then gripping each other again.

The mother in me wants to stop this, to clasp him into calm. But my arms halt at my side. C deserves this reckoning. His history, too, must be witnessed, held. Sunset leaks into the room, a murmur of red. In his terrified face I see a wild courage I have never known in myself. Here is a soul that risked *yes*, reached its earthy hands toward life, and so, toward death. He has named his love, daring to place it inside a flawed and mortal thing. Now, I see its mark on him. This choice, a rupture. A lavish wound.[47]

The crack of his sob. The sound of a tree as it falls.

After my first visit to Palestine, I moved with new weight, a budding sense of origins. *American* felt like even more of a misnomer, but *Palestinian* still felt only partially deserved. I saw my distance as indictment, shamed by my exemption from the hardships faced by those in Falasteen. Hardships that, I knew, I'd scarcely glimpsed in weeks of visiting. *Half-Palestinian* took on new meaning—there was so much I still did not know of us.

Despite my feelings of unworthiness, I continued to return, a shy suitor to our land. After my first year in college, I received a summer scholarship for advanced Arabic study in Aleppo, Syria. A few months before my departure, the Syrian uprising, and the brutal response by the Assad regime, rerouted my program to Amman. For years, I would watch in horror as domestic and interventionist violence ravaged the nation, stealing centuries of history and precious human lives. Beyond, the entire region smoldered, as revolutionary fervor and righteous discontent crashed against tyranny and long-standing exploitation by the West.

My post in Jordan landed me an hour from the border with Palestine. I crossed over twice. Each time, I faced a tougher interrogation, and each time, I deepened my resolve to haunt the Israeli regime with my return. I wandered from Jerusalem to Bethlehem to Ramallah to Jericho, riding my U.S. passport privilege. Like my father, I was grateful just to breathe there, a stealth pilgrim roaming mosques, streets, and souqs.

I stumbled upon direct violence a few times; one Friday, I watched Israeli forces spray worshippers with a water cannon, barring

Ramadan pilgrims from al-Aqsa Mosque. After the military vehicles and mounted police dispersed, I watched the crowds creep back, gathering cardboard to lay on the street, kneeling on this makeshift floor to pray. Another day, I watched, helpless and surrounded by guns, as Israeli soldiers slammed my friend Khalid to the ground. Despite my screams of protest, they hauled him away, imprisoning him for walking on the wrong side of the street in his own neighborhood. Before he disappeared into their truck, he turned back to me, flashing hazel eyes free of fear. *It's all right, Sarah.*

Stroke by stroke, my body absorbed the textures of our dignity, of our rage.

But these visits were fleeting, and my longing only grew. The next summer, I volunteered in the West Bank city of Nablus, joining a Palestinian charity to run a children's camp. Stationed in one place for several spacious months, I could finally experience Palestine as routine. In the long, almost mundane hours, I heard the hum of my own shadow life.

The organization provided lodging in a villa at the top of one of Nablus's many hills, which I shared with a rotating cast of foreign volunteers. The house was grand and crumbling beautifully, full of evening wind. I slept on the second floor, in a room with wide stone tiles and an unscreened window that opened to a quiet street. Across from me slept a French Egyptian woman who made long bilingual phone calls. In the morning, I boiled Turkish coffee in the tiny, second kitchen down the hall. Waiting for the steam, I pulled aside a fraying curtain to watch the slopes and buildings blooming pink.

My mornings brimmed, rich in children. I arrived early each day to greet dozens, ages three through eight. For the next several hours, I helped local teachers orchestrate art projects and games. Once shy around children, in Nablus I learned to kneel to their level, look them in the eyes. There, I glimpsed multitudes wide as any adult's, each one a shifting pattern of desires, questions, and moods. Emerging miracles, each one with their own terms.

This job was the first time since my own childhood that I moved fully in Arabic. While I had returned to the language years before, this had come in the form of classes or sporadic conversations. Those Nablus mornings, there was no classroom formality, no sense of scrutiny. Any stumbles in grammar or conjugation dissolved into the bright chaos, and the children's replies did not miss a beat. *Khaltu!* they called to me. *Auntie, look!* They waved fingerpainted pages, glitter on their elbows, in their hair. My Arabic tongue loosened, my throat filling with remembered, or inherited, words. I smiled for hours straight.

On my way home, I crossed the city center, past the fruit market, bakeries, and knafeh shops. I made the rounds often, filling bags with tomatoes, mint, pomegranates, and a few pieces of pita, their bellies still full of steam. I stopped for the thick, syrupy cheese pastry last. Knafeh was an indulgence I'd eat only partially, tucking the rest away in its wax for a later that might never come. Each bite was a delight so rich I'd wonder how it made me feel so innocent. I slipped my slice inside a pita, East Nabulsi style, laughing back at the shopkeepers who delighted at my taste. *Nabulsiya!* Many became friends, introducing me to their children and wives, hosting me for Friday meals. They claimed me, calling me *bint Ziyad*, though they'd never met my father. A signal of my honor, their respect.

Evenings, I sat with fellow volunteers on the stone balcony that wrapped around the second floor. As the hot air cooled to a marble breeze, I watched the hills drop into darkness. A moment later, they blinked back to life with the lights of nearby towns and refugee camps. In some, I could track headlights, their glow sliding along roads and slopes. Framed by the still dusk, it all felt close enough to hear the hum of these engines, the murmur of those neighborhoods.

But in the night, there was no way to know what web of obstacles lay between me and each glittering hill. Flying checkpoints, or the gun of a vengeful soldier, or an armed settler with bloodthirst. I spent several afternoons each week outside the city teaching in Balata, the largest refugee camp in the West Bank. There, I saw the evidence of Balata's famed, fierce resistance—posters of martyrs, faded and new, layered on bullet-ridden walls. The streets were narrow, poor, and overcast with its heavy history—decades of battle with Zionist forces, whose state-of-the-art weaponry has only intensified the rebellion in hearts and limbs.[48]

Back in Nablus, my Palestinian friends warned me to stay near home after dark. Raids were common in Balata, but Israeli soldiers might also enter Nablus by night, bursting into family homes. Boys and men often disappeared in this way, detained for months or years without recourse or charge. Nicknamed Jabal an-Nar* for its own ardent history of insurgency, Nablus could at times feel autonomous, but as all Palestinian cities, it remained circumscribed. Above us, the sky sometimes ripped with Israeli F-16s. They dove low enough to chatter our teeth, fast enough to break the sound barrier, just to thunder a reminder of their lurking might.

---

* Mount of Fire.

On the outskirts of the city, new settlement outposts were appearing atop hills, driving Palestinian families off their farms. Each encroachment created new frontiers for violence. Palestinians en route to school or work risked the bullets and dogs of settlers, and the soldiers who amassed to defend the illegal seizure of land. The safety I felt in Nablus was only as large as the space between human hearts.

◇ ◇ ◇

Late that summer, I took a car west. After a few winding, road-choked hours, we approached the crossing between the West Bank and '48.* I felt my body rolling up like a scroll. A thousand microclenches, the press of my back against the seat. My inner music, which had grown so free, dropped to static. I pushed my thoughts inside this silence, ejecting Nablus and Balata, erasing friends' faces, burying my family name. As if thoughts alone might reveal me, the truth wafting off me like a scent.[49]

The checkpoint came into sight. My veins burned like ice. As an American citizen, my presence in the West Bank was not illegal, but it would raise suspicion. Israeli forces often targeted foreigners suspected of solidarity with Palestinians. Just a few weeks before, one of my fellow volunteers, an Australian, had been detained, interrogated, and deported with a lifetime ban.

Still, it was my Americanness that I would rely on when I reached the soldiers. Here, for once, I was grateful for my blond hair, the native English on my tongue. It was not uncommon for an IDF soldier to flirt with me, and if I managed a smile, I was occasionally waved through. Such interactions made me sick, as did every mercy my passport afforded me. Yet some debasement seemed unavoidable, compromise built into the mechanisms that allowed me to be in Palestine at all.[50]

---

* *1948*, a common term to refer to the land inside the borders of the state known as *Israel*.

This time, I was lucky. Nearing sunset, the soldiers looked drowsy, bored as they stood around the small station where I submitted my bag to be searched. I waited somewhere outside my body as they scanned my documents. I tried to look un-Palestinian, to mimic their slack, entitled stance as I leaned on one leg, hip cocked. I passed through. On the other side, I sank into a soup of adrenaline. As I felt the prickling wash of relief, I spoke to my driver—we'd both been mostly silent, as if afraid to disturb the gods before rolling our dice.

I was so nervous . . .

I know. But don't be afraid.

But what if they kick me out, ban me?

Yes, they can do anything they want. But one has to try one's best. This is your وطن.* *Don't be afraid.*

---

* Homeland, ancestral land, country.

❖ ❖ ❖

My father and brother greeted me in Jerusalem. We hugged, the grit of worry slowly shedding from our foreheads. It had been an anxious day, the three of us facing the Israeli border separately— they'd come through the Jordanian crossing shortly before I entered from the north. My brother, two years younger than me, now taller, sat beside me on the bed. This felt like a miracle, as it did whenever one of us made it across a border created, first and foremost, to exclude us.[51] We slept early. The next morning, we would search for 'Ibdis.

The trip was my father's idea. It was rare for him to peer so intently toward the past—even in our first visit to Palestine together, it was the present he pointed to. But with his son interning with him in Saudi Arabia and his eldest daughter stationed, however briefly, in the West Bank, his imagination began to turn. That summer, we practiced a different life, glimpsed a hologram world. One in which we had not bound ourselves to Amreeka. One in which our bodies slept on this land.

I agreed to this search, but 'Ibdis was a word so unknown to me, even my curiosity was vague. On the two-hour drive south from Jerusalem, I watched the landscape shift from rich green to arid plains. Off and on, our route skimmed along the hulking separation wall that cleaved through the West Bank. Beyond, Jewish settlements, whole towns and cities of them, perched on Palestinian hills. My father sighed periodically, shaking his head and muttering angry appeals to Allah. *Astaghfur . . .* I felt the mixture of fury and impotence that had become familiar. Beside me, my brother said nothing.

I was dozing when our car moved off the highway and onto a rattling dirt road. I sat up to see a parched brown field. In the distance, a line of electrical towers partitioned the sky. Emerging from the parked car, my father squinted, scraping the landscape for clues. A few printed pages of directions, gathered from a crowdsourced Palestinian database, fluttered in his hand. *It's changed . . .* he murmured. Brittle, bleached grass clutched the razed earth. Pale watermelons dotted the dirt. Silence blistered our skin.[52]

My father fixed his sights on a massive, shimmering sycamore tree in the middle distance. He began to walk, my brother and I following, watching as he bent to pick up a stick. He flicked it left and right, the low wind carrying his murmured memories: *My mother would have walked this way, back and forth to the field* . . . My father's words summoned crops, ripples of green and gold from the cracked earth. We were sweating as we reached the tree. *This was our jamayza* . . . Unripe figs lay scattered at our feet. We bit into them and puckered at the starchy sour. I swallowed anyway, suddenly desperate to put this place inside me.

Most of the shattered houses my father had seen in the 1970s had disappeared—but only his eyes could measure this loss. We found a few overgrown, ruined walls. My brother climbed onto a scattering of stone slabs, his face quiet, studying. Understanding accreted, pearling into view. Our grandmother was young once. A beginning that was fullness, and from which we might have grown. We stood next to an intact stone well, its throat dark and dry. My father repeated the story his mother had told him while standing at its edge: *They bought this pipe from their Jewish neighbors—see the Hebrew on the side? The village had a party when the well was finished. The Nakba came the next day.*

And then my understanding began to stagger, disintegrate. It was not tears but tremble that filled me. Too much, too much to be ghosts this way, haunting what we will never see. My grandmother, by then, was dead, buried over a year. When she died, after a bitter bout with cancer, my father had to fight to obtain a grave. The cemetery where her husband was buried had since been declared *Saudi Only*. Palestinian bodies, stateless even in death, were to be sent to a separate site. Ziyad spent the first hours of his bereavement calling in favors from every influential Saudi he knew. As an exception, she was permitted to lie beside Musa, in a graveyard named after Eve.

In ʿIbdis, we searched for the shattered cemetery my father had seen on his last visit, but no trace now remained. Perhaps bulldozers had returned to finish what earlier invaders had begun. Perhaps the graves had been swallowed under new layers of soil. I stepped as lightly as I could. Somewhere, near or beneath my feet, my great-grandfather slept. Alongside him, generations, their bones stacking deep into the past. Family lines cut to sudden, ragged edges after 1948. Already, members of ʿIbdis had been buried in Deir al-Balah, Jordan, and Saudi Arabia; the living were even farther flung. I looked at my brother—where would our bodies rest?

We spent hours in the baking heat, though it felt like far less. We scattered, tracing separate aimless shapes inside the village grounds. There was nothing to do. There was nothing to say. And yet we lingered, knowing this moment was a glitch in empire that might not repeat.

The sun was retreating as we found each other back at the well. Bending over its stone edge, I felt the air shuffle, shift. Floating toward us, a white, round face. A pair of bottomless black eyes. I turned to stone. Its wings appeared, pumping once, twice, and the owl was over us. For an instant, her pale body was larger than the sun.

❖ ❖ ❖

Where do some hearts find the courage to move toward the knife? Taking the name of the beloved, do they bear, or ignore, how every love invokes death?

For days after the George Floyd protest, I skirt around C, flinching with apology each time I catch his gaze. I begin to grasp how my body has been, for him, an avatar of tragedy. For months, he studied my details with desperation and rising grief. While I faded beyond physical sensation, he scrutinized my too-cold skin, monitored its graying hue. When I was unable to hear reason, he caressed my flesh instead, transmissions of tenderness he hoped might recall me from the dead. On the street, he walked ahead of me to block the crowds or wind. *If I can keep her body safe*, he imagined, he prayed, *if I can buy us more time . . . she'll come back one day.*

As my decline drove others from my life, C drew nearer, shrinking his world with mine. Still claiming me, still calling himself by my name. This, even after he forced himself to begin planning for the end—he'd leave New York after my funeral, take up residence in his childhood home of Indonesia, plunge into solitude and surf. Even after *goodbye* wrapped me like a shroud, he refused to look away. Fighting for me as he knew how, he remained. Love, for him, was this simple. It was all of him, until the end.

◇ ◇ ◇

C took the first step toward me in the summer of 2016. Diverging from his usual spontaneity, he asked me a full week in advance to join him for drinks. That night at an outdoor picnic table, he paused before his first sip of beer. He looked suddenly unlike himself—shy, serene, and radiant at once. I'd learn later that what he spoke next were words he had pondered for months. Waiting, contending with possible consequences, and his personal doubt. Studying me, too, our bond growing until he decided his truth was worth the risk of utterance. *I like you. I'd like to ask you out.*

I looked back at him over my sweating tumbler of rosé, the air gauzed blue gold with dusk. For two years, we'd grown close as friends. He puzzled me—exuberant with others, toward me he was thoughtful and almost polite. I never saw him flirt with anyone, and found him impossible to read. I had tried, once, to ask him out, but on what I thought was a date, he brought a female friend.

Annoyed, I'd tried to shake him then, turning at last and with eager anxiety toward women instead. Still, C had hovered in my life, unresolved. This, in itself, left me confused. Before him, I had dated many kinds of men—but all of them, in the end, were men I was unafraid to lose. For them, I felt a bloodless love, one that did not threaten my essential solitude. But the instant I met C, I felt my soul nod. *I know you.*

Our first meeting was a single conversation, stretched for seven hours across a Brooklyn afternoon. I left for Jordan soon after. Two years later, moving from Amman to New York, I discovered my Bushwick apartment was, by chance, on his street. This news fluttered behind my ribs. The memory of C had clung to me, bewildering and soft, since that first day. But I clenched my stirring stomach, swore I would not make a move. I wanted the opposite of attachment. After a disastrous year of sexual harassment and assault, I arrived in New York at my lowest weight yet, hungry to be subsumed, anonymous.

As a grad student, I starved, studied, and worked, dropping exhausted in bed at night. Sometimes, a glass of scotch or wine in hand, I swiped half-drunk through dating apps. To show myself I was living, I went on serial first dates. I declined dinner invites, suggesting bars instead. There, I'd drink gin or whiskey quickly, trying to slide inside a haze that would allow me to be touched. Still, I found I could never leave the bar with any woman or man. The memory of my recent sexual assaults still roared in my skin. Beneath, a grief that eluded words. Human touch stirred up both. I could not imagine loving anyone more than I needed escape.

And so I lived headlong, the days blurred into sameness, flinging the hours away from me. Sometimes, in the dregs of early morning or a late train ride home, silence caught me, and I shuddered at my recklessness. I knew that this was all there would ever be—that these days, which I burned with such urgency, were all that made a life. *One must believe in the reality of time*, wrote Simone Weil in her diary. *Otherwise one is just dreaming.* Each night I fell asleep swearing that soon, but not tomorrow, I would step out of this dream.

That night at the picnic table, C's usual thrown-back posture reversed. He tilted toward me. The outdoor bar disappeared. Chest thudding, I felt the inrush of time, the staggering awareness that some moments come only once. I looked at his open face, tanned cheekbones rising with his smile. His gaze poured toward me like warm water or a song. Beneath it, my body relaxed a fraction of a degree—that familiar, bewildering ease. I was shocked to realize: those eyes would hold me as long as I allowed.

Notes of terror and longing ran opposite directions through my spine. My breath halted. To want, to care, to touch something good—these would mean the end of my self-hypnosis. Love, the antithesis to Weil's dreamy denial. Its language is attention, presence, vulnerability. I felt the threat of joy, too—joy, which I had avoided for so long, afraid of the way it hurled me into my body, into life. Afraid, too, of its fragility, how quickly it could cave to loss. I felt all these hover nearby, now, on the other side of my *yes*.[53]

◇ ◇ ◇

The Occupation has created a generation of us that have to adore an unknown beloved: distant, difficult, surrounded by guards, by walls, by nuclear missiles, by sheer terror, wrote Mourid Barghouti. *[It] has succeeded in changing us from children of Palestine to children of the idea of Palestine.* For years, this had been my truth. Palestine was a phantom photograph, a barely marked sliver on a globe. It was my father's voice gone suddenly thin. It was a silver pendant necklace, a portrait of al-Aqsa in every relative's living room. It was my grandmother asleep on the floor. On the TV behind her, stone-throwing children faced with Israeli tanks.

Returning after my summer in Nablus, I carried a Palestine that was, at last, more than its symbols. My body held its own memories, the weight of real time spent on the land. Now *Palestine* was texture, complexity. It was pomegranates, and it was pain. It was the names and kitchens of elder relatives and new friends. It was the hissing man who sidled behind me, following me to my door. It was Zafer, the Nabulsi coworker who chased him away—*Shame on you. And she is one of us!*

It was the silence of ʿIbdis. It was the occupation, the sense of being both stifled and exposed. It was a place I had only just begun to know. A place that had only just begun with me. *Homeland of my heart,* I wrote to myself on my final day, chest widening and bared. *Farewell for now. My heart tells me it won't be long.* With the vague certainty of the infatuated, I assumed I'd return, and return.

On my next trip, I arrived at a border crossing in the north of
Jordan, a small bag packed for what I hoped would be a two-week
visit. I arrived with a Jewish acquaintance who was traveling to visit
relatives in Jerusalem. She had agreed to coordinate our crossing in
the hope that a white American companion with Israeli connections
would sanitize my ethnicity. The guards waved her through. Next
in line, I stepped up with feigned confidence and a smile. A gun-
strapped man read my name, asking me to repeat it out loud. I
pronounced it quickly, dropping the gutturals. He frowned, then
slapped my passport shut. *Wait over there.*

My friend attempted a weak protest: *She's with me . . .* The soldiers
barked, *She has to wait.* With that, my companion gave up. *Good
luck*, she shrugged, and disappeared. I sat for three hours in the
tiny outpost, the sky inking with night outside. After a few rounds
of interrogation, they called me up for the last time. A middle-aged
man handed me my passport. *You are not going to Israel today.* A gale
blew through the back of my head. *Wait*, I said, trying to sound
calm. *I'm sorry, but why?*

Your name.

My name?

Yes, this name, it is a security threat.

My name?

Yes. You are not going to Israel today.

Words tried to form themselves between my suddenly numb lips. Behind the officer, I saw a door open, an idling vehicle beyond. The other soldiers were already filing out. *Goodbye,* he said, gesturing toward the front door I'd entered hours before.

I stumbled outside and discovered the shuttle back to Jordan had disappeared for the night. Before me stretched no-man's-land, armed borders on each side. In a fugue of grief and rage, I careened into the dark, moving through sand and brush in the vague direction of the east. Some moments later, I heard the sound of a speeding vehicle. A second later, a floodlight blasted my eyes white. *Stop! Who are you? Where are you going?* Despite myself, I felt a surge of relief. The voice spoke in Arabic.

They kicked me out, I answered, also in Arabic. *What?* The voice clearly found this answer absurd. The light lowered. A Jordanian soldier's face floated toward me. He frowned. *They made you walk?* He snorted, glancing west. *I'm Palestinian,* I explained. The lines of his body softened faintly. *Ah. Okay. I'm sorry.* He waved toward the armed truck. *Come, we will take you back.* A second soldier, who I had not seen, lowered his gun. The reality of his pointed weapon only registered hours later. Stretched out on a kind stranger's floor, I began to shake.

❖ ❖ ❖

Your question, wrote Kanafani, *was still revolving round the ceiling and reverberating in the trembling of my fingertips: "Am I Palestinian?"*

In our Brooklyn apartment, I stare at my own ceiling for weeks. Summer seeps into our brick walls, rises dewy on my skin. In the silence, Kanafani's question circles me, momentous and absurd. *Am I Palestinian?* The answer, technically, is simple. But my *yes* throbs at a distance. Exiled, ringed by sharpest hurt.

That night in the Jordan Valley was nearly five years ago. Since then, I have barely uttered its memory. I returned to the U.S., stumbling back into a life of safety that made my grief feel unearned. *Aren't you lucky? Aren't you blessed?* Quietly, I let half a decade pass without trying to return. As it had for my grandmother, Palestine had become unsafe for me to name, to love. *Palestinian* now meant *rupture,* a life cut in two.

The breach began as the Israeli soldiers forced me out into the dark. My legs swayed as they carried me away from Palestine, each step involuntary, a kick by some cruel boot. A scream flapped in my throat as I imagined the soldiers swinging guns to their backs, boarding their ride home. By now, their thoughts had turned to—what? Plans for a late-night meal? Some restless lust? How far would their commute carry them? To the nearby Beit She'an?* To somewhere near the sea? How many ghosts were their tires tearing through?

---

* A Jewish city established on the ethnically cleansed land of بيسان., Beisan.

I stumbled forward a few seconds more before full horror enveloped me. It was possible I had been banned; often, the Israelis blacklisted a person without giving notice or cause. Never mind that I had behaved carefully on all my visits, avoiding all but one peaceful protest in the West Bank. As a diasporic Palestinian, my returns threatened the core Zionist demand: that we all disappear.

On the dark earth between man-imagined borders, something in me began to cleave. Memories I had tucked in separate, sealed containers now surged, thundering. I saw again the Palestinian pilgrims I witnessed in Jerusalem, their bodies pummeled by water, then tear-gassed, on their way to prayers. I recalled the men with body parts missing, lost to settlers' guns. I was back in Hebron, watching Khalid slammed to the ground again and again. These, a few of the countless cuts meant to bleed us to defeat.

Inside me, these brutalities collided with a chorus of Nabulsi children, the brush of my great-aunt Sakina's fingers, the dropped figs in 'Ibdis, the plump white dance of sheep. More and more, the memories came, and I staggered beneath their weight. Multitudes, tender, difficult, and boisterous. Futures buried in ancestral ground. A vastness that, now receding, left a blue vacuum in the place of hope.

A distant homeland was being born again, Kanafani wrote, describing the scalpel working on his son's chest, *hills, olive groves, dead people, torn banners and folded ones, all cutting their way into a future of flesh and blood.*

I had not known love could feel violent this way—

—becoming intimate, engraved, as it was torn away.

✧ ✧ ✧

Horea's first visit to ʿIbdis was her last.

After their 1976 trip, she and my father returned to Palestine several more times. There, ʿIbdis hung on the horizon, silhouetted in the corners of their eyes. In Gaza, Ziyad now shared his elders' eastward glances, his mind's map tilting, remade. At home, when his father's radio sang homeland anthems, Ziyad's imagination filled with ʿIbdis's walls, rebuilt. Eyes closed, he returned to the cemetery, repairing the headstones one by one. In his daydreams, he roved, exulting in Jaffa waves, praying in القدس.* He ended his reveries back in ʿIbdis, finding his mother there. *A few more years*, he thought, as his body grew. *We'll go home soon.*[54]

But when relatives in Deir al-Balah offered to drive them to visit their ruined village again, Horea always declined. She did not speak of her reasons; even the name *ʿIbdis* grew fainter in her throat. My father would never know if she regretted their first trip, if it doubled or balmed her loss. Regardless, this was the shape her love took in its aftermath. Perhaps, in this way she guarded what remained. Perhaps this was how she tried to close, or survive, her wound. A memory resisted. A prayer not to know.

---

* *Al-Quds* or "the holiness," the Arabic name for Jerusalem.

My one memento from the hospital is a page torn from the guest book. The month of December 2019, each day a gap filled by C—

his name
his name
his name.

Every day, he returned, the lone visitor to the ward. Outside, New York dressed in its best lights, blasting *merry* into eyes and ears. Nightly, I heard the howl of the buzzers as the staff unlocked the metal doors one by one. His body gliding into the brittle quiet where I stood in the soft slippers he gifted me. He said *There's nowhere I'd rather be*, and this was a promise and a choice. His words conjured that dusk, that picnic table, the first time I caught that *yes* in his eyes. That night, we had looked the part of *carefree, young—* but there was such sobriety in his smile. Perhaps, even then, he sensed what it might mean to choose me.

Yes.

In 2020, pinned between Kanafani's question and a wounded C, I begin to grasp how a life may pivot on this slender word. How love and meaning are bound up in our once and successive yeses. *Yes*, which can mean *I see* or *I surrender. Yes*, which might also mean *I am claimed*—and so, *I will be hurt.*

This may be why C is unimpressed as I apologize for the pain my illness puts him through. By now, he has accepted that to love me is to live alongside his greatest grief. This is unchangeable: at twenty-eight and newly married, he touched widowerhood. There is no future without this rupture, no present that does not hold the memory of my death.[55]

At our kitchen table, we sit in silence, holding each other's gaze. I am startled to see his dark eyes flecked with icy blue.

He is beautiful.

How does one mourn an interminable event? asks Christina Sharpe in her book *In the Wake: On Blackness and Being.* It is the question that Sharpe asks on behalf of Black life inside *the afterlife of slavery.* But it is also the type of question that might follow Fayaz's tears. How to answer *the multiple and overlapping presents that we face,* asks Sharpe, when each one holds atrocity?

In my case, after that night in the Jordan Valley, the past-present of Catastrophe became too much to bear. Where Kanafani's son broke open with a yes to this inheritance, I ducked inside *no.* A no that forbade me to remember—both the rupture and the love that preceded it. A no that pushed Palestine back into the realm of symbol, the dim domain of ancestors, part of a neutered *past.*

This *no* colonized, spread. Joining, compounding my anorexic drive to silence the other, unbearable histories inside my flesh. Starving to murder time, to sever self from self. An addiction to barricades, walling every soft route back to the wound. The hypnosis of a fortress: from within, all the world appears a threat. And so my fear of love grew until all attachment appeared Trojan, tragedy in disguise. But Sharpe, standing in the midst of a longer disaster, calls for a courageous grappling, a *yes* to the weight of what we inherit, and the ruptures we live among. It is only through such reckoning that liberation might be found.

As a white-passing U.S. citizen, I come to Sharpe's work first to be reminded how I am bound up in the afterlife of slavery, responsible for the ways anti-Blackness supports a system that often benefits me. But Sharpe's model also offers wisdom for Palestinians and others living in the simultaneity of a violent past. She instructs us in *wake work*, a praxis of grief as well as power. *Wake work* as a position of deliberate attention, of present-tense memory. Wake work, a kind of vigil, writes Sharpe, but also *being awake*, a willingness to name our intimate aftermaths.

Am I Palestinian? I did not choose this question, but the choice to answer is mine. I must reply not in my father's voice, and not in innocence. To choose *yes* is to invoke, accept, the catastrophe of love.

It pins me to my bed. It storms, throttles, rips with the force I remember from that Valley night. Pours in, the blue gale I have fled as if from oblivion. And I see that it was only in my flight from rupture that my Palestinianness was partial, halved. Kanafani's son Fayaz was born, like me, to a white mother. But as I feel myself split again, I know that our share of Palestine is whole.

✧ ✧ ✧

I can tell you're trying hard to love me, C says to me as we wake side by side. I roll toward him and place my hand on his arm. It is July 2020, almost exactly four years since our relationship began. I search for the signs of time in his face. A few lines of weariness around his eyes? A little more bulk in his frame, now that he's quit cigarettes? In truth, it is hard to tell—for most of our relationship, I've struggled to do this very thing: to sit in quiet, rapt attention, soaking each other in.

A few days after C asked me out, I agreed to meet him at the beach. I still owed him an answer, and riding the A train to Rockaways, I still felt unsure. Disembarking, I walked toward the surf shop where we arranged to meet. The sun was sloping, golden, toward the west. I squinted as light filled my eyes, slowing my gait in the glare. In the haze, I saw C approach. His head was turned as he spoke to his friend, but the air between us seemed to gently tug. He had seen me. And wanted me.

For an instant, the clamor of my mind dropped. I felt a sudden sense of my body, the hot breeze on my bare legs and empty hands. An ache rose from my hips to the back of my throat, and I knew my armor had cracked. My heart pounded at this exposure, but for a moment, I breathed my own curiosity. I caught the scent of desire. A heady fizz, a slithering thrill reaching my fingers with sparks.

There were answers I would know only on the other side of his touch. The unknown licked my neck, and for once I did not recoil. Later that night, over beers again, I told him, *I'm afraid. I'm not sure where this will go. But I am saying* yes *for now.* Yes *to trying to find out. Is that good enough?* C replied with a grin I will remember all my life.

Each morning, the question returned—*Can I try loving, being loved, another day?* My life was beginning to warm. I learned again what it felt like to be on someone's grid. C knew when I stayed out late, checked in to see if I was safe. When a blizzard flooded New York with snow, he trekked over in rubber boots to sit it out with me. It felt absurd to be frightened by his tenderness, struggling to say *yes* to these acts of care. And yet, in my memory, our relationship has the shape of a skittish dance, each of C's gestures only half returned. Difficult, to reach, to touch him back, while also wanting to disappear. What love, I now ask myself, can a shadow hold?

In bed, our eyes hold as a sense of lost time swarms my throat. I ask him, *Trying to love you? What do you mean?* He responds, *I can see how you're trying to figure out how to really be here with me. Sometimes it's like you're role-playing, showing me love through actions that you think you're supposed to do. But I believe this is genuine love for you, right now. You've been so far away.*

There is only kindness in his tone. I feel the warm wash of safe embarrassment. I know, deeply, he is right. But I wonder about this man, who has chosen, for years, to love through a telescope.

Was I always this way?

Yes. You've been getting closer, slowly. But yeah.

I blink.

Why would you bother, then? Why choose me? Why choose someone so displaced . . .

His eyebrows rise. His answer quick.

Because I can see this isn't where it ends.[56]

◇ ◇ ◇

What is needed here is slowness, Barghouti wrote to himself, struggling to grasp his life stretched between multiple exiles, separations, and deaths. *The vibrations of the past will take their time until they calm down and find a form in which to rest . . . We have to live the new slowly and intensely.* Inching my way across the summer of 2020, I carry my vibrating body through one hour at a time.

Inside me, the portal, the knife-door remains. Through it, the blue wind continues, and I begin to name what it brings—the smell of kebab, grilled by Cousin Khalid on Jeddah's beach. The taste of fakhfakhina on a late Nablus night. A dozen مُؤَذِّنِين, sounding in a blushed sky. The wind carries the cries of my grandmother, too—but there is something precious even in this pain. It is a form of loving, trusting me with the most tender parts of her. And I am trying to love her back, offering myself as a home.[57]

In the absence of answers, this offers a place to begin. The first inkling of reverence for my ruins, which are also a monument to catastrophes outlived.[58] Palestine: an orientation toward a life that names, and holds open, the ruptures loving makes. Caring as refusing to forget. Caring as the willingness of the wound.

مقاومة

Resistance

Arabic Lesson ٥#

Resist lives uncomfortably in English. Two serrated syllables, grating the Western mind. Power does not touch this verb—the tyrant's vocabulary is smug, definitive: *strike, fire, bomb.* Sharp, even in its bureaucracy: *rule, order, deport.* And again: *fire.*

But *resist* is vernacular. It moves feral, zigzagging against the grain. Its rhythm, hard to trace, confounding those who sit above.

In Arabic, *resist* is a large and ardent tribe. Many are their tongues and tools.

نضال: from the root ن ض ل, charges forward. It thirsts *to surpass, defeating* its opponent in outward combat. نضال loves a weapon—*a horse, arrow, gun.* نضال wants to be known as *defeater of foes.*

معارضة: from ع رض, a root large as land. Its first meaning is, literally, *breadth.* Beginning with *to become wide,* عرض populates space with points of view—it becomes *to display, to expose, to inspect.*

Perhaps it is through these vantages that difference is born; as the etymology evolves, the word moves from *review* to *oppose,* or *sit opposite, to shun.* As if the natural outcome of growth is skepticism, critique of the place one once stood.

Or perhaps it is from a distance we most easily name enemies. معارضة rises in defiance, an agitation, *against.*

Among the many words constellating resistance, مقاومة is the most robust. Its root is sturdy, deep: قوم, meaning, at its simplest, *to stand.* It lives in the daily, first: قوم /قومي, a mother waking her sleeping child.

But quickly, the body begins choosing sides: قوم turns and means *to revolt, stand against,* but also *to stand with.* Perhaps the two are not so different: to raise a body is in itself an overthrow—of inertia, gravity.

قوم is a field of such dualities, stretching to encompass not only opposition but productivity, endurance: *to practice, to persevere, to exist, to keep one's word, to seize power, to take under one's wing. To raise from the dead.* Words of worth and belonging crowd in too: *to measure [the value of]. To pay one's debt,* but also, *people, nation, tribe.* It is from this sprawling, jostling place that مقاومة, *resistance,* arrives.

What to make of this strange chorus?

The answer is louder, off the page.

❖ ❖ ❖

The hot breath of summer exhales.* The one-year anniversary of my hospitalization arrives. I greet the day with a bittersweet ambivalence. It has been weeks since my last grandmother dream; now her presence is quiet, close as bone. With her, I am crowded by new clarities. In my body, a bend in grammar, a shifting syntax of the soul. I move awkward, alien.[59] Reality, now, feels mostly interior. There, under a blue sun, I fill with old new worlds. They enter through the welcome of the wound.

Some of these presences are explicit—Palestine, unburied, completing the arc of my internal sky. Other ghosts withhold their form, moving like breath or sound. I feel the march of them all, building like pressure between my wing bones, electricity in my neck. Sometimes, for an instant, the colors shift together and knit something like joy. In these moments, I am made dense. A pool reflecting stars I know but have not seen.[60]

But these flickers of vitality retreat with the opening of my eyes. On the far side of my skin, my senses fumble. Confused by my apartment, I trip and knock against the walls. My balance, off-kilter with this country in my chest. *Yama, Sittee,* I murmur. *How did we get here?* C comes home one day to find me lying on the floor, laptop at my ear. From its speaker croons آيَة ٱلْكُرْسِيّ on repeat. My grandmother's favorite sura, its cosmic rhythm silvering my veins. A tunnel in my ear full of dark, familiar dirt. These days, I am always searching for such portals. Picking at the paint on our walls, willing myself to fall through.

---

* The summer of 2020 was the second-hottest on record to that point.

We drive our new used car north in October rain. Upstate, we tumble through autumn gold. This is the majesty I missed last year, glimpsing only confiscated, crumbling leaves tucked in envelopes. Now, my eyes touch the shivering branches, read lattices of light. *Aren't you lucky to be alive?* Later, we celebrate my recovery anniversary gently, with our first restaurant meal since the pandemic began. In an outdoor booth, I wear my largest sweater, order leek soup and red wine. Liquids, always liquids, on the days I thirst to disappear.

I watch our meal from a distance—C's smile, candlelight. I try to bring my feet to the earth. *Breathe deep, touch the table.* We swirl and sip our wine, and I shyly ask C to take my photograph. The picture, a piece of evidence I examine before bed: a woman, amorphous inside her turtleneck, holding a smile and a glass. *Is this you?*

Fall grows steeper, slanting into dark. I wake from dreamless nights tangled in my own hair, trying not to feel bereft. My blue *yes* colors everything, but my days accrete around me, outwardly unchanged.[61] The blessed scalpel felt like a benediction, an exquisite wound I hoped would imbue an uncanny guiding power. I try to think from grief forward, to imagine a future in the wake. But my thoughts bounce off our apartment walls, slide down the edges of my brain.[62] Trying to conjure revelation, I chew apricot and mint. Tapping on my collarbone, calling my sittoo's name, greedy for enlightenment. Instead, I meet a different ghost. She saunters in one afternoon, sending my stomach swimming, sick.

I know her—she is me, two ragged years ago. It is her home I am sleeping in—the thin-legged fiancée who loved this converted attic the moment the broker turned the key. Outside, a snowing night. Inside, a gleaming stove and exposed brick, set-ready for a Brooklyn-transplant dream. A quick lap around the two empty rooms, and she sank cross-legged on the floor. Nose pricked by the smell of new paint, she smiled at tungsten lights and dialed C. *I found it. This is the one.* Around her, the dark wood shone so bright, it was almost warm.

Later, the fragile woman sits at our table, smiling behind another glass of wine. Around her, new friends, New York friends, jovial and rakish, mostly white *struggling creatives* who knew her as their *Arab American friend.* She worked in journalism and covered the *Middle East**—many took her as an assimilated Syrian or Saudi, rarely asking her to clarify.[63] In her work, she fought small battles over headlines and pull quotes, trying to resist simplistic framings of the so-called Muslim world. Editors commended her for *humanizing her subjects.* Her contentment was stretched thin as skin over teeth. Beneath, a frightening sense of being both stalled and swept away.

The man in her bed confused her the most. *Love* was a fear she tried to welcome, its body dark and dense. But a new word, *wife,* now trembled in the corners of her eyes, a light without heat. Wedding

---

* "'Middle Eastern,' 'Near Eastern,' 'Arab World' or 'Islamic World' . . . have colonial, Eurocentric, and Orientalist origins [which] conflate, contain and dehumanize. . .

. . . "We use SWANA (South West Asia and North Africa) to speak to the diversity of our communities . . . including but not limited to: Kurds, Nubians, Sudanese, Armenians, Circassians, Arabs, Iranians, Druze, Assyrians, Chaldeans, Turks, Yazidis, Azeris, Turkmen, Afghans, Copts, Imazighen, and other identities and their intersections."

—SWANA Alliance

gifts began arriving, stainless steel pots and ceramic bowls conjured from thin air. She tried to make their weight her own. She prepared C breakfast every morning, though this ritual puzzled him. *Thank you, honey? You don't have to do that?* Standing next to the sink, she smiled at him, her feet hovering above the floor.[64]

In the blue light, I can see so clearly—the origami of longing she tucked inside herself. I recall how, in the middle of a crowd, she might get a flash of green. A brief, rogue moment of remembering. Her heart crawling to the owl's well, wrapping a lemon tree. In moments alone, she smelled bakhoor, 'oud. Still, she bit her second tongue. She trusted no one with these fragments. They were all she had left of the land. She knew what Americans could do.

Now, she flutters in the kitchen, tending to another set of guests. Skimming through the air, she is proud as she serves her amateur desserts. And then I see it—slowly, almost imperceptibly, she is growing smaller. No, not smaller—she is retreating. Yearning, inching toward escape. *Of course,* I realize. *Of course she knew.* The betrayals buried in her frantic living. Her happiness a choreography, jarring with the beat of her own blood.[65]

But then—she boomerangs back, once again life size, near. After all, she never claimed to be *free*. Such a word would have been rubber on her tongue—synthetic, childish. Rather, she is *fortunate*. So *grateful*, as she settles back at the warm table, admiring husband and guests. Sometimes, it is possible to feel expansive, luminous, inside these chosen walls. Many afternoons she has studied those dark wood floors, westward sun splashing through the maple tree, puddling silver green at her feet. *It was enough, it was more than enough.*

There is no reason not to love these rooms—no reason, except that her life here feels like the opposite of imagination. Less chosen than the benign aftermath of other futures foreclosed. A few years ago, alone in Jordan, she'd camped on the edge of her solitude and tried to dream. An inner breeze stirred her then, the color of the hills. From her perch outside عين الباشا, she saw the land cascade toward Jericho, Ramallah, Nablus. How it swept so simply, the momentum of earth, illiterate in borders, boundlessly at home. Her mind, probing its own heart gently and finding motion, light. *Loose in the world*—it caught her, this phrase. Her wish. Equal in its allure and fear.

❖ ❖ ❖

As a teen in Illinois, I lived across from a cul-de-sac. It sat slightly uphill from us, its toothless mouth gaping bleached asphalt, lips aimed at our white-paneled home. On its corner, a tall pole where an American flag writhed and saluted in summer wind. For five years, I stood in my mother's front door and swore myself against dead ends.

Nearing high school graduation, my life had acquired a momentum that did not quite belong to me. My parents' dreams for my *bright future* had become my overwhelming responsibility. Strange, the way the talk of *big horizons* felt more suffocating, more constricting every year. *Opportunity*—in Amreeka, both promised and tenuous. An intricate ritual of merit—or was it luck? In private, my daydreams did not speak of professions—curiosity was its language, restlessness its shape. But I listened when adults said college was *the gateway to the world.* They insisted the elite schools would allow me to *go the farthest*—so I studied the profiles of prestige.

Online, these colleges appeared somehow both exuberant and languid, exquisitely landscaped playgrounds for the mind. These schools were also sadistically selective. At this, I felt Ziyad's fire climb my spine—*I'll show them.* I enrolled in a full load of dual-credit classes at our community college, bought SAT workbooks, learned to brew my mother's Folgers by the pot. At seventeen, traveling with an academic club to Philadelphia, I haphazardly fell in love with the University of Pennsylvania. Sun-dappled, ivy-laced and Ivy League, it enchanted my well-primed imagination, becoming my *dream school.* A year later, receiving my acceptance, I slid from my chair onto my mother's Afghan rug.

❖ ❖ ❖

The march to my American destiny was disrupted often. My teen years were bisected by summer and winter trips back to the Middle East. Disembarking into the humid heat of a Jeddah tarmac or the chalky dry of Amman's Queen Alia International Airport, I felt a film lift from my eyes. A clarity cohering my senses as a deep, cellular friction eased. The release of an anger so subliminal, only its absence had shape. I enjoyed but did not contemplate this pleasure, assuming it was merely the warmth of jogged nostalgia, not the call to return. This was reinforced by my younger cousins who, a few days or weeks into my visits, would chide, *What are you doing here? You like it? Why? The Middle East is* زفت, *it is going nowhere.*

My replying smile was mostly wince, my chest flashing, sharp. For all my visceral delight—in family, palm trees, عربي, and heat—I could not dismiss the tragedy infusing the air. These cousins, born in Saudi Arabia and Jordan, had been denied citizenship alongside their refugee parents. In Saudi, each faced an ever-escalating regime of taxes and fees to retain their residency. Though my father sent money to many, some were still forced underground when they became unable to pay. Beyond our familial horizons, the American occupation of Iraq was nearing its seventh year. Across the region, corrupt leaders, many installed or sustained by the West, appeared entrenched.

Entrenched, too, was the Zionist colonizing project, our شتات three, then four generations deep. In our family, hope was a weighty mixture of patience, sumud, and grief. Words like *return* receded. Longing, the architecture we learned to live inside. My

275

grandmother, by then in failing health, seemed to embody this—pallid, swollen, curled up on her mat. The time we shared had become mostly silence. Each time I kissed her goodbye, my lips came away cold.

It had not always been this way.

Once, in 1993, my father stood in his American living room and soared at the sight of Yasser Arafat, the aging leader of the PLO, onstage at the White House lawn. Arafat's eagerness was evident in his erect shoulders, the waves he tossed like favors at the crowd. A few yards away, the Israeli prime minister Yitzhak Rabin stood, his gaze fixed away from the Arab, radiating contempt.

U.S. president Bill Clinton loomed above the two shorter men, his arms outstretched behind them, pastoral and smug. After each signed a set of papers, Arafat stepped toward Rabin. His arm chopped forward, an offer of a handshake that might have been a dare. Rabin, who had almost refused to take the stage, met the Palestinian hand with his own. Arafat pumped the minister's limp arm to an eruption of cameras and applause.

On his side of the screen, my father felt a cheer rise too. Thirty-three, he had only ever known Palestine under occupation, under war. The last six years had been particularly bloody, and the deal the men just signed was murky and brief. But that morning, holding his week-old firstborn son, Ziyad's heart was woozy, soft. He was ready to let the symbolic stand in for substance, to squint and let the fanfare around the Oslo Accords imply victory. Though disdain practically dripped from Rabin, the sight of an Israeli prime minister side by side with a fedayee* was a shock that made anything—even freedom—feel possible to reach.

---

* فِدائي: male freedom fighter, literally "one who sacrifices for a cause"

My father let himself believe this was a comeback for Arafat, a reviving victory for the PLO of his youth. As the cameras flashed in the D.C. sunshine, Ziyad felt those years return. He could still hear it—the drumming anthems on his father's radio, the fedayeen's songs closing each night on Sowt Falasteen. In those days, out of the dust of 1967 losses, the resistance had risen with a fierce call for return.* A spirit of revolution was afoot across the so-called Third World, and the Palestinians aligned their struggle with anti-colonial movements from Latin America to Vietnam.

---

* *R.C. It does seem that this war, the civil war, has been quite fruitless.*

G.K. It is not a civil war. It is a people defending themselves against a fascist government, which you are defending.

R.C. Or a conflict?

G.K. It's not a conflict. It is a liberation movement fighting for justice.

R.C. Well, whatever it might be best called . . .

G.K. It's not "whatever," because this is where the problems start, because this is exactly what makes you ask all your questions. This is exactly where the problems start . . . This is a people who are discriminated, fighting for their rights.

R.C. . . . Why won't your organization engage in peace talks with the Israelis?

G.K. You don't mean exactly "peace talks," you mean capitulation. Surrendering.

R.C. Why not just talk?

G.K. Talk to whom?

R.C. Talk to the Israeli leaders.

G.K. That's a kind of conversation between a sword and a neck, you mean?

R.C. Well, if there are no swords and no guns in the room, you can still talk.

G.K. No. I have never seen a talk between a colonialist case and a national liberation movement.

R.C. But despite this, why not talk?

G.K. Talk about what?

—Interview between journalist Richard Carleton
and Ghassan Kanafani, Beirut, 1970

In this era, Arafat was one of a global chorus denouncing the hypocrisy of Western states that espoused *democracy* and *human rights* while upholding colonies and exploitative *free trade*. Twenty years before the White House handshake, Arafat stood at the podium of the United Nations General Assembly, the first delegate from a nonstate entity to give such an address. His invitation came at the behest of a number of former colonies, who, under the leadership of Algeria, had pooled their voting power.* There, his keffiyeh arranged in a piquant pile on his head, he invoked sister struggles from Zimbabwe to Laos.

He presented the Palestinian experience of Zionist colonization inside the history of Western imperialism writ large. He decried the centuries of antisemitism suffered by the Jewish people, and also the way that suffering had been instrumentalized to support a violent cause, adding, *We do distinguish between Judaism and Zionism. While we maintain our opposition to the colonialist Zionist movement, we respect the Jewish faith.* He envisaged Palestinian liberation as *one democratic State* from the Jordan River to the Mediterranean Sea, *where Christian, Jew and Muslim live in justice, equality and fraternity.*†

But he warned that, should his appeals to justice go unheeded, the armed resistance would endure. To thunderous applause, he ended his speech: *Today I have come bearing an olive branch and a*

---

* "This is totally wrong of the United Nations to treat the head of the liberation movement with so much respect."
　　　　　　　—Henry Kissinger, in response to the warm
　　　　　　　reception given to Arafat's speech

† "The Jews who had normally resided in Palestine until the beginning of the Zionist invasion *will be considered Palestinians.*"
　　　　　　　—Article 6 of the PLO charter, 1964 (emphasis added)

freedom-fighter's gun. Do not let the olive branch fall from my hand. I repeat: do not let the olive branch fall from my hand.

So went the stridency of resistance in my father's youth—a visible and vocal set of factions in exile, swearing themselves to return. Their sense of urgency was stoked by the fast-moving facts on the ground. After the Nakba, only 22 percent of historic Palestine had been left under Arab* control. In the 1967 war, Israel claimed the remaining enclaves. In their visits, Ziyad and Horea witnessed how the occupation was changing, choking Palestinian life from the river to the sea. En route to their relatives, they now navigated Israeli military posts, forced to zigzag around new, Jewish-only roads. They saw the new colonies erupting over Palestinian hills, heard stories of dispossessed farmers now forced into service or construction jobs for their usurpers, in effect erasing themselves.

Meanwhile, Israel was burnishing its image in the West, presenting itself as a modern, democratic outpost in an otherwise backward region.† Some Palestinian revolutionaries worked on the legal front to expose this hollow claim, including a successful bid to include *Zionism as a form of racism* in a UN declaration backed by the majority of African member states. Other fedayeen chose more dramatic tactics—for a period, hijacked planes became a tool of leverage to demand Palestinian prisoner release. Others launched

---

* Egyptian and Jordanian administrations of Palestinian populations.

† "[Supporting Israel] is the best $3 billion investment [per year] we make. Were there not an Israel, the United States of America would have to invent an Israel to protect her interests in the region."   —Sen. Joe Biden, 1986

cross-border strikes on Israeli targets, bloody attempts to make the settlers' status quo untenable.

The Zionist regime was swift and maximalist in its response, incarcerating hundreds of thousands of Palestinians within the territories* and striking fedayeen bases in neighboring nations. In 1982, with the backing of the United States, seventy-six thousand Israeli troops and one thousand tanks breached the Lebanese border, inciting a full-scale war. Three months later, an estimated seventeen thousand to nineteen thousand Lebanese, Palestinians, and Syrians were dead—mainly civilians.† Israel also maintained a steady pace of extrajudicial killings of both strategic and symbolic targets. Ghassan Kanafani, who never fought but wrote with a pen of fire, was assassinated by an Israeli car bomb at age thirty-six.‡

By the 1980s, Horea had ceased to follow the political play-by-play. Her measure of hope was her proximity to ʿIbdis, and each

---

* "Since 1967, Israel had detained approximately one million Palestinians in the occupied territory, including tens of thousands of children."
—UN Human Rights Council, "Special Rapporteur Says Israel's Unlawful Carceral Practices in the Occupied Palestinian Territory Are Tantamount to International Crimes and Have Turned It into an Open-Air Prison," July 10, 2023

† In addition, between 1,300 and 3,500 Palestinian refugees and Lebanese civilians were massacred in Sabra and Shatila by Israeli-supported mercenaries. The Israeli army lost between 300 and 700 troops.

‡ Kanafani's seventeen-year-old niece, Lamees, was also killed in the blast.

year was another road, closing. It wears on the body, to hold open possibility when none can be seen. In her long banishment, all lands were equal in their disappointment, their promises similarly thin.

And so she coaxed the years to smallness, treasured any mild hour. It was true, and it was also self-protection, that her family was both home and horizon, the scope of her sphere. She had delivered four of her five children to adulthood, intact. Thousands of nights she had borne them in her worries. Years of days, buoyed them with all the care her hands could dream. It was the work of a lifetime, to steal four out of five Palestinian children from the oblivion intended them.

Her fingertips, by then, were worn to silk, whorls and lines erased after countless kitchen burns. Her spine, her knees, bones ringed with the history of what she carried, built. She too was فِدائيَّة—*one who sacrifices*—if only to liberate one hour from hunger, one small body from the rain. She did not say revolution would not come. But she no longer craned her neck.[66]

From her, Ziyad learned dailiness, the pragmatism of *not yet*—time arranged like stones on borrowed land. A life balanced between the refusal to settle and the yearning for a roof. Living against two horizons—the fixed line of the land and the confounding shape of time. Toward the latter, Ziyad offered his studies and toil. For the land, his prayers.

The space between these two blurred when they drew closer to Palestine. There, visiting, Ziyad saw hope and resistance rhymed.

Beneath the long shadow of Nakba, each act of living pressed against enclosure and theft. Every garment adorned with embroidery, every poem passed teacher to child. All the olives snatched back from stolen groves—rebellion, the backbone of صمود, was everywhere. In these moments, it was not the headlines—or the world's silence—that determined faith. Something ancient renewed itself in each wedding, almond, song. A wordless conviction that all this could not, it could not be for naught. Each body, sensing the seeds of its own future, which no army could wholly destroy.

❖ ❖ ❖

By the mid-1980s, the PLO was weakening in exile. Soon, they would renounce their claim to the whole of historic Palestine, shrinking their vision of liberation to scraps of the West Bank[67] and Gaza. Permission to visit grew harder for Horea and Ziyad to obtain. Their trips grew shorter, tighter. Only they knew the colors they buried, planted, in the land each time they left.

In 1987 mass rebellion broke in occupied Gaza. Unlike the outside-in operations of the PLO, the first uprising rose from a spontaneous grassroots rage. نفض—an old Arabic root meaning to *shake off*. The first tremor, building, rattling the perimeter of possibility. نفض multiplying, finding إنتفاضة—*intifada*. A communal quake. Ziyad was a newlywed in Jeddah when it began, awed as his TV showed protest spreading to the occupied West Bank. Across Falasteen, patience set aflame. Thousands pitting stones against the lie of normalcy. He was awed, too, by the mass acts of nonviolent resistance—civil disobedience, boycotts, strikes—led in large part by the women of the land. This was Falasteen: freedom, fighters, not only the fedayeen.

And he was sick, sick in every particle, as Palestinian blood filled the streets.* The Israeli response to a mostly unarmed populace was so egregious, it proved a liability. In a new era of televised news, there was no amount of spin that could obscure the disproportionality of tanks charging children armed with rocks. For the first time in years, some in the West began to question the Israeli narrative of perpetual victimhood. The mass scale of the uprising was a lesson for Israel too. The Zionist state seemed suddenly aware of the sheer number of Palestinian bodies it had

---

* "During the first 31 months of the intifada, Israeli security forces killed over 670 Palestinians and injured many thousands more. Israeli authorities lay the blame for these casualties on the Palestinians, arguing that their violent resistance to Israeli troops has necessitated a forceful response to restore and maintain order.

". . . Our investigation found that, to the contrary, Israeli policies all too often encouraged a lack of restraint by IDF troops . . .

"The most glaring exceptions to this stated policy of restraint can be seen in aspects of the open-fire orders issued to IDF troops, the so-called rules of engagement. These rules explicitly authorize soldiers to use lethal force in response to certain situations that are not life-threatening to soldiers or bystanders.

"They include orders authorizing relatively liberal use of lethal force to stop fleeing Palestinians suspected of crimes that do not involve threats to life; orders authorizing the use of lethal force to shoot masked Palestinians who try to escape arrest, without regard to whether they are engaged in violent, let alone life-threatening, activities; and orders authorizing the use of plastic bullets, which are supposedly non-lethal . . . but in fact have resulted in well over 100 deaths during the intifada, in situations far short of threats to life. These permissive rules are the direct cause of many of the IDF killings of Palestinians during the intifada."
—Human Rights Watch, *The Israeli Army and the Intifada Policies That Contribute to the Killings,* August 1990

annexed along with the land.* Stunned, to discover each one possessed the power to rebel.

In large part, it was the ferocity of the intifada that spurred the Zionist regime to reconsider the arrangement of their control. The waning PLO stepped in to claim the newfound leverage, and the two sides met for rounds and rounds of secret, contentious talks. With little consultation of the Palestinian street, the parties struck a deal. Arafat recognized *Israel's right to exist* on 78 percent of historic Palestine. The Israelis recognized not Palestine but a demilitarized PLO, and pledged a future withdrawal from parts of Gaza, Jericho, and other unspecified territories in the West Bank.

Despite these concessions, for many, the figure of Arafat still carried a revolutionary aura. And for Ziyad, a brand-new U.S. citizen,[68] there was a particular seduction in seeing a Palestinian so close to American imperial power. Glimpsed through the eyes of longing, it was possible the White House handshake might be the just reward of long resistance. At long last, a step toward freedom, and peace.

In the opening this hope made, Ziyad glimpsed a wild, familiar sky. Its dome broad, flawless blue. Open, arcing, coaxing the body to recall desire. In less than an instant, he learned the actual location of his dream. At this truth, his breath stopped—then surged into every pore.

* The population of the occupied territories, not counting Palestinians inside "1948"/ "Israel," was approaching two million.

His brother Mohammed had seen it too. Within weeks, the two men had taken loans, wiring money to Palestine. Each one purchased a tract of land in Deir al-Balah, Gaza. As he called his mother, Ziyad's engineer mind was already pouring concrete. When she answered the phone, he told her what the future held.

I'm building us a house, Mama.

This home would have two stories. The first floor would be for his mother. The second, for his wife, daughters, and son. We would drink tea on the veranda. It would face the sea.

C, we have to move. The words rush out of me, exhaling a breath I hadn't known I held. We are walking down Eastern Parkway, rows of brownstones rinsed colorless by gray light. I am suddenly lightheaded, shocked by my own words. It is November, and for weeks my ghost and I have circled. I have watched her touch the sweet shapes of our apartment, motions harmonizing with the lines of her life. A smooth horror only I perceive. In me, the sinew of survival slowly clenching. My body taut, readying to run. *Haunting is a frightening experience,* says Avery Gordon, *but haunting, unlike trauma, is distinctive for producing a something-to-be-done . . . something else, something different from before.*

I am unnerved when C does not question my demand. His glance is surprise and feeble hope. All fall, he has watched me in my private silence, channeling his concern toward my food intake, waiting for me to speak. *Sure, S**. Whatever you need.* We arrive home and discover the apartment has shrunk by half, the warm walls and soft lamps so clearly a trap. *Almost right*—a particular danger. One I will not escape if I do not burn it down.

❖ ❖ ❖

A year ago we discussed moving cross-country, but now, in the nadir of the pandemic, even touring empty apartments feels perilous. We spend a Saturday in the chilly sun, walking to meet masked real estate agents and tour hollow rooms. At the final building, the agent texts that he mixed up his schedule—he will not be able to show us in. *Sorry.* We shrug, tired and cold, and begin trudging home. But a few blocks away, my body halts. *I think we need to go back.* Intuition is something so rare for me, I scarcely know how to give it voice. Though it feels absurd, we turn to walk back to the locked door.

We have almost reached the building when the agent texts us and says, *Actually, the super is there. If you still want to see it, he will let you in.* The place is lovely but modest—two bedrooms, honey-wood floors, windows facing trees. It is far from the neighborhoods we have known, less trendy than the other places where we have lived or looked. But the quiet in this place is different, deep. I feel something leaving my body. A rare laugh rushing in. I turn toward C. Arms out, I begin to spin.

In the week before our departure, I am gripped by a feverish desire to haul our belongings to the curb. I begin with my wardrobe, a strange malice rising in me as I comb through my clothes. My hands move with a sudden instinct to strip the closet of femininity, all things pastel and floral suddenly repugnant to me. I discard them in vehement fistfuls, unquestioning.

C catches the fever too. We are vaguely giddy as we rove the apartment, grabbing one object after another, nodding in unison toward the pile labeled *give away.* We decide to discard our furniture, much of our kitchenware and decor, all of it secondhand. We don't know how we'll afford replacements, but still, we shed and shed. Each item, placed on the wet sidewalk like an offering to angry gods. Our furtive gestures a prayer. A plea. *Please don't follow me.* In the morning, the skies still gray, our friend Hamzeh arrives to help us clean. When we leave, I snap a photo. The apartment, swept and empty, appears almost innocent.

On our first morning in the new apartment, I wake up on an air mattress that has slowly deflated beneath our weight. Empty walls blink back at me as I recall the night before. The snow that began to fall as we hauled our boxes in from the cold. The curry we ate cross-legged on the floor, every window swallowed in white. Later, lying belly down in sleeping bags, laptop beaming a nature documentary into the dark. With C's eyes fixed on the savanna, I slipped out my phone and took a selfie. Again, an embarrassing need to see the woman captured by the camera flash. This time: proud eyes and brunette brows, floating in deep black space. In her face, relief verging on mania at the touch of a new, strange place.

Now, my body lifts me off the floor, moves from room to room. I survey the chaos, a life uprooted, disemboweled. The pink longboard bisecting the floor, washed with uncurtained light. A forest of books and baskets our cat, Mowgli, now prowls. I bask in my domain of disarray, the subtle defiance of a shattered status quo. For the first time in years, I have moved with instinct and desire. Stepped out of containment, the loop of routine and fear. For the first time in long memory, I sense the movement of time. Exposed, for once, to the slither of each minute, hours a dark pressure building toward the shock of a new day.

When C wakes, we emerge from our building to search for coffee. In the Sunday silence, I hear the soft exhale our steps make, boots sinking in untouched snow. Shivering in my too-short coat, I watch

C's cheeks grow pink. On his buzzed head is a green beanie from a Boston skate shop, a piece of knitted fabric he has known longer than me. Out here, on what feels like an abandoned planet, our footprints seem precious and absurd. Our life, small brushes on a sidewalk that is already erasing us.

C is a few steps ahead of me as we head toward a strange street. For years, I have watched his movements with implicit trust; as I do with most people, I ascribed to him the certainty that always eludes me. I have followed, leaned on him as I saw many women do with their men—deferring to him in the bulk of our decisions, from finances to movies. I had never given a man such authority before, and each abdication twinged me with feminist guilt. But the work of living had grown heavy. His life was generous, full of sun and gentle confidence. Inside it, I felt legible. Derivative, and relieved.

Now, C is scanning our surroundings, uncertain. Young.

Of course, I think, *of course he has felt lost too.*

When C and I met, he slept on a futon in an apartment with two roommates, a half-built skate ledge, and one set of silverware. We agree I will have creative control of our new apartment. The project feels almost shamanic, as if objects, rightly placed, might reveal the self I must become. I compose our kitchen, living room, and bedroom, one painstaking piece at a time. Over the weeks, a home coheres. We acquire a couch, a beautiful secondhand bookshelf, a walnut table with slender, sloping legs. I buy cheap candles, consecrating our new surfaces with the scent of trees.

C sets up a makeshift desk and dives back into his new, full-time job—his income is our main lifeline, which fills me with gratitude and guilt. I work a part-time translation job, but mostly, I flutter inside the bright glass box of my doubt. I, too, might begin wading back into my career. 2020 is tapering to a close, and the initial, reeling months of the pandemic have given way to a taut misery that almost resembles calm. Some of my former editors have sent *feelers*, emailing requests for pitches, suggesting work that might enfold me once again.

This is the fruit of years of labor, a professional network I worked painstakingly to build. A past self would have been gratified, desperate for *gainful employment* to subsume the empty hours. But something in me hesitates, leaves the REPLY button untouched. As if my skinny ghost might be on the other end. Sitting at the thin rim of a web, waiting for the tug of silk, inviting her to close in.

◇ ◇ ◇

The summer before my freshman year at college, my first trip to Palestine left me blood-fresh and aflame. Returning to Illinois, I found myself both repelled by American convenience and newly wary of its allure. Too abruptly for my parents to refuse, I informed Penn of my decision to defer for a year volunteering overseas. Online, I discovered such endeavors were an industry of their own—ads depicted fair-skinned youth, arms slung around brown children, above a bannered price tag.

Instead, through a friend, I found a tiny NGO and persuaded them to take me on as a volunteer in Algeria. There, in the southern desert, 160,000 refugees from the Western Sahara live in camps after Moroccan and Mauritanian forces displaced them from their homeland in 1975. Hailing from *the last colony in Africa*, the Sahrawi people claim Palestinians as their kin.

My host family claimed me, too, and I soon grasped the obvious— that what service I could offer was far outstripped by the gifts lavished on me. Sahrawi sisters renamed me *darling*, and a piece of me was born there, in the poetry of sand and stars. I learned to tie a melhfa, growing gradually more graceful in the yards of vibrant cloth. My body acclimated to the austere Saharan dryness, the lunar chill of desert nights. I worked in the girls' school, had a daily standoff with the family goat, and ate endless meals of couscous prepared from World Food Programme grain. I grew conversant in the حسانية dialect, and over sweet-sweet glasses of tea, shared talk of empire, of homelands and hopes deferred.

The scarcity of clean water often left me violently ill. My days shivering on floor mats marked me more than any anti-colonial discourse ever could. I thought often of my father, his childhood in Gaza, and how unsanitary water brought blight to his young body, repeatedly. And when my friends' touch reached me through my fevers, I felt echoes of his mother's care. As I departed in the spring, my Sahrawi hosts asked me not to forget them. *We always remember Palestine.* With the gravitas of youth, I vowed to dedicate myself to working for both our peoples. In my ribs, a clarity of hope I did not imagine I would lose.

❖ ❖ ❖

My incoming class at Penn arrived to much fanfare. Repeatedly, the administration congratulated us for securing our blessed place among the future-makers of the world. Some of my peers seemed convinced—they came from wealthy families who owned hotel chains and congressional districts. Their smug boredom bewildered me— with my full financial aid package, every library book, free lecture, and cafeteria breakfast left me staggered by my luck. Unsure of my major, I zigzagged through different departments and recruiting fairs. Everywhere, I found *Career Opportunities* that served a world in which Africa was a research topic, and Palestine did not exist.

Midway through my freshman fall, I crossed paths with a handful of Arab and South Asian students standing by a table on our college walk. One of them was calling out something about Palestine, extending flyers to mostly dismissive passersby. I was stunned, this the first public mention of Palestine I'd seen on a campus festooned with advertising for free BIRTHRIGHT* trips to Israel. At a party my first week of class, a couple of Zionist boys,

---

* "Birthright Israel began with a bold idea—offering a free, life-changing trip to Israel for young Jewish adults between the ages of 18 and 26 and, in doing so, transforming the Jewish future. Today, Birthright Israel is the largest educational tourism organization in the world that has given over 850,000 journeys to the magical state of Israel . . . They come from 68 countries including all 50 U.S states, Canadian provinces, and nearly 1,000 North American colleges and universities. 80% Of [*sic*] participants consider Birthright Israel a life-changing experience—an approval rate any brand would envy . . . [It] also offers other opportunities in Israel such as: Exciting resume building opportunities . . . [and] a Highly [*sic*] selective business leadership fellowship."   —Taglit-Birthright Israel, 2021

fresh from their own BIRTHRIGHT trip, took personal offense at my ethnicity. Earlier the same week, a student told me her Israeli relatives were worried that she'd be unsafe with a Palestinian living on her dorm hall. *Which is funny because you're actually really nice!* she concluded with a smile.

At the time, I swallowed the cold lump her comments made. I was conditioned to expect every one of the assumptions she implied. In fact, her assessment—*You're actually really nice!*—would have struck my father as a success. *People have this idea about Palestinians, habibti,* he would explain, and by *people,* I knew he meant people in the West. *They think Palestinians are . . . bad.* I understood his allusions—I had seen how we were reflected on American faces and TVs.

By my adolescence, the mostly nonviolent first intifada had been eclipsed by its much bloodier successor.* Then, the once-rare figure of the suicide bomber dominated American media. Reports showed the Western-looking streets of Jerusalem and Tel Aviv scattered with Israeli bodies and debris. From this vantage, the hundreds of Palestinians killed by Zionist forces during and between uprisings were easily justified *self-defense.* In the post-9/11 world, we had

---

* "Of those killed in the conflict, 4,228 have been Palestinians, 1,024 Israelis, and 63 foreign citizens. For every person killed, approximately seven were also injured . . . the total number of Palestinians, both civilians and combatants killed by the Israeli security forces or Israeli individuals, remains relatively high. In 2007, for example, for every one Israeli death there were 25 Palestinian deaths compared to 2002 when the ratio was 1:2.5."
—United Nations Office for the Coordination of Humanitarian Affairs, *Israeli-Palestinian Fatalities Since 2000—Key Trends,* 2008

become the ur-terrorists—feral enemies of freedom, responsible for ruined peace.*

They think we're bad people, habibti, my father said, and always continued, *but if they get to know us, they'll see that's not true.* His eagerness to resist our poor reputation made sense to me. It hurt to imagine my gentle family so accused. But I internalized his words as instruction to make my life an advertisement for our humanity.

It was an objective that seemed at odds with Palestinian resistance. In the pursuit of liberal empathy, merit was afforded to those who proved themselves *civilized.* Any act of Arab unruliness— and especially any act of violence or armed struggle—instantly disqualified us from the esteem of our European and American arbiters. Thus excluded, we were declared unworthy—or at least incapable of handling—the privileges awarded the more enlightened nations: self-determination, freedom, and, never ironically, military force.

---

* "Diana Buttu, a Ramallah-based analyst and former adviser to the Palestinian negotiators on Oslo, told Al Jazeera: 'Everybody, including the Americans, were warning the Israelis that the Palestinians are reaching a boiling point, and you need to calm down. Instead, they turned up the fire even more.'

"Under the Oslo agreement by May 4, 1999, there was supposed to be an independent Palestine, Buttu noted . . . '[But] In fact, we saw that the number of settlers doubled from 200,000 to 400,000 just in that short period from 1993 to the year 2000. You can see that what was happening on the ground was designed to ensure that there wasn't going to be an independent Palestinian state,' she said."

—Ali Adam, "Palestinian Intifada: How Israel Orchestrated a Bloody Takeover," Al Jazeera English

Seldom did I attempt to speak of the contradictions, the disproportionate violence encompassed by this self-exonerating rubric. To suggest systemic causes for Palestinian resistance, let alone to call for nuance in the treatment of violence, was to *condone terrorism.* Our subjectivity—our rage, our throbbing desire for liberation and return—were likewise coded only as a threat to Israel's unquestioned *right to exist.* These accusations frequently cowed me to silence, whittled my language into a mere inventory of our suffering. Palestinian power appeared out of reach; the best hope seemed to be an appeal to pity, arguing our innocence as the merit on which we deserved, if not freedom, then at least to be left unkilled. I had accepted the burden of perfect victimhood.[69]

You're very diplomatic, my father once told me, and he meant this as praise.

Which is why I was almost a block past the Palestine group before I realized what I'd done—averted my eyes, skirting past their pamphlets, a vague thud in my chest. I glanced back, already losing track of them in the undulating crowd. My reflexive avoidance shocked me, then shaded me with guilt. I had not known I was a coward. But my body rushed onward, as if to outrun the conviction already setting in.

My first few months of college had been one long, fizzy romp, giving myself over to the confusing duty of having the *time of my life* while also working relentlessly. At Penn, it was *normal* to spend four nights stumbling between house parties, wriggling to music in a haze of Everclear—but also mandatory that all these nights add up to a *killer GPA/internship/career.* This unspoken imperative was doubled for the many of us who, like me, were born to immigrant parents. And so, even as I played cavalier, the weight of my *opportunity* bound my reverent feet to the earth. Grateful, skittishly obedient to the benevolent university. *From Gaza to the Ivy League!* my father had said. This was our chance.

The presence of the Palestine activists scrambled this frame. These students were disrupting the calibrated jocularity of campus, transgressing the unspoken borders of *diversity*. Later that semester, when the group hosted an anti-Zionist Jewish speaker on campus, the student newspaper reported not on the event but on its *controversy*. In the audience, I stood in the back and watched red-faced students stand and shout, calling the speaker hateful for his critique of the Israeli blockade of Gaza. Outside, Zionist students sang songs about peace, lamenting to the student reporter that the pro-Palestine students were *being so divisive*.[70]

But even before this incident, that first day on the college walk, I knew the group was taking social risk. I could not imagine myself among them—could not conceive how I would handle public, or even private, scorn. My body tensed at the thought of being anything but well behaved in the rarefied university space. And I worried, too, how the aura of *controversy* might narrow my horizons, mark me for punishment or exclusion, and so failure of my father's dreams.

And I saw all these concerns as insignificant, unforgivable, compared to the real stakes in Palestine. I walked faster, contradiction clutching my chest.

◇ ◇ ◇

You're so close, C tells me during an appointment with my nutritionist, *just a few feet from the shore.* My eyes fill with seawater. Lately, my weight has dipped, pulling me from my goal. From the Zoom screen, my nutritionist chimes in, *There's no way around this. Your body simply needs what it needs.* I lower my head. I feel this truth in every shouting cell, my mysterious nerve pain spiking, warning, in recent weeks. Deep down, I know I am only stalling, that this time, I will not spiral down and down. The love-pierce of my inner *yes* has marked me. I am sentenced to survive.

But after we end the appointment, I turn to C with my tears. *I just wish there was another way.* Until now, draped in too-large clothes, I have kept myself mostly separate from the reality of my returning curves. But now, I am haunted by the flesh knitting my corners soft. My hands wander ceaselessly, monitoring the disappearing angles. Walking, I reach back to touch my ass, its new bulk rippling, shifting from side to side.

And I cannot stop reliving a moment from a few months ago, my weight then dangerously low. Stepping out of the shower, I caught sight of myself in the mirror and was gripped by delighted surprise. *Oh God, there you are.* For an instant, my meager body looked taut and—boyish. At this, a secret part of me soared. I leaned closer, touching my sharp shoulders, circling the knob of my wrist. Entranced, almost aroused, by these hints of masculinity.

I pulled my hair back—the long waves I have worn like a duty, which I have always wanted to chop—and admired the strong line of my jaw. When I slipped on an oversize tee, the fabric swallowed my small breasts, making my chest look flat. I stared at the hollow space. It looked like escape.

A moment later, my eyes remembered their conditioning. I saw the whisper of hips again, the softness in my face. But my borrowed masculinity was a revelation, a flash of Otherwise.[71] My mind, tricked by lean lines, read not *she* but *me*. Mistaking myself for young and male, I felt limitless, flesh signifying nothing but flesh. With it, an awareness, long untouched by language, suddenly a blazing clarity: my gender feels terminal, futureless. Woman: the place where things end.

I was six when I first looked at a woman's body with fear. Tumbling down the stairs one morning, I halted, cold, at the sight of my mother, limp on the couch. She looked both swollen and thinned. Her sleeping face a wince, the opal sheen of her eyelids telling that some part of her had remained behind in the hospital bed. There, for months, I'd squeezed in next to her, accepting chocolate milk from nurses, my eyes avoiding the blue smear of bruise ringing her IV. Trying to believe the words adults said over the beeping of machines: *Mommy will feel better soon. Are you excited to meet your new sister?*

Slowly, my mother convalesced from her near-fatal pregnancy, but I could never unsee the new slope in her shoulders, never forget—forgive?—that I had seen her die. After her resurrection, my eyes followed her, swarming with concern. I began to see the sighs she released between laughs. I sensed what I thought was exasperation, an aura of weariness that hovered over her body, wilting her shoulders, dragging her slippers on the floor. *This is womanhood.* The impression formed deep inside me, without words.

This, though I had a father who applauded my independence, advised me to never rely on a man. My mother taught me about women's suffrage, told me I was lucky I did not live in the sexist past.[72] I believed them; middle class and fair complexioned, I seldom encountered people who said, outright, that I was inferior to men. But a different set of truths entered through my eyes and skin. I continued to notice how women seemed to work ceaselessly, their labor seldom accumulating power. I felt an acute injustice at the contrast I saw with men—whether in media, in the Midwest, or in the Middle East. Males seemed to move in a world that was made for them. Women outside the home were treated if not like interlopers, then as anomalies.

Least valuable of all, it seemed, were women like Sittoo. When I was a child, her exuberant love and domestic prowess made her the most miraculous person I knew. But too soon, I began to see how bodies like hers—soft, aging, ailing—were treated as pitiable at best, but more often, vulgar. There seemed to be such a narrow span of time and type in which women had worth. Lithe, productive, young, and desired by a man—some combination of these attributes was required. Women who transgressed or outgrew these traits seemed to be either invisible or ridiculed. Apparently, to grow up into *woman* was, at best, to achieve a brief niche of influence—and then expire.

Often, I turned to nervous numbers games, counting backward from eighteen. *I'm only seven*, I'd think, relieved.[73] Eleven years, or more, before I would be forced to become *them*. But adulthood did exist, and I knew I would one day be forced to relocate there permanently. Now, approaching thirty, I see the eyes of that anxious child as I scan my reflection. What I feel is not gender dysphoria but futility. A decades-old lament of a body deployed in its own betrayal. Saying: there is another life, hidden inside my own. A phantom made of everything I believed my gender foreclosed.

My grandmother never saw my father's dream-plot of Gazan land. My father visited the site only once, in 1996, during a hurried, solitary visit to Palestine. On the flight from Chicago to Amman, he still nursed the stir of wind, that glimpse of wide bright sky. But the journey from Amman to Deir al-Balah—less than a hundred miles—took him several days. His route, a ricochet between borders, hours of waiting to be cleared by one soldier, then the next. Each checkpoint a tunnel Ziyad pushed his hope through, trying not to choke.

The second round of agreements, called Oslo II, had been signed by Arafat and Rabin the year before. The framework made the unequal concessions explicit, granting Palestinians a vague promise of *broadened self-government . . . to conduct their own internal affairs*, while enshrining *Israel's vital interests, and in particular its security interests, both with regard to external security as well as the personal security of its citizens in the West Bank.**

Under the rubric of this *security*, Israel claimed full control of over 70 percent of the West Bank, including the majority of agricultural and grazing land, and initially granted the Palestinians

---

* "Since 1967, there had been one state authority in all of the territory of Mandatory Palestine: that of Israel . . . the Oslo framework was designed to preserve those parts of the occupation that were advantageous to Israel— the privileges and prerogatives enjoyed by the state and the settlers—while offloading onerous responsibilities and simultaneously preventing genuine Palestinian self-determination, statehood, and sovereignty."
    —Rashid Khalidi, *The Hundred Years' War on Palestine*

self-government over only 3 percent.* At the same time, it burdened the PLO with the contractual obligation of protecting the Israeli settlers and soldiers who continued to multiply on Palestinian land. Under the same logic, Israel refused to grant Palestinians a regular army and retained full control of all borders and airspace. The PLO, which had surrendered its leverage in 1993, could only comply.

Yet some, like my father, still resisted despair. He fixed his faith on the words of politicians, whose promises defied logic even as they extended hope. Against the disappearance of their map, they flung speech about *interims*, insisting an *independent Palestinian state* would still come. *State*—though the proposed borders would include less than a quarter of Palestine, this word still allured. Before the Nakba, Palestine had been porous, linked by tradition, tongue, and history to its neighbors in North Africa, بلاد الشام, and the Gulf. But the world of the 1990s worshipped borders, *nation* the dominant language of sovereignty, a sign of peoplehood and power.

Arafat's original vision of a single secular democratic state had long since faded. The *two-state solution* was now the only civilized formulation for *peace*.† It was an arrangement that relinquished

---

* The division by 1998 stood at roughly 60 percent full Israeli control, 18 percent "joint" Israeli-Palestinian control, and 22 percent Palestinian administrative control.

† "Repeating the aspiration for two states and arguing that partition remains viable presents Israel as a Jewish and democratic state—separate from its occupation—giving it a veneer of palatability and obfuscating the reality that it rules over more non-Jews than Jews. Seen in this light, the failed attempts at a two-state solution are not a failure for Israel at all but a resounding success, as they have fortified Israel's grip over this territory while peace negotiations ebbed and flowed but never concluded."
—Tareq Baconi, "The Two-State Solution Is an Unjust, Impossible Fantasy"

the right to return to hundreds of villages, including ʿIbdis. But millions of Palestinians languished in refugee camps and diaspora, caught in the cul-de-sac of statelessness. Others faced intensifying intrusion by settlers on their psyches and soil. Separateness, however improbable, sounded like relief. The partition of history and home, a wound many would now call their dream. A vision born of no Palestinian heart but tolerated by some beleaguered minds.

Arriving in Gaza, over ten years after his last visit, Ziyad was startled by a new loneliness. The Strip was changing. In 1948 the Nakba had flooded this small, sparsely populated enclave with two hundred thousand refugees, but now, nearly one million bodies teemed, straining limited resources, encroaching on fertile farmland. Deir al-Balah's famed date palms were growing thin.

Of the many elder relatives who had loved Ziyad into the world, only a few remained. In the streets, youth ran thick and loud. Ziyad wondered about these children, third—fourth?—generations enclosed in the cramped limbo of the Strip. The borders around Gaza had grown sharp; likely, these small bodies had never crossed beyond. *The moon is closer to us now than are the fig trees of our departed village*, wrote Emile Habibi in 1974. In 1996, when the moon poured on Gaza, it found—what map, what trees, what dreams?

My father's land waited for him, soil silent, dark-soft. Alone, he paced the four corners quietly, painting his future walls. Before taking his leave, he knelt and filled an empty water bottle with the earth.

◇ ◇ ◇

My first public act for Palestine happened one cold morning just a few weeks shy of winter break. On the campus lawn alongside others, I bent to the ground to plant rows of small white flags. Finishing, we surveyed the ghostly spread as it quivered in early light.[74] With campus permission, we built this display to mark the anniversary of an Israeli offensive in Gaza known as Cast Lead. Each flag represented one lost life—1,300 white for Palestinians, and, in the corner, 13 blue for the Israeli dead. My fellow organizers— most of them South Asian, Jewish, or Arab, but not Palestinian themselves—appeared pleased, calm. Meanwhile, panic rippled, pounded in my limbs. *What have I done? Is there still time to slip away before anyone sees me?*

I turned and looked across the lawn, at the wild disproportion of white flags, all those civilian deaths. A swoon of sorrow sailed through me, my resolve hardening into tentative confidence. To me, this display defied partisan dismissals. It was an entry point built from the most basic humanist assumptions—that a death-ratio of one hundred to one would offend any reasonable mind. A memorial, but also a place to begin discussion on the nature of Zionist domination and the occupation's endless, violent grind.*

---

* "While the Israeli Government has sought to portray its operations as essentially a response to rocket attacks in the exercise of its right to self-defence, the mission itself considers the plan to have been directed, at least in part, at a different target: the people of Gaza as a whole . . . The Mission concludes that what occurred in just over three weeks at the end of 2008 and the beginning of 2009 was a deliberately disproportionate attack designed to punish, humiliate and terrorise a civilian population, radically diminish its local economic capacity both to work and to provide for itself, and to force upon it an ever-increasing sense of dependency and vulnerability." —Goldstone report (*Report of the United Nations Fact-Finding Mission on the Gaza Conflict*), 2009

I squared myself toward the college walk, clutching a stack of flyers printed with meticulously annotated facts about regional history, the occupation, the blockade. As the first hour of classes neared, foot traffic swelled—bleary jocks in sweatpants, hungry-looking STEM students, English majors with feline eyes. My insides screeched with fear and embarrassment, but I made my lips move. *Would you like to know more about Palestine? Would you like to know about the occupation?* Slowly, the pamphlets moved from my hand to theirs.

I would forget the face of the white woman who accosted me, though I would remember forever the sound of her voice—a shriek both condescending and juvenile. She swerved off her path and advanced toward me. I caught the sparks in her glare, but my chest did not have time to close. *Palestinians aren't real!*

Something deep inside me wobbled, dropping in shock. I was unprepared to be erased. *I'm . . . I'm Palestinian,* I stammered, and knew instantly this was the wrong starting place. *Palestinians don't exist,* she repeated, her voice louder, skidding, sharpening as she drew closer to my face. But I was no longer seeing her, my eyes filling with the multitudes of Palestine, which this woman seemed to both hate and deny. A multitude I knew I was failing as my tongue froze, dry.

This encounter was an initiation, this woman the first of many strangers who would declare my existence both unreal and offensive. It happened frequently, as fellow students disrupted our documentary screenings and speaker events or accosted us at the displays we set up outdoors. I grew better at holding my ground in the face of their rage. I knew the barbarian they expected to see—the hot-blooded Arab, biting back, teeming with emotion and hate. Under my cool exterior, I trembled, the weight of the anti-colonial cause narrowing to a point on my tongue. My body itself becoming argument: *See me smile! See me, nonviolent, civilized!*[75] Those who confronted me did not seem to feel such pressure for politeness; they let their heat and spittle rise. It was as if they knew their position in humanity was guaranteed.

I remained mostly poised in a state of agonized deference, contorting, redacting, trying to compose *Palestinian* in a form sophisticated and tame enough to be heard. Sometimes, I saw something turn behind their eyes, a sudden flood of presence between their irises and mine. They could see me. I was real. But mostly, neither language nor human hearts behaved as I had once believed they would. I watched words like *international law, ethnic cleansing,* and *colonialism* drop from my mouth to the floor. I invoked Palestinian bodies, describing them in terms of all they did not have: *water, safety, sovereignty.*

When this failed in the abstract, I offered my family's precious, private things: stories of my grandmother's hardships, my father's poverty. The rejection of these bids for empathy stung the worst.[76] I had lifted the small Gazan boy and his mother from the tenderest corner of my heart. Dragging them into American rooms, trotting them before refusing eyes.[77]

◊ ◊ ◊

On a colorless winter morning, the name *Trayvon Martin* erupted across my social media feeds. I clicked and read one report, then another, struggling to understand. *Why would a man shoot a boy?* I knew about *racial profiling* but had not yet learned the unique American mechanisms that code the Black body as *threat*. More clicking. More news stories, stacks of language flat and cold. In my other tabs, my Black friends proclaimed sorrow and shock, but none of my surprise. *Again*, they lamented. It had happened *again*.

The only protest I'd ever seen was in my former hometown—*pro-life* clusters waving gruesome posters outside a women's health clinic. But when I heard of a march organized by Black students, it was obvious that I would be skipping class. At the rally, I saw a friend standing on a planter, speaking to the crowd. Around dorm rooms and dance floors, I knew him as lively and carefree. That day, he looked ten years older. His eyes both stone and heat. When he shouted *They are killing us*, I felt how that *us* was expansive, haloed by veteran grief. When he screamed *I am Trayvon Martin*, I wanted to scream *No!* Instead, I drank in the shame that I had not known *he was*.

Later, the crowd became a roaring stream of young bodies screaming anger, screaming life. We passed rows of police, their SUVs a flashing barricade. As I walked between two Black friends, the armed formations struck me with a new, lethal chill. The martial cut of their uniforms, their bodies hung with metal and a disdain I realized I knew.*

In view of law enforcement, the leaders signaled us to lift our sweatshirt hoods over our heads. On their cue, we shouted, *NOT SUSPICIOUS*.† I had never imagined myself this way—my body a disruption, unruly in the streets. But in this moment, civility would be an affront. As for *nuance, context*—I had much to learn, but it was simple too. Children do not die this way—not before they are marked for killing, and their killers for innocence.[78]

---

* "It is beyond dispute that there are some very serious human rights problems in U.S. policing, including in relation to the use of force and respect for equality of all before the law . . . Many of the abuses documented, parallels violations by Israeli military, security and police officials . . . Hundreds of [law enforcement officials] from [Maryland], Florida, New Jersey, Pennsylvania, California, Arizona, Connecticut, New York, Massachusetts, North Carolina, Georgia, Washington state as well as the DC Capitol police have all traveled to Israel for training. Thousands of others have received training from Israeli officials here in the U.S. Many of these trips are taxpayer funded while others are privately funded."

—Amnesty International, "With Whom are Many U.S. Police Departments Training? With a Chronic Human Rights Violator—Israel."

† Zimmerman: Hey, we've had some break-ins in my neighborhood, and there's a real suspicious guy . . . This guy looks like he's up to no good, or he's on drugs or something. It's raining and he's just walking around, looking about.

Sanford PD Dispatcher (Sean Noffke): Okay, and this guy is he White, Black, or Hispanic?

Zimmerman: He looks Black.

Dispatcher: Did you see what he was wearing?

Zimmerman: Yeah. A dark hoodie, like a grey hoodie, and either jeans or sweatpants and white tennis shoes. He's [unintelligible] he was just staring . . .

—Transcript of 911 call by George Zimmerman, February 26, 2012

I do not want to harm myself. I am trying to borrow logic—from my nutritionist, from C, from the close friends to whom I am, slowly, disclosing fragments of myself. In different ways, each one of them asks, *Haven't you punished yourself enough?* I know wiry limbs are a crude rebellion, a sloppy use of my contempt. Pummeling my softness will not make me impervious. I release the blade of hunger. My weight stops dropping but flutters ungracefully between *emergency* and *health.* Our apartment remains half-finished, a series of empty white walls. I evacuate my wardrobe further, leaving only amorphous garments in black, white, or gray.

There is some relief in this inchoateness. *The future* is a shape my mind still refuses. *Femininity* a question I still do not address. But in my sleep, it is all Woman. In watery dark, I wake to the touch of soft, long thighs. A glimpse of waving hair. Her presence leaves a halo. A silk whisper across my knees, tracing itself to my navel, a hot chuckle behind my ears. Under the covers, my back arches, lips parting halfway to a reply. I feel the drag of a receding tide, waves undulating through me, escaping at my toes. When all is still again, I lie with eyes open as my bones slowly dry.

Are you and S like, a serious couple? M leaned over me in the drunken dark. I was stretched on the gritty carpet of a ramshackle row house. On the fringe of campus, it was home to an ambiguous number of Penn students and a hub for what passed as the school's alternative scene. As a junior, I found solace in the motley group of activists, neohippies, and artists that had enfolded me. Around them, I did not need to describe the flame in my throat, the grate in my veins as I strived for excellence at a school that felt like an antagonist. I did not have to explain *Nakba* or *colonization*; instead, I learned from them—they introduced me to bell hooks, experimented in nonhierarchical living, and worked on unionizing campaigns.

Like, are you and S exclusive? M leaned closer. I gazed up at her, my rum-thick head groping to understand the look on her face. S was my long-distance boyfriend, a man of startlingly conventional values I knew from back in the Midwest. As with most of my relationships, I had slid into this one with a mixture of curiosity and ambivalence. S was different from other men I'd dated—he was an athlete, burly, older than me, uninterested in books. White. But there was something seductive in his cloying masculinity. After a lifetime as an eldest, parentified daughter, it turned me on, sometimes, to be infantilized. He picked me up compulsively, carrying me around like a prize. I found novel pleasure in feeling small.

And I loved that we were long distance. It suited me to have a small dose of abstract romance, which reserved most of my energy and time for the more alluring pursuits of studies, friendship, and work. It was nice, too, to arrive at a party and dance, prepared to deflect approaching men by invoking the name of another man. I had done it just moments before—when everyone's favorite anarchist blocked me in a hallway, grabbed both my wrists, and leaned in. *Ugh, come on, you've met my boyfriend, man,* I muttered as I slipped his grip.

But now—I looked at M's hovering face, and her meaning reached me all at once. Not only gentleness in her eyes—there was desire too.

The moment halted. Silence swarmed my every cell, submerging me in the speechless dark where I kept my core secret from myself. There, pristine, untouched by thought, were all the elevated heart rates, the hot nocturnal aches, all the times I'd studied another woman's lips. Inward murmurs so impossible, I strangled them without a thought. This self-rejection was so automatic I registered no hypocrisy in my *radically queer-affirming* politics. It was simple— my own queerness was inconceivable, so I could be nothing but straight.

I had never cheated on anyone. It was for this reason—I would tell myself—that I gave M the sad smile I'd regret for years. *Yeah, we're exclusive,* I said apologetically, and watched her face change. Disappointment—but was that pity too? Had she seen it—all that crowded between us as I considered her? Did she know that, turning my face from hers, the man I saw was not S but my father? Could she tell that, in my body, his desires were more real than my own?

M's own parents were brown and immigrant—did they, like mine, insist *family is everything*? And did she catch an echo of grief there, too? In my father's profuse love, I heard horizons lost and stolen, until his hope rode the thin spines of his children in a country not his own. It was this weight I felt, my body heavy as it shifted away from M. An anchor so familiar, it rarely registered as anything but common sense. Some things simply couldn't be.

◇ ◇ ◇

Neither of my parents had ever spoken to me about queerness; in our family lexicon, sexuality scarcely existed, except to be obliquely warned against. In this silence, I grew up illiterate in my body's appetites. Intimacy came to me in reverse, a set of responses to moves that others made. Beneath this, queerness lived naturally in me—ambiguous daydreams, innocent tingling between my legs—until it had a name. Then, as a preteen feeling my first whispers of a same-sex crush, I responded with what I knew. *Girls can't kiss girls!* It was impossible—something I'd never seen, never heard.

By the time I began to encounter, and then befriend, people who identified as *gay, lesbian, trans,* the possibility of claiming these names myself had been effectively erased. I had already slipped in and out of several straight relationships—each of which had caused considerable dismay to my parents. At this point, their faiths remained sincere and conventionally preoccupied with female chastity. There was no world I could imagine in which romance with a woman could coexist with my family's happiness—and so I continued to not-imagine it.

M's overture endangered my precarious contentment, leaping me from the imaginary to the real. In the moment, the decision to deflect her kiss felt easy, preordained. But waking the morning after the party, I felt a whirring, a subtle revolution in my chest. Forced to acknowledge that I had not recoiled but dragged myself away from M. Out of my tight silence, rising color, fear, and thrill.

I'm . . . bi? I reached quickly for this word, less as an epiphany than a way to halt one in its tracks. *Bi* might be forbidden, but there was a subtle comfort in it too. A word that invoked plurality in others, *bi* for me was a demarcation, a way to fraction my sexuality and leave half of me innocent. Construed this way, this term seemed to offer both conflict and a truce. Maybe I could partition my unacceptable desires. Feed them nothing, hold them still in the dark. Outwardly, inwardly, the status quo would go unharmed. Perhaps I would forget, with time, that this peace was contrived. Maybe, with practice, it would not feel like loss.

❖ ❖ ❖

My father did not plan to keep his plot of land in Gaza secret from me. It was a slow stifling. When he returned to the United States with his bottle of soil, I was barely past toddlerhood. As I grew, he kept his Deir al-Balah plans mostly silent, biding time until he had the money to begin constructing our future home. Then, as the *two-state solution* devolved and violence spiked, *Palestine* invoked more horror than dreams.

Yasser Arafat had been outmaneuvered, and then—as the Israeli army besieged him in his headquarters—disgraced. As the second intifada raged, Israel had begun erecting miles of walls and fences through the West Bank, on a route that illegally annexed another 10 percent of the land. As settlement in the West Bank expanded, Israel withdrew from Gaza and sealed the Strip inside a cruel blockade.* By 2005, Deir al-Balah indeed seemed farther than the moon.

----

* "The significance of the disengagement plan [from Gaza] is the freezing of the peace process, and when you freeze that process, you prevent the establishment of a Palestinian state, and you prevent a discussion on the refugees, the borders and Jerusalem. Effectively, this whole package called the Palestinian state, with all that it entails, has been removed indefinitely from our agenda. And all this with authority and permission. All with a[n American] presidential blessing and the ratification of both houses of [U.S.] Congress."—Dov Weisglass, senior adviser to Israeli prime minister Ariel Sharon, October 2004

"In early 2006, Dov Weisglass, then a senior advisor to Prime Minister Ehud Olmert, explained that Israeli policy was designed 'to put the Palestinians on a diet, but not to make them die of hunger.' In 2012 it was revealed that in early 2008 Israeli authorities drew up a document calculating the minimum caloric intake necessary for Palestinians to avoid malnutrition so Israel could limit the amount of foodstuffs allowed into Gaza without causing outright starvation." —Institute for Middle East Understanding, "Putting Palestinians 'On a Diet': Israel's Siege and Blockade of Gaza," August 2014

By then Ziyad was living alone in Jeddah, tending to an ailing Sittoo. They seldom spoke of Gaza; perhaps he knew that she would not visit Palestine, in the flesh, again. The things she asked for grew smaller by the day. Tea with her son in the morning, a changed channel on TV. A dark room for napping, and help when she bathed. My father's aspirations grew smaller too. He worked sixty-, seventy-hour weeks, storing up savings for his children's *future*— that is, for American college bills. As I approached adulthood, I still knew nothing about my father's Gaza field. By then, he saw no reason to speak its name.

✧ ✧ ✧

My senior spring, after I'd lost track of the times I'd been told I did not exist, I attended an outdoor party. Our graduation was weeks away, the overcast air moist with scents of beer and recent rain. I was crossing the lawn toward some friends when I felt a set of steel fingers grab my arm. In an instant, I was jerked backward, dragged into a circle of white students. The grip belonged to a tall stranger, his neck stooping to put his beer-blowing mouth next to my face. *Yo, yo, listen up*, he said to his audience, *you guys want to hear a joke?* His hand anchored me in place. *This girl—she believes that Palestinians should have equal rights.* The group roared with laughter on cue.

I felt my cheeks flame. I tried to retrieve my arm, but he was not finished yet. His face came closer. *Isn't that right? You think Arabs and Jews are equals. Right?* I tried to hold my head up, to burn him with my glare. *Yes.* I might have stammered something else, too, but by then I was exiting my body, expelled. I heard the group laugh again. The boy had said something sexual my ears refused to hear. I finally broke his grip. My breath rattled back into me. I fled.

The party was several miles from campus, but I walked the entire way, dragging my failure behind me.*

---

* It would be less than a year later that I was refused entry to Palestine. Stumbling across the Jordan Valley, I remembered that drunk, steel-fingered boy.

I could swear I heard his sneer.

◇ ◇ ◇

The assault at the party changed me. After, trying to recover my pulse of defiance, I found only a hot, wincing wound. Somewhere in me, the scales were tipping toward futility. What haunted me was not the man's aggression but the feebleness of my defense. It was not only that the crunch of his grip throttled me back to the night a West Point student forced himself on me my freshman year. It sickened me to know that he might have undone me almost as easily without bothering to use his hands. Behind my limp reaction was years of practiced contradiction, claiming to reject male superiority while diminishing myself around men. Once again, I had proved: I was weak, unlike those assertive, confident women I secretly envied and desired.

Worse, it had begun to overwhelm, how the Nakba—irreducible and ongoing—pulsed simultaneously with the drunken laughter of college boys. College boys who would likely ride their elite education into the halls of wealth and power. At several points, the defamation of me and my fellow organizers—by Penn students, administrators, and faculty—had stoked violent threats that forced us to hire private security for our events.

Meanwhile, I lived and studied inside buildings named for dead men who still ruled. Out of sight, the Israeli occupation grew,* calcifying with every Palestinian future it foreclosed. My father's

---

* "Adjusting for inflation, US aid to Israel from 1951 to 2022 totaled $317.9 billion, making it the largest recipient of American foreign aid since World War II." —USAFacts

middle age ebbed under borrowed skies. My anger grew inward, blunting, a smoldering sense of defeat.

I might have turned to others, confessed this encroaching doubt. Perhaps I would have learned how rage and grief galvanize when processed, when shared. Perhaps I would have seen how *American* my metric for hope had become—impatient, tethered to results. Maybe I'd come to question why I'd sought liberation in English at all. Instead, I tucked into myself, and my despair grew florid, sprawled. يَأْس: a hopelessness that is also a capitulation, a renouncing of former efforts or belief. يَأْس, as in *I forfeit, the cause is lost.*

When I received word of my Fulbright award to Jordan, I greeted the news as confirmation: the U.S. held no future for me. The air itself had begun to drag, grate my skin with its indifference.* Moving would not answer my deeper sorrow, but my body begged for a different field.

As with every arrival in the Middle East, I grew two shades more vivid as I stepped off the plane. The first months in Amman unfolded like a fond memory. I woke up to a familiar electronic jingle in the street below, the siren of the propane salesman blasting from his bright blue truck. Still on crutches, my broken pelvis less-than-healed, I hobbled to the stove each morning and boiled maramiya tea. I acquainted myself with the local khudarji and dukan. I ate a little more regularly, eager to taste the land, the sweet flesh of

---

* Years later, a Palestinian therapist would explain to me: *In the U.S., we live in a Zionist state too.*

karaz, درّاق, mish-mish. I worked mornings, then spent my free time, and my stipend, in Arabic immersion classes. This, the reflex of my bruised heart—a spiritual thirst for the language, a healing touch that still allowed me solitude.

I arrived to class like a disciple, eager to be bathed in its sounds. Though I was already fairly fluent, these classes swept me deeper into instinct. My craft moved beyond mere meaning, toward beauty, dexterity. Four hours a day, I lost myself in the music of making, tuning to linguistic lineages and textures, experimenting in different registers and strokes. Between work and classes, I piped Palestinian radio into my ears, eavesdropping on a parallel life. Arabic grammar laced my synapses, slanting the patterns of my thought. Soon, the language usurped English, prevailing in my dreams, moving like water on my tongue.

In these months, I inhabited a different skin. With my inner music tuned to Arabic, I discovered a private sway in my hips. In conversations, I spoke in bolder colors, my arms stirred to choreographies, gesturing shapes around my speech. With its elliptical syntax, meaning woven across sentences and paragraphs, I felt myself become lush, beautiful. Each utterance, a return. An antighourba. Arabic was healing me.

During this year, I often escaped the bustle of Amman to my ʿamu Ibrahim's house in عين الباشا. There, a taxi dropped me in front of the villa my family had built from a single floor in the 1980s into a three-story multigenerational home. I softened into their sofa or sat beneath their grape trellises, accompanied by cats. In long, gentle afternoons, I sat with my uncle, aunt, and cousins, sipping Turkish coffee and nipping an argileh pipe. Occasionally, I rented a car and drove to the hills between their home and the city of As-Salt. There, my gaze flew over imaginary lines, roamed free on the sand and green of Palestine.

Rarely did I permit myself to imagine a future, or freedom, there. Without noticing, I boxed my aspirations in the hard corners of experience. There were remembered punishments—on my campus, among Americans, and on our occupied land. *Revolution* was a word I'd mostly encountered in books, and , the cry they called Arab Spring, had faced the wrath of counterrevolutions both imperial and homegrown. By then, I looked only for a small, private peace. I felt I could continue indefinitely this way—a single woman *loose in the world*. Bound to no man. Sharing exile among kin, under a sky almost our own.

❖ ❖ ❖

Perhaps this is the reason why I could not name the sexual harassment, or rape, for so long. It was a double devastation, being harmed by Arab men for the first time. Until that year, only white men had hurt me. All my life, brown skin had meant *family*.[79]

But those two men read my body otherwise. For the year he hounded me, my sexual harasser made my *mixed blood* a fetish. He drooled over my *Arab eyes* while fixating on my blond hair. Frequently, he hinted at my presumed promiscuity. *I know how girls are in America*, he purred, eyes climbing me toe to crown. He refused to believe I spoke Arabic, carrying on obscene conversations about me in my presence. Once, at the sound of puerile laughter, I turned to find him and an older colleague thrusting their hips at me. When I tried to rebuke them in the same language, they acted as if they couldn't hear.[80]

My rapist cackled at me in English.

✧ ✧ ✧

The decision came like a stone, dropped in a lake as it froze. I would *move back* to the United States. At the mere thought, I felt myself fade, recoil. But my rape came just after my expulsion, and possible ban, from Palestine. I had nothing left in me but يأس. Desperation, concession, abandoning the last last dregs of desire.

The Israeli soldiers had convinced me the border belonged to them. Palestine, a hostage I would not see again. Jordan would not be my horizon, either; though I had loved this place since childhood and called it home for nearly two years, the violations of a few men had altered everything. It was not only that the glance of any stranger now snapped me in half. It was the primal sense of rejection—my abusers had targeted me because they did not see me as fully Arab. My visceral sense of belonging was illegitimate. I was irredeemably American—or so my broken heart assumed.

Life in the U.S., I knew, would be partial, compromised. But at least, I thought, I could be translucent there. I had spent my life learning how to vanish inside assumptions, behind conformity. I had already begun starving myself again, racing once more to disappear. I spent my last, shattered months in Jordan sketching a future, outlining a story with generic, shiny shapes. *New York. Journalism. Brooklyn.*

✧ ✧ ✧

2021 begins dimly, the world too exhausted to celebrate. Six days
later, I am watching a live stream of the U.S. Capitol swarmed
by white outrage.* Two weeks later I watch, numb, as the White
House replaces one white ruler with the next. But in our home,
the days are toddlers, small and tender steps. Some nights, C and
I cook together. Out of the corner of my eye, I watch him bathe
vegetables, lower pasta into steam. His motions meticulous, each
meal a kind of prayer.

Each time I eat, a kind of answer. I am still swallowed in large clothing
but moving against the impulse to be my own casualty. I take long
walks in the snow-washed park. The sky has been cloudy for weeks,
and I love the way it bleeds milky into the ground. I could circle for
years in the blankness, relishing the false sense of nowhere, no place.

When I emerged from the hospital, one question haunted above
the rest. How am I supposed to return to the same world that
sent me searching for death? Even then, I sensed the mismatch
between *personal breakthroughs* and the structures that wound. How
to love inside the Nakba, breathe within the wake? To wear the
curves of a woman among unrepentant men? But I halt at the rim
of these questions. I feel sputtering, childish. Here, someone else
might speak of revolution—but toward what alternative? Trying to
envision it, silence blows against me, my mind blizzarding blank.

---

* "Those charged were overwhelmingly white (659 of 716, 92%) . . . Men comprised 81.3% (625 of 716)."
    —Michael Ricciardelli, "A Demographic and Legal
    Profile of January 6 Prosecutions"

❖ ❖ ❖

At night, I drop into sleep, into ravishment. Touched, taken by women who live only in my dreams. I wake each morning and wait for dawn, watching black go blue, then gold. I feel I am a stranger, and a long-lost friend. In the tide pools of my bed, I float, relishing the quiet alignment taking place in me. *Oh, there you are.* Recognition washing backward through my memories, clarifying them one by one. Radical relief—to have a name for my inward dullness, the gnawing unfulfillment in so many *good relationships*. But as the sun finds me each morning, relief succumbs to guilt.

Vowing myself to C, I imagined this part of me would, could, be closed for good. There was something so different about this man—who himself feels like a memory, a part of me I have always known. Caught up in my first true romance, I thought our love large enough to render my banished queerness moot. For a time, it did seem to disappear from view, obscured by the life building around our bond. Secretly, I was grateful to have found a partner who fit, roughly, the mold of my parents' hopes. My father had dreamed I'd marry an Arab but with time was calling C *my son*.

A happy ending for everyone, I thought, pressing my ring to my lips.

But now, I feel traitorous as my rogue yearnings return. *I'm queer*, I mentioned to C years ago, but my tone implied past tense. Surely, I reasoned, this inward fact was irrelevant in a relationship with a cis straight man. Now, as the morning overthrows the lingering shadows, C begins to stir. Inwardly, I move to disperse the hovering reveries, brushing kisses from my skin. *This is your beautiful life*, I think, looking at the walls of our small bedroom. It is more than enough.

C rolls over and wraps his arms around me. I take his face in my hands. *I love you so much,* I tell him. An ache sits in my lungs, but he doesn't seem to hear. *Love you too,* he murmurs, smiling, then laughing, at my earnest look. *I. really. love you,* I repeat, almost in tears. He chuckles. *S!* My pet name gurgles in his sleepy throat.

◊ ◊ ◊

Maybe we realize it would have been possible to live one's life another way, reflects Sara Ahmed. *We can mourn because we didn't even realize that we gave something up.* But there is one mourning I forbid myself. I know how fortunate I am.

◇ ◇ ◇

One night, a different dream arrives. An image of a fellaha, a rural Palestinian woman dressed in red and gold. Her arms are strong, her thobe hiked slightly, as she works the soil. I wake under her spell and, following a strange instinct, tumble to the computer. I type search words related to my vision, and by some trick of Google, I locate her. The same woman, same scene, rendered in mixed media by a Palestinian artist who shares my sister's name. Title: *Woman Digging Thorns out of Field, Palestine, circa 1900-1920.* I order a print from Amman, Jordan. I pay over one hundred dollars; a wild amount to spend on beauty, but I do not hesitate.

The last time I saw my grandmother, it wasn't her. She was lost in a sick body, pricked by needles and wrapped in tubes. In a hospital bed in Jeddah, doctors tried to protect her from pain. They filled her veins with morphine, dizzying her head so that she screamed, confused. A college student, I had flown to Saudi Arabia to spend winter break at my father's side. The two of us spent unbearable hours watching her writhe between bouts of sleep. When she woke, my father leaned over her bed, softly pleading with her to see him. *It's okay, Mama. It's okay*, he murmured, trying to convince them both. I sat in a corner, my own body throbbing, ice. The horror was larger than I knew how to be.

Later, we shuffled into the cluttered apartment where he lived alone. The air waited for us inside, thick and hot as blankets. Against one wall, a thin Yemeni mattress where Sittoo once slept and which I now called my bed. I ached to stretch out on it, my limbs too heavy to shed my abaya or jeans. In the darkness, I heard a soft thud as my father dropped to the couch. I turned, then braced. His body was slumped over itself, his shoulders gone boneless, small. From above, I saw only thick black hair, his face burrowed into his palms.

The weeks since my arrival had been one long, dim day. It was just the two of us. I woke early to make my father eggs, copying Sittoo's style, swimming the yolks in olive oil. He emerged from the shower hair wet and skin smelling of deodorant and ʿoud. I served the eggs with crisp pita, fresh vegetables, and cheese. He ate, I nibbled. We both gulped coffee and blinked at the TV. Each morning at the door, he gave me a kiss, and I pulled him in for a hug. As he walked to his car, we traded the Arabic blessings his mother once called after him.

In the dark, my father's sobs wrested from clenched lungs. He gasped and sucked inward, then heaved again. I halted for an instant, then moved to his side. Placed my arm around him, thankful the darkness granted him some privacy. There were few words between us, but from his lips I could make out *I should have done more. I should have done more for her.*

You're a good son. Baba.

You're such a good son.

She sacrificed—

suffered—

She knows you love her.

Her life was so much—

suffering—

You're a good son. Baba.

—I should have done more.

◇ ◇ ◇

We were so similar, my father and I. Ready to withstand anything but the pain of those we loved. This, we resisted on every front we found. We scrabbled, stretched, stubbornly salvaged joy. *A good year, a happy childhood.* Borrowed, private safety inside our larger loss. Sometimes, a heart cannot bear its own limitations. So we lived as if we—son, daughter, father—could outweigh a violent world. Such tender desperation. Such humane hubris.

❖ ❖ ❖

They're bombing Gaza again. The news hits my mind as a memory. Brutal and familiar flames. It is May 2021, and from the moment Israeli armed forces stormed al-Aqsa Mosque, a desecration of bullets and dirty boots, I have waited for this news. Brutality, searching always for its pretense. Provoking it. From Jerusalem to the West Bank, intifada shook the streets. From Gaza, Hamas issued a deadline for the Israelis to stand down in al-Aqsa and Sheikh Jarrah.* When this warning was ignored, rockets rose from the Strip.† Zionist planes commenced dropping death.

Every cell in me crackles, asphalt smoking, heat. This is the fourth military assault on Gaza in fourteen years, and a decade since I

---

* "In May 2021, Palestinian families in Sheikh Jarrah, a neighbourhood in occupied East Jerusalem, began protesting against Israel's plan to forcibly evict them from their homes to make way for Jewish settlers . . . In response to the demonstrations in Sheikh Jarrah, thousands of Palestinians across Israel and the Occupied Palestinian Territories (OPT) held their own protests in support of the families, and against their shared experience of fragmentation, dispossession, and segregation. These were met with excessive and deadly force by Israeli authorities with thousands injured, arrested and detained." —Amnesty International, "Israel's Apartheid Against Palestinians," February 1, 2022

† "The Hamas armed wing and other Palestinian armed groups launched rockets and fired mortars toward Israeli population centers that resulted in the deaths of 12 civilians in Israel and injuries to dozens of others. Munitions apparently directed toward Israel that misfired and fell short killed and injured an undetermined number of Palestinians in Gaza.
". . . Israeli authorities said that their aerial defense system, known as Iron Dome, intercepted about 90 percent of the rocket attacks." —Human Rights Watch, "Rockets in May Killed Civilians in Israel, Gaza," August 12, 2021

helped plant 1,300 white flags. Then, we were commemorating Palestinians killed by *Operation Cast Lead*.[81] Now, a new host of dead are rising from this, *Operation Guardian of the Walls*.

I feel my grandmother fall, fall, falling.

❖ ❖ ❖

It is only after the war ends, but doesn't end,* that my father tells me of his land in Gaza. He speaks of the house we would have had there, and for a moment I hear him as he might have sounded, almost twenty years ago. *There were going to be two floors. One for Sittoo, one for us.*

A balcony.

The sea.

But the present catches us. I am in Prospect Park on a wet May morning, staring at a man-made lake. His voice grows smaller, slows. A pause. A silence so full I want to reach through the phone and help him carry it. *I wish I sold it,* he laments—

implying,
I think—
but don't want to think—

---

* "[From May 10 to 21, 2021,] 256 Palestinians, including 66 children and 40 women, were killed in Gaza, according to OHCHR; and almost 2,000 others were injured, according to the local Ministry of Health. In the West Bank, 26 Palestinians were killed and about 6,900 were injured."
—United Nations Office for the Coordination of Humanitarian Affairs, "Protection of Civilians Report," June 4, 2021

❖ ❖ ❖

A package from Jordan arrives; I hang *Woman Digging Thorns out of Field* on our otherwise empty walls. It glitters, gold leaf and barbed wire crisscrossing the fellaha's form. Punctuated by bright poppies, backdropped by Arabic script. One word lifts, larger than the rest: الأرض. *Earth, land, ground.* On the ground of my apartment, I sit and think of fields. The dunums of ʿIbdis, ripe with wheat and mish-mish. My uncle Ibrahim's garden in عين الباشا, its miniature echo of his mother's harvest. My father's unused plot in Deir al-Balah. The soccer field outside my Brooklyn home, thick with soggy grass. Is this the lineage of losing, or keeping, dreams?[82]

The body is our first field of knowledge, said Ngũgĩ wa Thiong'o, and I see how mine is contoured by imaginations not my own. One way to tell the story of a life: list the order and number of ways you learned you were unsafe. For me, *girl* came first, then *Palestinian*. *Woman* and *queer* were tangled together, one overdetermined, the other gagged. Each one of these words a border, a frontier that told me: *Lose yourself, or disappear.*

Some boundaries were sharp, horrific. Others looked to me like love. Perhaps, inside this enclosure, I could be no one but that skinny ghost. خيال: one word for *phantom* that also means *imagination, illusion*—silhouetting belief. I could not exceed what I imagined, becoming more shade than substance, haunted by dismissed dreams. Yet *hope* was the name I gave my life as it moved. This was our family way—measured against catastrophe, we could only be the lucky ones.

And there was pride in refusing to *give up*. For decades, my grandmother and father defied annihilation, made *survival* into *life.* Yet now I see how their aspirations were both courageous and compromised. How their desires shrank with their circumstance. My grandmother's heart held ʿIbdis. My father's swam to Gaza's beach. But their bodies moved to a different geography. With their children, they turned toward the disappointments of *realistic, safe.* This was not surrender but protection, love. Their bodies bore the evidence of borders.[83] History, a landscape of too many graves. Each funeral is costly. A heart seeks its rest.

So our maps became abstract. We traveled toward subsistence, then schooling, careers. In a world owned and dreamed by others, we found islands of shelter, and even privilege. *Exile* became *immigration,* the *refugee* a *citizen.* Perhaps we did not—or dared not—recognize how death had crept inside our hope. How our horizons contained less and less of us.

And yet. I feel it in the soil of me—how somewhere, I have always sensed this. The haunting in our happiness. A rumble in the ground beneath, a shadow crossing the wrong way. Another set of ghosts— the figures of our forgone futures, an ever-present otherwise.[84] Sometimes, they stole into our flesh—a shiver, a reverie. A midnight flight to Gaza, where, on a balcony, someone's mother is pouring tea. Insistent, small and exorbitant transgressions of the *real.* Come daylight, their marks lingered on soft patches of our skin.

Perhaps if our language had allowed, we might have uttered what we'd seen. Calling our phantoms in daylight, and letting others overhear. Perhaps we'd find our secrets rhyming. Combining, incitements to desire and discontent. To do this would be a violence against all tamed forms of hope. A heart, once well fed, is twice as hard to starve. And shelters may be revealed as prisons, with a single glimpse beyond.

Here, hollow optimism must redouble—or die. *In this moment of sorrow of mine, I see [the Israeli apartheid wall] as strong and immortal,* wrote Barghouti. His lament was corporeal and full of ghosts. His body had known Palestine before the Nakba, lived a lifetime before the wall. And like every Palestinian, his body knew the land willed always toward open skies. This, his ground of being, from which Barghouti viewed the wall. With this vantage, no occupation, however brutal, could be accepted as fate. And so his lament continues, branching defiance out of sorrow—

> *But I am confident [the wall] will disappear one day . . . This wall will be demolished by our refusal to become used to it. It will be demolished by our astonishment at its existence.*

What if despair were this—a bracing bewilderment.[85] The lie of the *ordinary* perforating, exposing the horror beneath its skin. يائس need not mean only defeat. *Despair* could also be the moment we name the distance between our bodies and their dreams.[86] The scandal of this chasm and its many vicious walls. Brazen, brutal, banal—astonishing.

I was in love with her. The sentence catches me as I lie in bed. I hear C on the other side of the wall, turning on the sink. *I was in love with her*: maybe the most amazing thought I've ever had.

Before C, I had privately wondered whether I was capable of *falling in love*. For all the men I professed to *love*, I had never swooned. Even—I realize with shame—even with C, it was less *falling* than skittish descent. Later, as I finally released to the bright swirl of romance, a corner of me remained unmoved. I was embarrassed by my deficient passion, this pocket of dullness that felt almost like deceit. I decided it was residual depression, the melancholy that still lurked, gutting sweetness with gray.

But now—*I was in love with her*—and I am awed by the secret powers of my heart. This recognition shimmers with loss, yet with it, every love I've ever felt revives, swells, each one remembering, traveling its own river in me, rising, rushing to the brim.

❖ ❖ ❖

My grandmother was failed. She was failed by *Humanity*, a regime that claims *oneness* while dividing, disposing of those like her. Failed, too, by would-be protectors, Arab countries and kin. Her husband, hardened by the Nakba, was a wound she never closed. And she found failure in her own body, which endured the unendurable, but not without defeat. And I see myself failing, too—all those years I loved but did not treasure her.

There were so many times she chose to make these disappointments small. I feel it in my shoulders—how all she now holds for me is forgiving love. And I remember, too, how she found ways to rebel. I squint at memory and see defiance there. How even family that revered her sometimes grated against her will. Her stubbornness was legendary. Her grudges, stone. And long after illness should have stopped her, she dragged herself from room to room. Her hands, walking her toward that propane stove, reaching for oil, eggs, and flour.

And there were consolations too. Some were obvious, communal. There were the cats she named and cherished, the neighbors who shared her middle age. The visits to Palestine and Jordan, where surviving family nourished a sense of home. And there were her scores of offspring, one generation becoming two, then three. Sickly babies she spoiled, healthy ones she blessed. The one with her sense of mischief, and the four—odd and beautiful—born to her favorite son.

But there was one delight that she chose, and treasured, all her own. Um Awni, from بئر السبع near Gaza, a refugee since 1948. Um

Awni: *Mother of Awni,* her first name, Zeinab, shrouded by mothering. Only they would know exactly how the air felt when their eyes first met. Perhaps something like the nod my heart made, seeing C. *I know you, soul.*

For years after, in Jeddah, they began their days as one. Breakfast, gossip, delicious stillness in the absence of husbands and sons. They stretched these meals for hours, delaying their cooking, chores. They met again in the afternoon, once the housework was complete. As a couple, they roamed, visiting one friend and the next. Um Awni was something of a mother to Ziyad. And when her daughter Saba entered the world, it was into Horea's waiting hands.

I met Um Awni often. She was kin, and something like Sittoo's foil: my grandmother, stout, her skin clear olive, a fellaha to the bone. Um Awni was darker, slender, and Bedouin. Around her best friend, my grandmother transformed. Her limbs grew lax, her corners softening. Their voices volleyed back and forth or swirled in overlapping mirth. Their fingers fiddling a hem or reaching, caressing the other's arm as they spoke. Stirring, sugaring a lifetime's worth of tea. Between their bodies, a private archive. The first time I saw them together, I glimpsed Sittoo in a fullness I didn't know I hadn't dreamed.

◇ ◇ ◇

Queerness is that thing that lets us feel that this world is not enough, that indeed something is missing, writes José Esteban Muñoz, describing queerness not only as a set of acts or dispositions but *an ideality . . . the rejection of a here and now and an insistence on potentiality or concrete possibility for another world.* Queerness, like hope, as a thing that leaps ahead of itself, swept up in the wonder of its not-yet-realized dream. A loving recklessness, freely renouncing a *reality* that has never been home.

For years, I have despaired secretly. Mine was a hopelessness so global that it felt meaningless and cliché. *Yes, the human world is ruled by riches and atrocities. Yes, history is drenched in blood. Yes, the future looks like climate nakba, class catastrophe.* I kept these convictions quiet and burned with my hypocrisy. I was embedded in the structures I decried, and, worse, lost my faith in alternatives. Disciplined into believing critique was illegitimate unless it mapped a straight line to reform.[87] *Reform*, a word that is itself captive, built inside the status quo.

But what if the first word hope utters is *no*? What if this word is not only a negation but an opening? After all, if this word is forbidden, can any choice be free? *Refusal is the shorthand for what can't be named within the conceptual field of the enclosure*, declares Saidiya Hartman. *It expresses our unwillingness to be conscripted to man's project or world . . . the propertied earth.* And if *the first field of knowledge* is the body, *no* may be the sound of our deepest knowing, calling from the far side of the wall.

Gaza is devoted to rejection, wrote Mahmoud Darwish,
  hunger and rejection, thirst and rejection, displacement and rejection,
  torture and rejection, siege and rejection, death and rejection.
  Enemies might triumph over Gaza (the storming sea might triumph
  over an island . . . they might chop down all its trees).
  They might break its bones.
  They might implant tanks on the insides of its children and women.
  They might throw it into the sea, sand, or blood.
  But it will not repeat lies and say "Yes" to invaders.

The honesty of Gaza is a glory born of curse. There, violence wears no bureaucracy, *progress* a lie thrown bare.[88] Such pretenses are reserved for the realm of nation-states, where the right to kill is indexed as *lawful governance*.[89] Paradox is required when the objective is both dominion and innocence. But Gaza is made to stand outside this formulation. Rendered *abject* and *barbarian*, a warehouse of excess, native flesh. Every frontier needs its savage, the reviled Other as foil for colonizer, or field for conquest.[90]

Sentenced to this unlife, Gaza can only exist as *no*. This *no* is total; she is long past the desperation of appeasement or appeal. Gaza, called أم المقاومة, mother of resistance, daily births her refusal to succumb or disappear. *When we meet [Gaza]—in a dream—perhaps it won't recognize us, because Gaza was born out of fire*, marvels Darwish, contrasting Gaza's embodied struggle with the comfort and compromise of many outside the Strip. *The relationship of resistance to the people [of Gaza] is that of skin to bones.*

Raised at a remove from her, I too marveled at Gaza. Her aura breathed warm in family sitting rooms, pulsing stories, the touch of palms and cheeks. On television, I ached over images of Gaza at peace—my father's beach teeming with swimmers, silhouetting children against a liquid sun. But in my eyes, these glimpses were always warping, marred by outsize suffering. My love for her was wistful, often limp, always stricken by a sense of helplessness. Israel's siege accomplished more than punishment—it convinced most of the world that Gaza was, if not depraved, then irrelevant. Left behind.

But what if the precise opposite is true? What if our future itself begins on such forsaken strips of land? Perhaps nothing is more haunting than to know: Gaza's sky is our own. There is no innocence for we who dream ourselves separate from her fate. We are co-substantive, creating and sustaining, entwined realities. The distance between us is more temporal than material. Gaza is racing ahead of us, showing where our trajectory must lead—or end.

I won't follow you to "the land where there is greenery, water and lovely faces," wrote the protagonist in Ghassan Kanafani's short story "Letter from Gaza." Addressing a friend who had left the Strip for the bright shores of California, he declares, *No, I'll stay here, and I won't ever leave.* Here, the story's narrator compels us to imagine the world in reverse. What would change if Gaza were not excised from our horizons? What if my map had always had her at its heart?[91] Would I have subjected my dreams to the same discipline, banishing my discontents, throttling my inner *no?* Or might I have grown up unruly, unwilling to accept borders drawn by force? When presented with the captive promises of English, I might have made Refusal my mother tongue.[92] Rejection, turned not on myself but against a killers' world.

Gaza's suffering is not theory, never poetry or myth. It is flame. I cannot know how it burns, but I can offer my imagination as student to hers.[93] *Out of the queerest of spaces, the ugliest of beings, the most extreme forms of abjection, beauty and revolution abound,* notes Palestinian writer Tareq Baconi about Gaza. What will we know when we move toward the margins, sacrificing poison comfort, learning from the abject and the queer?[94]

Perhaps we will find a relentless woman digging thorns out of her field. *No*[95] her weapon and her seed. Banished from the brutal order, mother of resistance, of those who dream beyond.

I should have sold it, my father said.

But still he has not.[96]

Morning, I stand barefoot in the doorway of our east-facing room. Months, and I have still not furnished it. Empty, apart from the painting of the fellaha and a hand-me-down desk. Here, I watch the sun meet the wooden floor beams. Alone, I track the glide of dawn, my belly full of fertile dark. The rays, liquid and sweet as music, warm my mammal arms. At my back, the splash of cool night lingering in the hall.

Something fleshy and brazen opens in my chest. A brief wideness, broad enough for just this silence, ground, and light. For an instant, I am ancient and almost new. My cells hold it—a startled love, a sharp awe arriving with the precision of a name. With a courage I do not recognize, I let it take my breath away. A life—exquisite and terrifying the instant you begin to treasure it.

For days, I return to this doorway. I practice holding the sun.[97] Here in the hush of the unwaked world stands a woman who might be me. Imagine: I was never meant to meet her. Imagine: that we might stay.

In this sweet shelter, the mourning begins. A tremble in the pleasant walls, a crack in the snug abundance I have only begun cherishing. Through the breach, a fatal knowing spills—*it is not enough.* The touch is electricity, white hot ripping my spine. Ears ringing, I fight the urge to run—or else to grab the four corners of this moment, tying the morning to itself, clutching its gold bundle to my chest. *I'm sorry. I'm so sorry,* I want to say, stricken by my own audacity. But—*it is not enough.* I brace myself for punishment. *It is not enough*—this must be betrayal, ingratitude—or—

I have been ambushed by hope—

ض

❖

We must not mistake Palestinian return as something that will occur in the future. Rather, it occurs and has been occurring throughout this present moment *to enable a future* . . . Some returns are spectacular revolutionary moments, others are conspicuous and modest in imagination, but they all bring us closer to liberation, feeding into one another. These moments accumulate in the negative, because we count them in reverse, we count them down.

—Adam Hajyahia, "The Principle of Return"

We will continue to know how to be Palestinian, together, when we are free. We will know better how to be Palestinian, together, as we are free.

—Sophia Azeb, "Who Will We Be
When We Are Free?"

ض

Sometimes survival requires a brief act of insanity.

ض

Thank your wise mind, beloved. Glory to sumud, to the soul in you.
Praise the protest your body became, how it thrashed against your
hunger, refusing escape. You will make it this far, but—

Sometimes survival requires a brief act of insanity.

We know, after all, how some days come like death.

ض

Not all miseries are useless. You held yours so long; don't ask your
heart to explain. Let your remorse have its bed, even for a thousand
nights. Bring it fresh water. Food. There is enough cruelty in the
world—or, to use your father's word: قسوة. That guttural, that hiss.

ض

In your own bed, you will dream in third person for a year. Over
and over, you drop from sleep to disbelief. But the story of *her* will
be the envelope you ride back into time.

ض

What is unsayable, you will say. Don't bother planning for it. The
day will come when you have no choice. It will start with C: his

gentleness the perfect temperature. Thawing you in the dead of winter. A long drive, melting in the passenger seat.

ض

Never underestimate him. Do not believe you have measured the field of love.

ض

It is just what Lorde said: the erotic is where power begins. Pleasure and desire: these are Palestinian too. Wisdom, wisdom in your cravings. Guidance your mind could never find.

Once you were trying to be good. One day you will be vigorous instead. Trust.

ض

A new adolescence: not only breasts but petulance. Clumsy anger, learning its own intelligence, searching for the proper size. For months, you will seem to do nothing but yell. It has taken so long to grow your lungs. A good sign: when you are able to both rage and apologize.

It will be necessary for you to start this way. You will think you are wasting time. But *alive* is a skill you must hone. Do it between storms. Practice; court yourself.

ض

You will spend eleven months in monochrome men's clothing, until one day you slide inside a red satin dress. Both will feel like home. Learning, for you, it was always about touch.

ض

Sometimes it will feel like water. Skin skimming warm silk, remembering it was seas that made you, that your first name was called by earth. Recall how, for a year, you were convinced you were a mermaid. How you floated for hours in the Red Sea. Diving, shimmying your wild skeleton, waiting for your fins.

ض

Many nights, you will come to the table with simple anticipation, a fringe of greed on your tongue. Full, you will want, you will become. Learning the width of your own neck, the cost of swallowing. Letting life slide into you, make hollow into place.

These are the good days. You will cross impossibilities to meet them. But when they come, it will not feel as impossible as it sounds.

For years, memory will make these small graces large. Wonder. Private thresholds. —*Is this me?*

ض

I don't have to tell you what the bad days will be like.

ض

When it is ready, your body will take you east.

In Amman, alone, you will arrive bracing for the old fear. This city, in which you almost became yourself, before the violence of those two men. Six years later, you return to sleep in a small apartment, its veranda perched over a hill. The landlady will greet you in Arabic. You will open your mouth and return.

I think they see her, you will tell C on the phone a few days in. Somehow, you are no longer a spectacle, ajnabiya. In stores and on the streets, people address you as their own. *I think they see Sittoo, maybe. Her aura?* Or perhaps it is you. Each interaction will be a small repair.

ض

You will rescue a blind kitten. Your Jordanian neighbor names her Snow. Each night, opening the door to find her, tiny and toddling, you crouch to feed her and think: *This is what bodies are for.* For years, you will do this. Rebuilding a dictionary for your skin, your eyes, your limbs.

ض

Your Arabic will stir, breathe. Like a romance, it is restless and adorns the mundane. The day you are picking up parsley at the corner store and recall that there are two words for *bunch*—رزمة and ضمة. A total of seven letters, delicate beyond measure, gossamers of meaning gliding up from the void. *Where do they rest, in our long periods of silence? Do they hold any bitterness for your neglect?*

ض

In Amman, you will cook Horea's foods. In the souq, her hands
gently squeezing the tomatoes, slipping silk onions into your bag.
Her spices, cheap and abundant, powdering your counter. Megla
is where you start. A poor woman's meal, so basic and felahi that
its recipe does not exist on the internet. You will replicate from
memory and intuition, watch savory golden batter crackle and
brown. The air, thickening with the aroma of your first morning
together, on the sun-washed kitchen floor. Thick, eggy pancake,
wet chunks of feta on its sizzling, oily crust. You will eat it on the
floor, grease coating your fingers. A smile seen only by her.

هذا بطن!

ض

As you return to the U.S., an ending is underway. In your pores, an
old frequency, rising. It gives your heart a murmur. It makes your
body leave rooms. Every dark ceiling a valley rainfall, a tank turret,
owls.

I need to go back. You will say it because you are afraid to, and because
you are beginning to recognize the sound your life makes when it
speaks. You will spend almost a year simply practicing those words.
I need. عودة.

Your body a war with itself, terrified to imagine you might try.

ض

Sometimes survival requires a brief act of insanity.

ض

When you arrive at the airport in Tel Aviv, your bones will turn translucent green. Your phone offline, your bag almost empty, you will try to be a ghost. At first, your blond hair will work its stupid magic. The first officer will be polite. But when they open your passport, the music stops. *What kind of name is this?*

You have nothing to hide, but their small, too-white interrogation room will almost convince you otherwise. They will type and type into your file. Try not to hate yourself. Remember what is theater, and remember who is you.

ض

Hours later, each step toward the taxi line will be a full rotation between rage, elation, and fear. So many notations they attached to your name. Familiar horror: *This might be the last time.* A taxi driver will address you in stiff English. You will answer with dry lips. But when you see his license hanging over the back seat—*Mohammed*—you will almost burst into tears. The two of you will tumble into Arabic. A doorway at which you remove your shoes, crossing to sit inside.

ض

You will spend the next month there—a chilly, windy March. It will be more excruciating than you recalled. There is no preparing for the way the colonies have multiplied, how things have grown more ruinous, more cruel.

The light in the West Bank is not blue but white. Garish, almost unbearably clear. There are almost no pockets of pure life. Everything perforated, murder peering in. Where the occupation was once a ponderous shade, you will find it wanton, burly, swift.

The land, its groan. تعبنا، تعبنا! The strain on even the youngest faces too. You will wonder if childhood has a price. You will almost hate yourself for having the money to buy fresh vegetables and fruit. Your friends warn you not to approach Nablus. صعب، صعب, they tell you. There have been more murders than usual, settlers and soldier wrath.

The air will feel red, wet.

ض

But what will hurt even more than the horror is the joy. It is the reason you never stopped running from the Jordan Valley: it breaks you, all the beauty happening inside this wound. A reminder of all you have learned to live without. A terror, to know what is left to lose. How intricate, how coarse the ways the occupation barricades Palestinian grace from the world.

Still, you will try to be wide for all of it, to love it though sorrow blows inside everything. Your body will give you this: the chance to steal things back. The rain that soaks your shoes in Bireh. Fresh dates in Jericho. The makdous man in Manara Square. The shared taxi at Damascus Gate, with disco lights inside.

الكعك القدسي اللي ابوكي بحبه. الناس بتقول ان السر في الماء ، مستحيل بتلاقي نفس الطعم في اي مكان ثاني.

ض

You will take photographs and delete them. The flatness of the screen, the constant threat of confiscation. Palestine is Palestine, not pixels or words.

ض

An irreplaceable week when your brother and his wife join you in Ramallah. You will share a balcony brushed by trees and learn the names of birds. You will walk old streets and feel small, enter cafés and feel the past slipping out the back door. The knafeh will be just as sweet, but the final bite is queasy each time.

ض

At first, you are sure you cannot bear looking for 'Ibdis. But after few weeks under occupation, you are growing feral, losing your fear of loss.

It will take many hours, many checkpoints, many shekels to reach the place. Passing through Qalandia, its cattle chute and metal heart. Crossing al-Quds, squinting to hide the mission in your eyes. A frazzled taxi driver, startled when you ask him to turn off the road into a field. Chaos: your father on speakerphone—your brother trying to read topographical and archival maps—you translating two directions—collectively trying to navigate from memory.

Everything will be changed. Again. Changed for the less, as it always is. Sittoo's village replaced by commercial almond trees.

Automated sprinklers, bland obscenities. I don't have to tell you
how that will feel.

ض

But there will be one consolation. Two. A set of fraternal twins,
nakhla and جميزة, remaining. Their trunks gnarled and dense with
history. Hearing this, your father will crack to tears.

That's your land, kids. Ohhh.

ض

Time holds its breath that afternoon. The sky lending a soft palm
of clouds to shade the sun. In the halted light, you will swear you
smell the sea. In twenty minutes, you could be in Gaza. *Get a little
stronger, and we'll go, habibti,* your father has begun to say. You both
believe it more each time. *You need to be ready. It's not easy. But you'll
see. It's different. It's just a different world.*

ض

On your brother's last day in Ramallah, something in you breaks.
Your gushing will rattle you both, fistfuls of water on each cheek.
The words will be sidewise, imprecise. *I just have this bad feeling.*
Something in your body telling you: it might be a long time—
perhaps a different life—before you are able to return.

You will stay together an extra day. The last night will feel like a
raft in the sea.

Your final week is in Haifa. Beautiful Haifa, where you will not sleep well. Haifa, the city Western liberals love for its gently ethnic bar scene, for the way its Arab remnant *coexists*. The breathlessness of this boast: *They don't even need leashes here.* But there should be another word for civility without equality. (The United States has a few.)

You will have nightmares each night. On this side of the wall, you will find it much harder to eat, to breathe. Asphalt and invasive foliage where Palestinians should be. Still, even from here, you will not want to leave. Your first flight home will be canceled when Israelis go on strike. Their reason: they are worried the right wing is *ruining their democracy.*

ض

Your last day: عكّا. You will take the train just to see the Palestinian boys jump off the ancient walls into the sea. You have treasured their memory since you first glimpsed them, many years ago. Standing next to your father, you saw him in each leap—the smallest ones cannoning, older ones flaunting with somersaults and flips. All of them laughing as they gave their bodies to the blue.

Your train will be crowded with teenagers and their guns. Disembarking on a street swarmed with Israeli flags, you enter a shop. The cashier will be playing Arabic music. He will turn it down when you walk in, then back up when you say salaam.

The old city will be shabbier than you remember. *Or is it just that it's low season?* From sky to water, a palette of silver and peach. You will find the wall, but no boys.

ض

Coming back from Palestine, you carry a fever that will last all spring. You drank the wrong water in Bethlehem. And that ache in your marrow—the doctors will diagnose you with a rare disorder incurred by extreme starvation. History's half-life, your bones eaten from the inside out: *serous fat atrophy.* But you will know it by a different name.

They hate us so much, you will whisper to C. *I really believe they would kill us all if they could.*

ض

You were born knowing this. But history has a way of moving, changing shape.

ض

Sometimes survival requires a brief act of insanity, but there will come a day when you realize the loop has closed. And you feel it—how the time for opening has come.

You will almost give the oppressors credit. It was love that you turned back. But it is the fight that accelerates your return.

الديوان / Diwan

And all these people, they're in my head and they're in my body,
you know, they're sort of animating my flesh, disrupting the body
I guess I thought was mine. —Fred Moten

Part I: صمت / Silence

1. Inhabitants of silence . . . circumnavigating absence. For a moment it
was a sweet country. —Dionne Brand, *A Map to the Door of No Return*

2. Do we exist? What proof do we have? . . . The Palestinian predicament:
finding an 'official' place for yourself in a system that makes no
allowances for you . . . We need to retell our story from scratch every
time, or so we feel. What we are left with when we get to scratch is not
very much. —Edward Said, *After the Last Sky*

3. Modern man no longer communicates with the madman . . . There is
no common language, or rather, it no longer exists; the constitution
of madness as mental illness, at the end of the eighteenth century,
bears witness to a rupture in a dialogue, gives the separation as already
enacted, and expels from the memory all those imperfect words, of
no fixed syntax, spoken falteringly, in which the exchange, between
madness and reason, was carried out. The language of psychiatry, which
is a monologue by reason *about* madness, could only have come into
existence in such a silence. —Michel Foucault, *Madness and Civilization*

4. You must always remember that the sociology, the history, the
economics, the graphs, the charts, the regressions all land, with great
violence, upon the body. —Ta-Nehisi Coates, *Between the World and Me*

5. Over time, with experience, you sense that something is wrong or you have a feeling of being wronged . . . a body in touch with a world can become a body that fears the touch of the world . . . It is too much.
—Sara Ahmed, *Living a Feminist Life*

6. The magic of apricot
   my daughter blurts out
   the three unprompted words
   "I love you"
   in Arabic one   —Fady Joudah, "The Magic of the Apricot"

Part II: لسان / Speech
غربة / *Ghourba*

7. There is no line that can be drawn from one Palestinian to another that does not seem to interfere with the political designs of one or another state.   —Edward Said, *After the Last Sky*

8. You've punctured my solitude.   —Maggie Nelson, *The Argonauts*

9. He who was born in a country that does not exist . . . does not exist either. If you say, metaphorically, that you are from no place, you are told: There is no place for no place.   —Mahmoud Darwish, *In the Presence of Absence*

10. What I'm saying is that there is more other, scarier other, translated other, untranslatable other, the utterly strange other, the other who can't stand you. Those of us allowed to speak are the tip of the iceberg. We are the cute other.   —Rabih Alameddine, *Comforting Myths*

11. I write because life does not appease my appetites and hunger. I write to record what others erase when I speak, to rewrite the stories others have miswritten about me, about you.
—Gloria E. Anzaldúa, "Speaking in Tongues: A Letter to Third World Women Writers"

12. If you don't know anything about the history of a place, the rise and rise and genocidal history of a place that is that place—if you don't know anything about the people who were killed and the people who

did the killing and the people who neither killed nor did the killing but did the killing—if you don't know anything about the history that is the present moment and vice versa and the next, and the bodies underneath your feet and the bodies in the air you're breathing, that is America.

—Brandon Shimoda, "Notes for National Corpse Month, Part Five"

13. Displaced is where we moved to, displaced is where I grew up, displaced is where I am from.   —Thirii Myo Kyaw Myint, *Names for Light*

14. When the United States and Britain denied their non-propertied classes and their female citizens suffrage, or when the US operated a colonial system of slavery, genocide, and racial apartheid, no culturalist arguments were advanced to explain this grave democratic deficit among white Euro-American property-owning Protestant Christian men.

—Joseph Massad, *Islam and Liberalism*

15. Are you sure, sweetheart, that you want to be well? . . . Just so's you're sure, sweetheart, and ready to be healed, cause wholeness is no trifling matter. A lot of weight when you're well.

—Toni Cade Bambara, *The Salt Eaters*

16. The experience of immigration itself is based on a structure of mourning. When one leaves one's country of origin, voluntarily or involuntarily, one must mourn a host of losses both concrete and abstract. These include homeland, family, language, identity, property, status in the community—the list goes on. In Freud's theory of mourning, one works through and finds closure to these losses by investing in new objects— in the American Dream, for example.

—David L. Eng and Shinhee Han, *Racial Melancholia, Racial Dissociation: On the Social and Psychic Lives of Asian Americans*

17. The most powerful state in history has proclaimed, loud and clear, that it intends to rule the world by force . . . Apart from the conventional bow to noble intentions that is the standard (hence meaningless) accompaniment of coercion, its leaders are committed to pursuit of their "imperial ambition" . . . They have also declared that they will tolerate no competitors, now or in the future. They evidently believe

that the means of violence in their hands are so extraordinary that they can dismiss with contempt anyone who stands in their way.

The doctrine is not entirely new, nor unique to the US, but it has never before been proclaimed with such brazen arrogance.

—Noam Chomsky, address to the World Social Forum, 2003

18. We must remember that [the word] terrorism does not describe an objective reality; it is, like other pieces of language weaponized to murder, an ideological word used by ideological powers, with specific legislative and carceral bodies attached to its use.

—Fargo Nissim Tbakhi, "Notes on Craft: Writing in the Hour of Genocide"

19. Someone should write about the role of the older brother in the Palestinian family. From his adolescence he is afflicted with the role of brother and father and mother and head of family and dispenser of advice. He is the child who has always to prefer others to himself. The child who gives and does not acquire. The child who keeps watch over a flock of both older and younger and so excels at noticing things.

—Mourid Barghouti, *I Saw Ramallah*

20. But an agitated mind does not know any road to peace except the one away from home.

—Yiyun Li, *Dear Friend, From My Life I Write to You in Your Life*

رؤية / *Vision*

21. My body knew what was going to happen, because it, and only it, knew what I'd made it do, and what I hoped it would forget. —Kiese Laymon, *Heavy*

22. Thus the struggle for the liberation of Palestine, like any other liberation struggle in the world, becomes a struggle against world imperialism which is intent on plundering the wealth of the underdeveloped world and on keeping it a market for its goods. Naturally Israel—and the Zionist movement as well—have their own characteristics, but these characteristics must be viewed in the light of Israel's organic link with imperialism. —Popular Front for the Liberation of Palestine, *Strategy for the Liberation of Palestine*, 1969

23. Marginality [is] much more than a site of deprivation. In fact . . . it is also the site of radical possibility, a space of resistance.
—bell hooks, "Marginality as a Site of Resistance"

24. Resistance, yes, but other capacities too. Like quiet.
—Kevin Quashie, *The Sovereignty of Quiet: Beyond Resistance in Black Culture*

25. A woman must continually watch herself. She is almost continually accompanied by her own image of herself . . . From earliest childhood she has been taught and persuaded to survey herself continually . . . because how she appears to men, is of crucial importance for what is normally thought of as the success of her life.

One might simplify this by saying: men act and women appear. Men look at women. Women watch themselves being looked at. This determines not only most relations between men and women but also the relation of women to themselves. The surveyor of woman in herself is male: the surveyed female. Thus she turns herself into an object— and most particularly an object of vision: a sight.
—John Berger, *Ways of Seeing*

26. The English language is the most violent technology mankind has ever invented, so whatever it's certain of, I reflexively distrust.
—Kaveh Akbar, interview by Claire Schwartz, "The Wide Question"

27. One hides something for two reasons: one feels protective of it or feels ashamed of it.
—Yiyun Li, *Dear Friend, From My Life I Write to You in Your Life*

28. I've been thinking a lot about flinching, stuttering, tantrums, con-vulsions—involuntary reactions of aversion. An eating disorder is akin to a very long flinch.
—Nina Puro, quoted in JoAnna Novak, "On the Literature of Eating Disorders"

29. We demand for the right to opacity for everyone.
—Édouard Glissant, *Poetics of Relation*

30. This most enduring and efficient rite of passage into American culture: negative appraisals of the native-born black population.

Only when the lesson of racial estrangement is learned is assimilation complete. —Toni Morrison, "On the Backs of Blacks"

نكبة / *Nakba*

31. I've never had a yard but I've had apartments
    where water pipes burst above my head where I've scrubbed
    a lover's blood from the kitchen tile   such cleaning
    takes so much time you expect there to be confetti at the end
    —Kaveh Akbar, "What Seems Like Joy"

32. There is a danger in associating becoming disabled with a violent and oppressive history, because disability is already conceived of as "abject" (Kristeva, 1982).
    —Nirmala Erevelles, *Disability and Difference in Global Contexts*

33. My poetry is a reckoning with the disembodiments of the many selves housed within my body; the selves I survived to work towards the self I am becoming. The selves I had to kill to become.
    —George Abraham, "Teaching Poetry in the Palestinian Apocalypse"

34. We have to break the state of denial with which the world confronts us. We shall tell the tale the way it has to be told. We shall tell our personal histories one by one and shall recount our little stories as we have lived them and as our souls and eyes and imaginations remember them. We shall not let history be the history of great events, of kings and officers and books on dusty bookshelves.

    We shall recount what happened to us personally and the life stories of our bodies and our senses, which to the naïve will seem trivial, incoherent, and meaningless. The meaning is etched upon each individual woman, man, child, tree, house, window, and on every grave . . . A history of the obstinacy of our bodies and of our souls, no record of which is to be found in archives or registries. We shall make the two-hour electricity cuts to our houses important events because they are important events . . . I shall make of every feeling that ever shook my heart historic event and I shall write it.
    —Mourid Barghouti, *I Was Born There, I Was Born Here*

35. Is it possible to construct a story from "the locus of impossible speech" or resurrect lives from the ruins? Can beauty provide an antidote to dishonor, and love a way to "exhume buried cries" and reanimate the dead? Or is narration its own gift and its own end, that is, all that is realizable when overcoming the past and redeeming the dead are not? And what do stories afford anyway? A way of living in the world in the aftermath of catastrophe and devastation? A home in the world for the mutilated and violated self? For whom—for us or for them?

—Saidiya Hartman, "Venus in Two Acts"

36. تَضِيقُ بِنَا الأَرْضُ تَحْشُرُنَا فِي المَمَرِّ الأَخِيرِ، فَنَخْلَعُ أَعْضَاءَنَا كَيْ نَمُرَّ
The Earth is closing in on us,
Forcing us through the final passage
And we tear off our limbs to get through
—Mahmoud Darwish, "The Earth Is Closing on Us"

ذكر / Remember/Invoke

37. How can a century or a heart turn
if nobody asks, *Where have all*
the natives gone?   —Natalie Diaz, "Manhattan Is a Lenape Word"

38. عَلَى هَذِهِ الأَرْضِ مَا يَسْتَحِقُّ الحَياةُ
—محمود درويش

39. What is it like, to be born in a place, to stay and live there, to know that you are of it, more or less forever?
—Edward Said, "Reflections on Exile"

40. But you can write about what has been erased from this landscape—those trees don't disappear from the language, and that way, they almost exist.   —Adania Shibli, interview by Claudia Steinberg,
"Palestine as a Position of Witnessing"

41. Spaciocide is the objective of Israel's colonial project, and suffocation, the constriction and snuffing out of Palestinian nafs, is its intent.
—Lara Sheehi and Stephen Sheehi, *Psychoanalysis Under*
Occupation: Practicing Resistance in Palestine

42. When a woman decides to leave their country, something quite miraculous, in my opinion, happens in that they have to decide what to take out and leave behind in the archive of their self and what to salvage and carry forth because the memory is a limited archive.

    —Ocean Vuong, interview by Tonya Mosley
for *Fresh Air*, April 2022

43. This is the city of our senses, our bodies, and our childhood . . . The city of our little moments that we forget quickly because we will not need to remember.   —Mourid Barghouti, *I Saw Ramallah*

44. I belong to memories that do not belong to me.

    —Dao Strom, *You Will Always Be Someone From Somewhere Else*

45. You think there is absolutely no way you can get to it. Do you see how close it is? How touchable? How real? I can hold it in my hand, like a handkerchief.   —Mourid Barghouti, *I Saw Ramallah*

46. That's the history that most Americans don't want to remember or to recognize. For most refugees and immigrants, when we say we come here for the American dream, we are also saying we're coming here to be a part of settler colonialism, whether we know it or not.

    —Viet Thanh Nguyen, interview by Eric Nguyen, "For Viet
Thanh Nguyen, Writing Is an Act of Beauty and Justice"

47. And when two people have loved each other
see how it is like a
scar between their bodies,
stronger, darker, and proud   —Jane Hirshfield, "For What Binds Us"

48. The event of return does not take place after the fact, in a "post"-temporality where the Zionist regime no longer exists. Instead, the act springs from within the time of its reign, cracking its walls and fracturing its frame.   —Adam Hajyahia, "The Principle of Return"

49. I don't know what they thought I was capable of;
I wish I was more capable of it.

    —Zaina Alsous, "Violence"

50. Saving the argument
    I am let in
    I am let in until   —Solmaz Sharif, "He, Too"

51. Zionist opposition to Palestinian return and belonging is predicated on a zero-sum view: Israel is if Palestinians are not; Palestinians are not if Israel is. Perhaps instead of asking what it will take to overcome Zionist opposition to Palestinian belonging, we should ask, what possibilities does the return of their belonging create?
    —Noura Erakat, *Justice for Some: Law and the Question of Palestine*

52. My grandfather died with his gaze fixed on a land imprisoned behind a fence. A land whose skin they have changed from wheat, sesame, maize, watermelons, and honeydews to tough apples.
    —Mahmoud Darwish, *Memory for Forgetfulness*

53. And love will simply have no choice but to go into battle with space and time and, furthermore, to win.   —James Baldwin, "Nothing Personal"

54. The dreams of the colonial subject are muscular dreams, dreams of action, dreams of aggressive vitality. I dream I am jumping [above the wall], swimming [near the shores of Akka], running [in the streets of Jaffa], and climbing [the trees of Birzeit]. I dream I burst out laughing, I am leaping across a river and chased by a pack of cars that never catches up with me. During colonization the colonized subject frees himself night after night between nine in the evening and six in the morning.
    —Frantz Fanon, *The Wretched of the Earth*, with additions by Adam Hajyahia, in "The Principle of Return"

55. There is nothing more vulnerable than caring for someone; it means not only giving your energy to that which is not you but also caring for that which is beyond or outside your control . . . To care is not about letting an object go but holding on to an object by letting oneself go, giving oneself over to something that is not one's own.
    —Sara Ahmed, *The Promise of Happiness*

56. In order for me to speak a truer word concerning myself, I must strip down through layers of attenuated meanings, made an excess in time,

over time, assigned by a particular historical order, and there await whatever marvels of my own inventiveness.

> —Hortense J. Spillers, "Mama's Baby, Papa's Maybe:
> An American Grammar Book"

57. As a custodian for the soul passed down to you through your mothers, you might make it a little easier for it this time around . . . why not treat it with real tenderness? It has been through so much already—why not let it rest? —Sheila Heti, *Motherhood*

58. Palestine is a mode of living . . . if you are listening, it becomes so natural that you care, and you create a connection of care.

> —Adania Shibli, interview by Claudia Steinberg,
> "Palestine as a Position of Witnessing"

مقاومة / *Resistance*

59. What is surrealism but ancestral memory? —Aja Monet

60. Feeling real is not reactive to external stimuli, nor is it an identity. It is a sensation—a sensation that spreads. Among other things, it makes one want to live.

> —Maggie Nelson, on D. W. Winnicott, in *The Argonauts*

61. ?memory of figment a merely not are you know you do How

> —Zaina Alsous, "Birth Right"

62. This is how one pictures the angel of history. His face is turned toward the past. Where we perceive a chain of events, he sees one single catastrophe which keeps piling wreckage upon wreckage and hurls it in front of his feet.

> —Walter Benjamin, "Theses on the Philosophy of History"

63. Colonial mimicry is the desire for a reformed, recognizable Other, *as a subject of a difference that is almost the same, but not quite.*

> —Homi Bhabha, "Of Mimicry and Man"

64. Haunting is an animated state in which a repressed or unresolved social violence is making itself known. [It is] the singular yet repetitive instances when home becomes unfamiliar, when your bearings on the world lose

direction, when the over-and-done-with bones alive, when what's been in your blind spot comes into view.　　—Avery Gordon, *Ghostly Matters*

65. Best advice I ever got was an old friend of mine, a black friend, who said you have to go the way your blood beats. If you don't live the only life you have, you won't live some other life, you won't live any life at all. That's the only advice you can give anybody. And it's not advice, it's an observation.　　—James Baldwin, interview by Richard Goldstein, *James Baldwin: The Last Interview and Other Conversations*

66. Tent #50, on the left, that is my present
But it is too cramped to contain a future!
And—"forget!" they say, but how can I?
　　　　—Rashed Hussein, "Tent #50 (Song of a Refugee)"

67. The pollution of language can get no more blatant than in the term West Bank. West of what? Bank of what? The reference here is to the west bank of the River Jordan, not to eastern Palestine. The west bank of a river is a geographical location—not a country, not a homeland. The battle for language becomes the battle for the land. The destruction of one leads to the destruction of the other. When Palestine disappears as a word it disappears as a state, as a country and as a homeland . . .
　　Can verbicide lead to genocide?　—Mourid Barghouti, "Verbicide"

68. Belonging does not interest me. I had once thought that it did. Until I examined the underpinnings. One is misled when one looks at the sails and majesty of tall ships instead of their cargo.
　　　　–Dionne Brand, A Map to the Door of No Return

69. Is it not curious, one might ask, that the very sympathy shown to Palestinians appears directly proportional to their perceived inability to confront the uniform machinery of settler colonialism?
　　　　—Abdaljawad Omar, "Hopeful Pathologies in the
War for Palestine: A Reply to Adam Shatz"

70. All of our speech acts are objectionable if their demand is freedom. Our putative saviors who keep instructing us to be nicer don't oppose bad optics; they oppose Palestinian liberation.　　—Steven Salaita,
"Down with the Zionist Entity; Long Live 'the Zionist Entity'"

71. Sometimes when I walk down the street wearing men's clothing, I wonder if I am threatening the gender binary or if I am helping to reproduce the idea that to look masculine is to be liberated.
—Genevieve Hudson, "Hunger Inside My Queer Body"

72. So much inequality is preserved through the appeal of happiness, the appeal to happiness. It is as if the response to power and violence is or should be simply to adjust or modify how we feel; for instance, by transforming a social relation of exploitation into a personal feeling of empowerment.
—Sara Ahmed, *Living a Feminist Life*

73. The child poised on the threshold of a door in a desert is also the ghost going the other way; they are one action immortalized by a single position towards the world: *not there.*
—Franny Howe, "My Father Was White but Not Quite"

74. If we return now to the historical roots of our cause we do so because present at this very moment in our midst are those who, while they occupy our homes as their cattle graze in our pastures, and as their hands pluck the fruit of our trees, claim at the same time that we are disembodied spirits, fictions without presence, without traditions or future.—Yasser Arafat, speech at the United Nations General Assembly debate on the question of Palestine, 1974

75. How can decolonization manifest itself without disrespecting the colonial enterprise, they ask, while they [employ] hermetically sealed structures of sustained colonial terror, which inevitably reduce all decolonizing efforts to nothing less than abolition and rupture of the structures' non-penetrability.—Adam Hajyahia, "The Principle of Return"

76. Pity is a fragile and feeble foundation for building movements. Our strength does not lie in eliciting pity but in inspiring through various acts of resistance.
—Abdaljawad Omar, in "Palestinian Resistance and the Path to Liberation," panel at the People's Conference for Palestine

77. Not only do [Palestinians in Gaza] have the right to live, but they have the right to contempt, they have the right to feel angry, the right to fury,

the right to not want to forgive, to not want to be graceful, to not want
to be perfect victims.   —*The Listening Post*, "Mohammed el-Kurd
on the Media's Complicity in Genocide"

78. How many of my brothers and my sisters
    will they kill
    before I teach myself
    retaliation?
    Shall we pick a number? . . .
    WHAT IS THE MATTER WITH ME?

    I must become a menace to my enemies.
    —June Jordan, "I Must Become a Menace to My Enemies"

79. Here the story becomes complicated: it is a feminist of color kind of
    complication. When we speak of violence directed against us, we know
    how quickly that violence can be racialized; how racism will explain
    that violence as an expression of culture . . . We must still tell these
    stories of violence because of how quickly that violence is concealed and
    reproduced. We must always tell them with care.
    —Sara Ahmed, *Living a Feminist Life*

80. For most right-wing and liberal readers, [this] is why such books exist.
    Will the author address the way Arab and Muslim sexual repression
    plays out . . . Or will she prevaricate and justify and relativize and decon-
    struct to the point where any essential difference between misogyny
    as practiced in the West and East is erased?
    —Lina Mounzer, "Going Beyond the Veil"

81. Repetition is a Nakba.   —Lena Khalaf Tuffaha, "What Happens Next"

82. O kind friend, if you visit my house,
    bring me a lamp, cut me a window   —Forugh Farrokhzad, "The Gift"

83. It is psychotic to draw a line between two places . . . It is psychotic to
    submit to violence in a time of great violence and yet it is psychotic to
    leave that home or country, the place where you submitted again and
    again, forever.   —Bhanu Kapil, *Schizophrene*

84. if I know anything, it is that "here" is a trick of the light, that it is a way of schematizing time and space that is not the only one available to some of us.

—Billy-Ray Belcourt, "If I Have a Body, Let It Be a Book of Sad Poems"

85. We have to make violence unthinkable.

—Mariame Kaba, We Do This 'Til We Free Us

86. This is what our ruling class has decided will be normal.

—Aaron Bushnell, age twenty-five, spoken before committing self-immolation in front of the Israeli embassy in protest of the genocide in Gaza, February 25, 2024

87. This does not seek a remedy
this does not need a balm
this needs an ending   —Dionne Brand, *Nomenclature*

88. Because when your body is buried underneath tons of concrete and metal and barbed wires, in front of this overwhelming truth, if left to sensory and rudimentary cognitive capacities, confronting this reality might lead you to madness. And madness under a deranged reality is the culmination of cognition, where the imaginative mind creates another reality that bypasses the prison walls.

—Walid Daqqa, *Searing Consciousness*

89. Every nation hates its children.   —Solmaz Sharif

90. There is a Gaza—an unwanted and dominated population—behind most stories of democratic rule, which is why the truth that Gaza embodies has the potential to dismantle our world order. It is no coincidence that Gaza has become a stand-in, a shorthand, for the major travails that plague our times, be they refugees, barricaded populations, overpopulation, police and military brutality, or ecological disasters.

—Tareq Baconi, "Confronting the Abject"

91. All flourishing is mutual.   —Robin Wall Kimmerer, *Braiding Sweetgrass*

92. I need to speak about living room
where the talk will take place in my language . . .
I need to speak about living room where the men
of my family between the ages of six and sixty-five
are not
marched into a roundup that leads to the grave . . .
—June Jordan, "Moving Towards Home"

93. If you are reading this, it means I have died and my soul has ascended to its creator . . . I walk to my fate, satisfied that *I have found my answers* . . . Why should I answer for you? You should search for it. As for us, the people of the graves, we seek nothing else but God's mercy.
—Basel al-Araj, *I Have Found My Answers*, quoted in translation by Hazem Jamjoum

94. Long ago
I turned away invader's horses
Deep in my soul
I know
I will turn them away again
—Mahmoud Darwish, *Lover From Palestine*

95. Decolonization, which sets out to change the order of the world, is, obviously, a program of complete disorder. But it cannot come as a result of magical practices, nor of a natural shock, nor of a friendly understanding. Decolonization, as we know, is a historical process.
—Frantz Fanon, *The Wretched of the Earth*

96. This obscure feeling that you had as you left Gaza, this small feeling must grow into a giant deep within you. It must expand, you must seek it in order to find yourself, here among the ugly debris of defeat.
—Ghassan Kanafani, "Letter from Gaza"

97. I wait for those lights, I know some of you do too, wherever you are, I mean when you are standing by an ocean, alone, within the calmness of your spirit. Be planetary. —Etel Adnan, *Shifting the Silence*

Acknowledgments

This book begins and ends in gratitude. For survival: Sittee, YaBa, we were never meant to make it this far. Thank you for the gift of your unbitter, abundant living, your steadfast loving and dreaming, always and despite. It is the honor of lifetimes to carry your name and blood. Habibi C, survival was a gift you gave me too. Neither this book nor this body would be here without your fierce faith, your sweet hands, your mighty patient heart. Thank you, and I love you, then, now, and to come.

Thank you to my agent, Elias Altman, who read early, raw pages of this book and called me to tell me, *Your grandmother is the North Star.* Thank you for your sharp editorial eye, for trusting this book to become what it needed to be, and for your tireless work to bring it into the world. Thank you also to my editor, Alicia Kroell, who read my first published piece about Sittoo and reached out to inquire about the rest of the story. I could scarcely imagine writing a book then, but years later, you helped make it possible—even in the midst of genocide—with your keen and gentle guidance.

Thank you to the rest of the team at Catapult, where this book has been treated with seriousness and care. Thank you to Kendall Storey for your early support, along with Alyson Forbes, Elizabeth Pankova, and the rest of the editorial department. Thank you to

Laura Berry, Wah-Ming Chang, and the whole production team for your meticulous work on this multilingual, unorthodox manuscript. Thank you to Megan Fishmann and especially Vanessa Genao for all you did to introduce this book to a world often hostile to Palestinian stories. Thank you also to Rachel Fershleiser and Alyssa Lo for your enthusiasm and labor in getting the book into people's hands, and to Lily Philpott for your compassion and intentionality around events. Thank you also to Elyse Lyon for your invaluable copyediting, Bridget Carrick for proofreading, and Katharine Meyers for all you did to champion this book.

To my early readers: Kiese Laymon, your words were the first to call me from silence back to the page. Thank you for sharing your abundance with me—through your art, your friendship, your generous reading and feedback. George Abraham, my sibling in the apocalypse, you are shelter, and you sharpen me—thank you for taking time with this manuscript in the midst of our ending world. Abdelrahman ElGendy, brother of the huge heart and sharp pen, I am grateful for your insights on this manuscript, and all things. Ghinwa Jawhari, my g, I would not be okay without you—thank you for reading, for raging and laughing with me through the darkest year. Nadia Owusu, thank you for the example of *Aftershocks*, and for your thoughtful, heartful advice. Hala Alyan, habibti—thank you for all you do for our community, and for cornering me at an open mic when I was still trying to hide. Kaveh Akbar, gratitude for the conversation we had when this work was yet embryonic, and for your subsequent generosity. Marcelo Hernandez Castillo, thank you for pushing me from the workshop to pitching. Elise Mitchell— thank you for your companionship as we both learn what it means to walk with and carry ancestors. Thank you and يعطيكم العافية to Roger Allen and Khaled Al Hilli for your invaluable insights on the exquisite, harrowing subjects of Arabic etymology, grammar, and morphology.

Thank you, Tin House—and especially to Lance Cleland and A.L. Major, who saw something in my project before I fully dared. Thank you for the month in Portland, and all the ways you've supported me since. Gratitude to the *Margins* magazine and fellowship, and to the Asian American Writers' Workshop for being a haven and advocate for many, including me. Thank you to Café Royal Cultural Foundation, the Sachs Program for Arts Innovation, and Millay Arts for material support during the writing of this book. Thank you to the Literary Reportage program at NYU, and especially Robert Boynton, Liza Featherstone, and Ted Conover, for your guidance during my first years as a writer in New York City. Thank you also to the Comparative Literature department at NYU for investing in my research and study. To my therapists and nutritionists: B, L, L, and R, as well as the entire staff at the Columbia Center for Eating Disorders—your work was lifesaving.

And to all those who have made it possible to stay: Bethany, the rigor of your love changes lives—how did I deserve you? (Check my heart.) Maryam, my sister-dreamer, thank you for sharing life deeply and tenderly, and for being the first to see I had a book. I love you. Hamzeh, there were storms we shared with no one but you. Deep love and gratitude, always. Kate, thank you for your strong, bright presence, especially through my silent years. Stodder, I hope we never finish talking, or writing, or laughing. Angbeen, grateful for your generous, creative heart. Sarah C, Aaron, Marrisa, and Lisa— thank you for loving the odd girl from across the ocean all those years ago. You are family. Aqsa, whether you like it or not, you continue to inspire me. Lara, thank you for your care, your cooking, and your wit. Thank you, Liz Bishop and K Goff, for listening for the story in my physical pain, and believing I could heal. And Mowgli, our literal angel, thank you for giving us years of snuggles, laughter, and pure love.

There are innumerable others—friends, elders, editors, neighbors—who have taught me, who supported my work, and who revive my reasons to remain. They include: Noor Hindi, Hannah Bae, Ladan Khoddam-Khorasani, Liz Simakoff, Chase Berggrun, Ahmad Sahli, Emilie Alongi, Camille Bromley, Fariha Róisín, Fargo Nissim Tbakhi, Jess Snow, Afnaan Moharram, e.jin, Hilary Sun, Gigi Tiwari, Mathew Rodriguez, Julianna Hedberg, Hamed Sinno, Hazem Fahmy, Hannah Gann, Natasha Jahchan, Sarah Leonard, Cora Currier, Ali Gharib, Zach Webb, Writers Against the War on Gaza, the Palestine Festival of Literature, Mizna, the Palestinian Youth Movement, and so many more—deep thanks, and much love.

To the rest of my family—Mom, my first writing teacher and first reader! I love you and am humbled by your heart; thank you for your bottomless grace. Dana: you are my hero. I will always dream big dreams for you, and I love you to the moon. Tariq: who you are sustains me. You have my endless admiration and love. Laura: you are exquisite. I am lucky to love and learn from you. Victoria: I love and am so proud of you; grateful for who you are. Jamie and Donna—thank you for your generosity, your unwavering faith and love. Ben and Jacob—we treasure you and yours. To my family in Falasteen and especially in Gaza—Zuhair, Sabah, Haneen, Nabil, Basil, Ibrahim, Haitham, Heba, Samir, Mahmoud, and our hundreds more:

انتم الأفضل بينّا. إن شاء الله بنتقابل قريباً وفلسطين حرة.

Writing is a profoundly physical act, and would not be possible without the material sustenance granted by the earth and rain, the bodies that sow and harvest and deliver, the labor that keeps me sheltered and fed. This book was conceived, written, and edited across many spaces, in sickness and in health, including on the A, Q, B, 2, 5, G, F, J, and M trains, in doctors' offices, emergency rooms, Prospect Park, my yoga mat, airplanes, Jordanian kitchens, Italian hostels, Mexican cafés, and at a Spanish beach, to name a few.

My writing and living has also overlapped with unceded and occupied lands, including that of the Munsee Lenape, Canarsie, Schaghticoke, Mohican, Očhéthi Šakówiŋ, Myaamia, Hoocąk (Ho-Chunk), Kaskaskia, Bodwéwadmi (Potawatomi), Kiikaapoi (Kickapoo), Peoria, Sewee, Kusso, Lumbee Stl'pulmsh (Cowlitz), Clackamas, Cayuse, Umatilla, and Walla Walla peoples.* The movement for a free Palestine can never be separate from the struggles for land back and self-determination for Indigenous people around the world, and our collective survival depends on the liberation of all beings, human and other-than-human, everywhere. And so I thank the global resistance, our many martyrs past and present, for the profound love that is their, our, fight.

Acknowledgment of Translators

1. *The Secret Life of Saeed the Pessoptimist*, Emile Habibi, translated by Salma K Jayyusi and Trevor LeGassick (Arabic)
2. *History of Madness*, Michel Foucault, translated by Jonathan Murphy (French)

---

* Native Land Digital

3. *In the Presence of Absence*, Mahmoud Darwish, translated by Sinan Antoon (Arabic)

4. *Borderlands / La Frontera: The New Mestiza*, Gloria Anzaldúa, self-translation (Spanish)

5. *The Earth Is Closing in On Us*, Mahmoud Darwish, translated by Sarah Aziza (Arabic)

6. *I Saw Ramallah*, Mourid Barghouti, translated by Ahdaf Soueif (Arabic)

7. *Strategy for the Liberation of Palestine, 1969*, the Popular Front for the Liberation of Palestine, translated by Foreign Languages Press (Arabic)

8. *Poetics of Relation*, Édouard Glissant, translated by Betsy Wing (French)

9. *I Was Born There, I Was Born Here*, Mourid Barghouti, translated by Humphrey Davies (Arabic)

10. *Memory for Forgetfulness*, Mahmoud Darwish, translated by Ibrahim Muhawi (Arabic)

11. *The Curiosity of A Child or . . . The Predestiny of Man?*, Ghassan Kanafani, translated by Jenan Abu Shtaya (Arabic)

12. *Illuminations*, Walter Benjamin, translated by Harry Zohn (German)

13. "On the question of Palestine," speech at the United Nations General Assembly, 1974, Yasser Arafat, official translation by the United Nations (Arabic)

14. *The Gift by Forugh Farrokhzad*, translated by Sholeh Wolpé (Persian)

15. *Searing Consciousness*, Walid Daqqa, translated by Ghina Abi-Ghannam (Arabic)

16. *Enemy of the Sun: Poetry of the Palestinian Resistance*, edited and majority-translated by Naseer Aruri and Edmund Ghareeb, with translation of "Tent #50" by "Mrs. Rashad Hussein" (Arabic)

17. *Silence for Gaza*, Mahmoud Darwish, translated by Sinan Antoon (Arabic)

18. *The 1936–39 Revolt in Palestine*, Ghassan Kanafani, translated by Tricontinental Society, London, in conjunction with Committee for Democratic Palestine (Arabic)

19. *The Wretched of the Earth*, Frantz Fanon, translated by Richard Philcox (French)

© Natasha Jahchan

SARAH AZIZA is a Palestinian American writer, trans-
lator, and artist with roots in ʿIbdis and Deir al-Balah,
Gaza. The recipient of a Fulbright fellowship and numerous
grants from the Pulitzer Center on Crisis Reporting, she
has lived and worked in Saudi Arabia, Algeria, Jordan,
South Africa, the occupied West Bank, and the United
States. Her award-winning journalism, poetry, essays,
and experimental nonfiction have appeared in *The New
Yorker*, *The Guardian*, *The Baffler*, *Harper's Magazine*, *Mizna*,
Lux, *The Washington Post*, *The Intercept*, *The Rumpus*, NPR,
The Margins, and *The Nation*, among other publications.